Information Technology and Traditional Legal Concepts

Information technology has served to revolutionise the use, exchange, and protection of information. The growth of the internet, the convergence of technologies as well as the development of user generated and social networking sites has meant that significant amounts of person data as well as copyrighted materials are now readily accessible. Within this changing cultural landscape the legal concepts of privacy, data protection, intellectual property and criminality have necessarily had to develop and adapt. In this volume a number of international scholars consider this process and whether it has merely been a question of the law adapting to technology or whether technology has been forced to adapt to law. As technologies have wrought a culture shift it is therefore apposite to ask whether legal concepts, as reflections of culture, should also change. It is in this volume where papers on privacy, data protection, intellectual protection and cyber crime begin to address this question.

This book was previously published as a special issue of *International Review of Law, Computers & Technology*.

Richard Jones, Associate Editor, *International Review of Law, Computers & Technology*, has taught in areas of intellectual property and information technology law. He was invited by the Council of Europe to work in this area and awarded a Research fellowship with IBM to investigate legal expert systems. He was Chair of the British and Irish Legal Educational Technology Association (BILETA) and a Council member of the Society for Computers and the Law.

Roksana Moore, Lecturer in Law and Intellectual Property, School of Law, University of Southampton is researching in vendor liability for software defects. Her research interests also include software patents, ICT standardisation and traditional knowledge and intellectual property.

Information Technology and Traditional Legal Concepts

Edited by
Richard Jones and Roksana Moore

Routledge
Taylor & Francis Group
LONDON AND NEW YORK

First published 2011
by Routledge
2 Park Square, Milton Park, Abingdon, Oxon, OX14 4RN

Simultaneously published in the USA and Canada
by Routledge
270 Madison Avenue, New York, NY 10016

Routledge is an imprint of the Taylor & Francis Group, an informa business

This book is a reproduction of *International Review of Law, Computers & Technology* 23.1&2 The Publisher requests that those citing this book use the bibliographical details of the journal issue on which the book is based.

Typeset in Times New Roman by Taylor & Francis Books

British Library Cataloguing in Publication Data
A catalogue record for this book is available from the British Library

ISBN13: 978-0-415-61485-6

Disclaimer
The publisher would like to make readers aware that the chapters in this book are referred to as articles as they had been in the special issue. The publisher accepts responsibility for any inconsistencies that may have arisen in the course of preparing this volume for print.

Contents

INTRODUCTION

An uncomfortable marriage: The challenges 'new' technology is posing to 'old' or established legal concepts?

Richard Jones[a] and Roksana Moore[b]

[a]*Liverpool JMU;* [b]*Queen Mary College, London*

BILETA 2008 '*Law Shaping Technology; Technology Shaping the Law*' was organised at Glasgow Caledonian University by Michael Bromby and took as its main theme the security and privacy of personal information. The conference's first keynote speaker, David Flint, a Partner in MacRoberts Technology Media & Communications Group, is an independent expert under the UK Domain Dispute Resolution Procedure. He tackled the conference theme head on. How can the right to free speech be reconciled with the right to privacy, particularly with the rise in social networking technologies and user generated content? Have for example sites such as Facebook and YouTube responded in a timely and effective manner to safeguard our data, while promoting our rights to free speech? The topics of information and privacy have featured regularly in the writings of legal scholars for over a century, not least because of ongoing debates and obscurities with regard to definitions and applications of the terms. This edition capturing several privacy-related papers from the conference, which go some way to meeting David's challenge.

One of the key hurdles in creating the law of privacy has been the disagreement of what constitutes an invasion of privacy and it is generally accepted that this is further dependant upon cultural, and other, perspectives. Karen McCullagh, in 'Protecting "privacy" through control of "personal" data collection: A flawed approach' acknowledges the absence of key definitions with regards to privacy, seeks to identify whether or not the term privacy is synonymous with the term personal (UK Data Protection Act 1998), and adopts empirical research to assist in determining this. McCullagh's findings and discussion is important in demonstrating that an agreement upon a common ground of the invasion of privacy seems to exist.

Continuing on the theme of definition within privacy, Dan Ritchie in 'Is it possible to define "privacies" within the law? Reflections on the "securitisation" debate and the interception of communications', considers privacy within the context of surveillance and the interception of communications. The definition of privacy is reviewed with an emphasis on informational privacy, providing an interesting account on how the public perception of what is private can differ in context of modern technology. Richie puts forward his own questions that should be addressed to further the debate on privacy, and in so doing proposes that individual approval or disapproval is the crux of personal feelings of privacy.

Issues affecting children are generally high on most agendas and privacy is no different. In her paper Emmanuelle Bartoli performs a comparative analysis of the provisions in place to protect children's personal information online within the EU and USA, and highlights several difficulties, challenges and loopholes within legislation.

In their paper, Cannataci and Mifsud Bonnici consider how a minimalist approach to law-making was the foundation of bad policy and bad law that left the UK's data protection Commissioner virtually toothless and under-resourced for many years until the recent moves to grant him wider powers in 2008 and 2009. They evaluate the soaring number losses of personal data in the UK in the context of such constraints and then move on to examine whether the new Coroners and Justice Bill 2009 would remedy the situation or is simply more evidence that the UK has not entirely escaped from problems of bad policy and bad law in the field of data protection. Their paper includes summary tables documenting nearly a hundred different cases of losses of personal data across the world which the authors have researched during the period 2007–2009.

Within our Current Developments section Sophie Stalla-Bourdillon revisits European Directive 2000/31/EC and the Communications Decency Act and the Digital Millennium Copyright Act within the context of Children's Privacy – a timely intervention given 2008 developments and reports on children and the Internet. Bourdillion questions whether self-regulation or co-regulation form the basis of future regulation and subsequently how that regulation should take place with regards to standards setting, monitoring and enforcement.

As with all BILETA conferences parallel sessions are the norm and this edition has also captured papers from some of the other sessions. Technology to combat crime and technology to assist in crime was another significant theme of the conference. David Wall delivering the second of the conference keynotes (not included in this edition) mapped out the conceptual origins of cybercrime in social science fiction genres enabling him to explore the relationship between rhetoric and reality in the production of knowledge about it. Clare Sullivan in her conference proper 'Is identity theft really theft?' tackles this increasingly worrying problem. While figures show cybercrime increasing year on year by up to 10% indications are that identity theft may be declining. The credit crunch of 2008/9 may see an end to this decline and Sullivan considers the key question of what is identity. In conceptualising identity the author asserts that identity is emerging as a new distinct, legal concept. Spanning the crime and privacy debate is spam. In '"Spam, spam, spam, spam ... Lovely spam!" Why is Bluespam different?', Eleni Kosta, Peggy Valcke and David Stevens of the Interdisciplinary Centre for Law & ICT (ICRI) at the Katholieke Universiteit Leuven consider how technological progress, has created new types of spamming, including Bluespam, the action of sending spam to Bluetooth-enabled devices, such as mobile phones, personal digital assistants (PDAs) or laptop computers. Although, at first sight, it would seem that Bluespam should be considered as any other kind of spam and would therefore fall under the ambit of Article 13 of the ePrivacy Directive, closer examination enables the authors to question this assumption and conclude that Bluespam may not be covered by the ePrivacy directive. They speculate that the scope of the regulation on unsolicited communications needs to be broadened in order to cover networks like Bluetooth, or indeed new regulations covering the sending of unsolicited Bluetooth messages should be enacted. In a timely intervention Wiebke Abel in 'Agents, Trojans and tags: The next generation of investigators' considers the issues in and around the use of technology by the investigatory and enforcement agencies as a strategy to more effectively combat cybercrime and the increase in crimes committed using computer technology. In a statement issued in 2008, the Council of the European Union has recommended that member states should undertake clandestine remote searches of computers of suspects, if provided for under national law. Such powers will no doubt to significant challenges.

The conference again brought forward a large number of intellectual property based papers. Intellectual property law continues to be a dominant preoccupation for information technology lawyers. This is not surprising given that the cultural impact of intellectual property has been stoked, and in part driven by developments in technology. Copyright's origin in the Statute of Anne's preamble states 'An Act for the encouragement of learning, by vesting the copies of printed books in the authors or purchasers.' The Act, at first limited to printed materials, was introduced to deal with the challenges of the printing press, so beginning a close relationship between copyright and technology. In 'Technology and the cultural appropriation of music', Richard Jones considers the interplay of music, technology and intellectual property. The paper considers how developments in information technology can now be used to offset the expansion of copyright. After reviewing some of these developments, particularly the Creative Commons, and considering evidence now analysed from a Europe-wide survey of musicians and publishers completed in 2008, the paper concludes that these fixes, rooted in intellectual property, unfortunately offer little by way of solution. Technological solutions not so closely tied to intellectual property may offer more appropriate and workable solutions. Continuing the intellectual property–technology link Hasina Haque in 'Decentralised P2P technology: Can the unruly be ruled?' returns to an issue that has dominated intellectual property this century, the role of the Internet, peer to peer file sharing systems, digital rights management (DRM) and secondary infringement. Courts in the USA have added a third theory, namely, inducement theory into the genre of secondary infringement. The article examines the prospect of implementing inducement theory into the UK context. After examining the legal issues, the paper suggests that instead of adding a new theory into the domain of secondary infringement the challenge of decentralised peer to peer (P2P) technology should be addressed through technology by way of device protection. Our third intellectual property paper is by Neal Geach, 'The future of copyright in the age of convergence: Is a new approach needed for the new media world?' The author considers the new Audiovisual Media Services Directive that aims to provide the regulatory framework for television without frontiers. Geach concludes that while convergent technologies have created opportunities for the media industry it has also created threats in that the same technology is also being used to infringe the copyright of content producers on a far greater scale. The conclusion then is that the Audiovisual Media Services Directive's biggest weakness may be in not addressing the link between converged media platforms and the potential for increased copyright infringement. Finally in this section a paper on computer contracts. Computer contracting is a complex and often challenging area for lawyers, the complexity in part arising from the interface of contract with intellectual property. Here Ruth Atkins considers the extent to which permitted acts under copyright law can be varied by contractual arrangement and conversely, the manner in which proprietary interests can override contrary stipulations expressed in a contractual agreement.

The Conference would not have been complete without some examination of the broader challenges of regulating cyberspace. It was in the mid 1990s when academics first ventured into the murky waters of cyber-paternalism or cyber-liberalism. In his book Andrew Murray in *The Regulation of Cyberspace: Control in the Online Environment* (2007)[1] argues that the debate is now more complex, the regulation of cyberspace is not simply the imposition through a top-down system from regulator to regulatee, a number of actors and elements come into play. Cyberspace according to Murray is not a static regulatory universe into which an intervention would be made, 'cyberspace is a challenge, because in cyberspace, it is not always clear who the regulators are.' There may be competition between nation states or in some examples in the dynamic world of cyberspace, regulatees can become regulators.

We hope you enjoy this special BILETA 2008 edition of the *International Review* and we hope you will be better able now to appreciate the challenges 'new' technology is posing to 'old' or established legal concepts. May we take this opportunity of thanking Michael Bromby and Ken Russell for all their help in selecting authors, to the large number of anonymous referees who provided immensely helpful feedback and of course to the long suffering authors who had to cope with our numerous and varied requests.

Notes

1. Andrew Murray, *The Regulation of Cyberspace: Control in the Online Environment* (Abingdon: Routledge-Cavendish, 2007).
2. Johnson, D. R. and D. G. 'Post, Law and Borders – The Rise of Law in Cyberspace', *Stanford Law Review* 48 (1996): 1367.

Law shaping technology: Technology shaping the law[1]

David Flint

Although the original Data Protection Act in the UK was 1984, it was really only with the 1998 Act that data protection ever raised a murmur in the public consciousness.

> Privacy is about our 'right to be let alone'. (Louis Brandeis)
> Protecting privacy is about protecting our sense of self.

The question has been raised: 'What are sites such as Facebook doing to protect our data and our privacy?' Consider a politician who takes all steps including injunction to prevent newspapers printing pictures of his children in order to protect their privacy, yet sends out thousands of Christmas cards showing those children – is that privacy, or hypocrisy? Maybe social networking sites have no obligation to protect our data – at least insofar as we have chosen to make it publicly available on those sites. Should law and society protect such blogs as free speech or protect those mentioned therein from having their information and exploits retained in perpetuity? I have focussed here on some of the data protection and privacy issues which appear to me to merit consideration. If the purpose of legal protection is to encourage creators, how does a music industry company such as Sony or Universal owning all the copyrights facilitate this purpose? How should the monopoly rights of content owners be reconciled with the rights of users? Is DRM compatible with permitted use under copyright law? If breach of data protection law should be punishable by financial penalty, how should breach in the public sector be handled, given that any penalty would simply be recycled? Should ISPs be required to police IP rights – and if so how does this fit with privacy concerns?

The subject of this year's (2008) BILETA conference is described as 'Security and privacy of our personal information is becoming a central theme with the rise in social networking technologies and user generated content. Have sites such as Facebook and YouTube responded in a timely and effective manner to safeguard our data, whilst promoting our rights to free speech.'

Over the 12 months since March 2007, it is clear that data protection has reached a new level in the psyche of the individual citizen and that, increasingly, the public are turning to lawyers seeking redress from some actual or perceived breach of their rights and of their privacy; nor, however, is this a purely British problem. Obviously from a legal perspective much of the pressure for data protection has been driven by European Community Directives, they in turn being a necessary implementation of a Council of Europe recommendation on privacy. Having had the opportunity over the last few years to conduct a project for a client looking at implementation of the Data Protection Directive over 16 of the EU member states, and having had for interest and general information needed to consider the rules in many of the others, the only thing that can be said is that it is possible for 25+ countries to take a single text and turn it into national law in 25+ different ways; indeed, other than the Data Protection principles with which you will all be familiar, the national systems have little in common. For a business person there would seem to be irrefutable logic in trying to implement these types of regimes in a more consistent and coherent system. I am far from convinced that the system I would choose would be the UK one, and equally I doubt that our business community would thank us for the German system, although Germans seem to find that wholly acceptable to them.

As someone who travels a great deal on business according to my family and colleagues (and who 'occasionally is out of the office' according to me!), it has been a very fascinating exercise to watch how public and political perception to data protection and privacy has shifted in the last 10 years.

Although the original Data Protection Act in the UK was 1984, it was really only with the 1998 Act that data protection ever raised a murmur in the public consciousness. Outwith Europe, data protection and privacy as we understand it was confined to some of the Commonwealth and, in a very specific regard to celebrities in California who needed protected from the very people who had made them celebrities in the first place. I can recall some 7 years ago having the pleasure of chairing a conference in Adelaide on data protection where the then Australian Privacy Commissioner, Malcolm Crompton gave a keynote speech which had a number of buzz phrases which in the years since I have shamelessly recycled – albeit usually with attribution – and I make no apology for doing so again as I believe that these simple concepts underpin or should underpin everything that we strive to achieve in this important area.

- My Privacy ... My Choice
- Privacy is about our 'right to be let alone' (Louis Brandeis)[2]
- Respecting Privacy

This may appear overly simplistic but as lawyers are accused of making things overly complicated – actually lawyers crave simplicity and clarity despite what some clients may erroneously believe; unfortunately the quality of legislation over the past quarter century has declined as with general educational standards to a level that it is often almost impossible for the trained legal mind, let alone the man on the proverbial Clapham omnibus, to comprehend what the legislator intended let alone how it should be applied. However, I digress.

These three simple concepts may seem uncontroversial to you and perhaps in a democracy they should raise few eyebrows; however, let us step back for a moment and look at the reality of the world in which we live. Very quickly we see that anonymity and privacy are fast becoming a luxury or at least something which we cannot take for granted. Probably one of the most famous cartoons ever is a cartoon from the New Yorker which has a dog at a computer keyboard and the caption reads 'On the internet no one knows you're a dog'. While that is true to some extent, the fact that one were a dog might be readily ascertainable by a search of the IP address from which the messages emanated, a subpoena to the ISP for the traffic records and a match between user details and that IP address, thereby showing that the computer was connected to the dog pound or a kennel!

Protecting privacy is about protecting our sense of self:

- who we are
- what we know

- what we think
- what we have done
- what we want to do

Orwell in *1984* described a society in which 'Big Brother' watched everything that the individuals did or thought. In 2008, the position is reversed and individuals watch everything that contestants on Big Brother do – although I have to say that watching people fast asleep for hours at a time is far from my idea of entertainment.

I can remember in the 1960s and 1970s, reading *1984* and thinking that it was something so far in the future as to be irrelevant along with such other classics as *2001 – A Space Odyssey* and *Space 1999*; and, perhaps I was right – however, the fact is that if Orwell wrote his sequel and called it 2020 would any of you see it as fiction or as a technical guide? Our perceptions of privacy and expectations of personal privacy have been radically changed by the events of the last two decades; the present debate about ID cards seems emotive to those of us in the UK but in much of the rest of the world it has not been an issue for over half a century. Of course one cannot expect the Briton (and I suspect more the Englishman than the Scot) to have to carry an Identity Card; that is of course unless you have in mind travelling by plane. If you do not have a passport or a photo driving licence, travelling by Easyjet to Barcelona is as possible as building a set of wings and flying, Icarus-like, to the sun.

So we need to look more deeply at this question. Clearly we do not mind carrying identity cards of some description for some purposes. My colleague Val Surgenor presented a paper at this conference on RFID tags and privacy – those of you who travel in London will have seen, and may possess, an Oyster Card. That is an ID card of sorts and it knows where you are; M6Toll and DartTag are both ID type cards in that the system knows where the tag is. Millions of citizens are prepared to sacrifice some of their privacy for the extra convenience (or in the case of Oyster, substantial saving) that these systems bring. Back to Malcolm Crompton's first principle – 'My Privacy ... My Choice'. I do not have to carry an Oyster Card; I do not have to cover my car in Toll tags, I may choose to do so but I cannot be compelled so to do. It is that fundamental difference which underpins much of the rational opposition to ID cards and the like.

The argument that it will in some way make us safer is perhaps a convenient argument for a system bereft of real value; indeed, if the system were of great value, most people would want to have one. If I suggested that my carrying the new card I have invented, 'the BILETACard', you would automatically be allowed to travel free on airlines first class and pay a maximum tax rate of 2% I would be killed in the stampede for the sign up. Therefore it must be that the populous has still to be convinced first that the card will be of value and second that the information that it will contain or provide the access key for will be kept safe by those who will collect it.

That brings me to the next part of this keynote, the rise of social networking and user content and the privacy and security issues which this raises.

Personally, I have never seen the attraction in FaceBook, Bebo, YouTube and the like but perhaps that is a generational thing. However, the fact is that for millions of young (and not so young people) these are major parts of their lives; indeed in a culture which sociologists might describe as having a lack of one-to-one face-to-face human resource interfacing many people conduct their entire lives through the filter of a social networking environment, arranging their social calendar, lives and loves in the ephemeral world of cyberspace. Those of you who know me will be aware that I am a shy, retiring sort of person – or at least a private person (to some extent). I believe strongly in privacy and private information – not because I have anything to hide (or nothing more than anyone else) but rather because it is none of your business. I therefore have a conceptual difficulty in coming to terms with the information which is imparted on the social networking sites by the individuals themselves.

I know that we have questioned what sites such as Facebook are doing to protect our data and our privacy. However, I question (as I am allowed to do in a keynote) whether Facebook has any obligation to protect us from ourselves. If I choose to have a Facebook page on which I publish my name, address, bank details, PIN, mother's maiden name and the like, should Facebook have any responsibility to protect the integrity of that information from abuse. Perhaps more relevant might be the ease, or rather lack of ease, with which one can withdraw from social networking sites and expunge all information about one.

Facebook has recently come in for criticism for retaining information even after someone closes their account; some information may still be accessible and much will never disappear. At least, however, the information was originally mine and I must, at some time, have wanted it to appear. YouTube type sites are somewhat different in that much of the information posted does not relate to the poster but to others and how is their privacy to be protected?

It may seem to have been a good idea to upload a video of your student colleague in an inebriated state behaving in an anti-social way; he/she may even have found it amusing . . . at the time. Unfortunately, in five years time when the reality dawns that one cannot be a student for ever and that gainful employment must be sought, will that video enhance one's attractiveness to a potential employer, and have no doubt about it, employers are routinely carrying out online searches using Google/YouTube/FaceBook/Bebo etc. to get a real idea of a candidate and a video of you being sick over a cat is not generally perceived as being a plus point.

This brings us to one of the dichotomy of BILETA 2008; how can the right to free speech be reconciled with the right to privacy. The issue is that, in our western democracies, each of these is given an equal importance – albeit that there may not be any specific right of privacy in UK law. I am delighted to say that the question of the existence or otherwise or a right to privacy in UK law is a subject for another day, or at least another time. It is however curious that many of the individuals who seem desperate to establish and protect their right to privacy are the very same individuals who have based their celebrity status on self promotion and for whom the requirement for privacy is more to protect the perceived value of the 'exclusive' they have signed with a 'Celebrity' magazine than any real desire to adopt a Mae West posture of 'I want to be alone'. Consider a politician who takes all steps including injunction to prevent newspapers printing pictures of his children in order to protect their privacy, yet sends out thousands of Christmas cards showing those children – is that privacy, or hypocrisy?

Maybe social networking sites have no obligation to protect our data – at least insofar as we have chosen to make it publicly available on those sites. I understand from those younger than I, that it is possible to make one's page hidden from all but those to whom one has chosen to grant access. However, I know of individuals who cannot add more friends as they have reached the limit for friends on Facebook (10,000 I believe). Luckily, as a lawyer, having more than 10,000 friends is unlikely to be a problem any time soon. Are these people friends? I am not sure how I would describe them. Perhaps it is part of the desire to belong and to be wanted that spawns this reciprocal sycophancy.

Possibly it is all part of a greater social phenomenon of self publicity; in a world in which for many career aspirations include winning the lottery and appearing on Big Brother, and where everyone is told that they can achieve everything, individuals have the mistaken belief that others have any interest in them, what they say or do or what they think. According to a quote in *Blog Herald*,[3] 'Technorati currently states it is tracking over 112.8 million blogs, a number which obviously does not include all the 72.82 million Chinese blogs as counted by The China Internet Network Information Center'. I do not wish to be unkind but I doubt that many of these 185 million people are saying anything to which I would wish to listen; indeed, looking at many blogs shows that the only people reading them are the authors.

Turning back to the wonderful New Yorker cartoons sees February 2008's calendar entry with two dogs, one of whom is saying to the other 'I used to have a blog, but now I've gone back to pointless incessant barking'.

Should law and society protect such blogs as free speech or protect those mentioned therein from having their information and exploits retained in perpetuity? In the pre-Internet age (as can be seen from the old films shown on cable and satellite) it used to be that the cub reporter was sent to the dusty archives for the local newspaper to see if they could find information about someone – generally a well known person, good or bad – and come back to the office clutching a copy of some dusty clipping. Today the reporter would probably never leave his desk; everything that has been said or written about anyone in any public media in the last 20 years is almost certainly on-line. Yesterday's newspaper used to have a limited value as a wrapper for fish suppers; if I did not see a story in a newspaper because I was away, the chance of ever seeing it was almost nil. Today, I come back to my desk (assuming that I was not reading the paper online on the beach somewhere) and after a few keystrokes I have everything I need to know in front of me. BILETA 2008, itself, returns 153 entries from around the world.

The 2008 conference was very timely; the four tracks that were chosen to be addressed were all topical and complex issues for many of which there are as yet few issues. I have focussed in this keynote on some of the data protection and privacy issues which appear to me to merit consideration. A similar focus could have been made on any of the other streams, all of which interact and cross-over; indeed looking at the many papers that were presented, there are many which could have fitted in more than one stream.

The second stream that was considered was that of Copyright, although many of the papers there would fit equally into a Technology stream.

Of all the IP rights with which we have to deal, Copyright is perhaps both the best known and the most contentious. I do not have to remind an academic audience of the issues of file-sharing in an academic environment although I know that the Glasgow Caledonian University has a robust Information Transfer Policy which prohibits P2P sharing and trafficking in copyright material.

Clearly none of us (and of you) would want to break the law; but many today do not see P2P filesharing as infringing; there is little recognition of a connection between creativity and copyright infringement; perhaps this is because most of the infringement action worldwide has been taken by the behemoths of the music industry with little apparent benefit for the musicians.

Copyright within an academic environment is almost a *sine qua non* given that academia is supposed to be a hotbed of creativity. However, Universities are supposed to be about information dissemination and exchange of ideas. Particularly in the UK (but also over much of Europe) the role of the academic in information exchange seems to be lost. The ideas which exist in the USA of 'fair use', alas seem to have no place in UK law and, indeed, recent changes in the law have made the limited fair use exceptions even narrower. This matters to you as academics as you must be able to refer to or incorporate (under attribution obviously) other work in your theses and papers.

Copyright is supposed to be a compact between creators and society as a whole; in return for making one's brilliance available to society, society gives the creator a limited period of monopoly in respect thereof.

The problem is that as copyright has become longer and longer (allegedly to prevent Mickey Mouse ever becoming public domain) this compact has been irreversibly slanted in favour of the content industry (as opposed to the creator); work is now protected for longer than the true economic life of the material. However, whether it is life +50, +70 or something else – the USA has the longest potential period of 120 years – at least if one can live long enough, a work will become public domain at some point.

Step in technology in the form of DRM; most national copyright laws prohibit the removal or circumvention of any DRM control device or technology. This has a number of serious consequences for you and other users of copyright material. First, after the copyright period, you still will not be able to have unfettered access to material as it will still be DRM'd and if experience is anything to go by there will be no way of reading it; think Betamax, 8-Track and more recently HD-DVD; second, DRM and other similar measures are simple and unselective – these have no knowledge or understanding of such fair use rights as you might have. Perhaps Creative Commons is a way forward.

Nevertheless one must query whether the existing law (and the proposals to 'improve' it being touted by the content industry) meet or continue to meet the requirements of the creator/society compact ... or whether major change is needed. If the purpose of legal protection is to encourage creators, how does a music industry company such as Sony or Universal owning all the copyrights facilitate this purpose?

The government and the EU Commission have both been consulting on this matter recently and will no doubt do so again. We put in comments – did you? If not, perhaps you should; have no doubt, the content lobby will be putting in its arguments that, absent more draconian rules, it will be the end of civilisation as we know it – if you do not agree, do something about it!

You will be pleased to know that I do not intend to deconstruct the other streams in the same way as I have done with privacy and copyright but, as an academic audience, there are clearly matters which I would hope you would address. Unfortunately for many of these issues there is no real debate and the agenda is being driven by very powerful vested interests which conflict with academic and individual interests and with the interests of society as a whole. In closing I leave you with some thoughts and a few questions to ponder over:

- How should the monopoly rights of content owners be reconciled with the rights of users?
- Is DRM compatible with permitted use under copyright law?
- What ever happened to fair use?
- If breach of data protection law should be punishable by financial penalty, how should breach in the public sector be handled, given that any penalty would simply be recycled?
- Should ISPs be required to police IP rights – and if so how does this fit with privacy concerns?
- How in a global world do we reconcile different social norms and standards where a single Internet page can be seen anywhere? Are we confined to the lowest most conservative standard?
- How do we/can we ever recover trust in government to look after our data?

Notes

1. Keynote speech presented at BILETA 2008, 23rd AnnualConference on 'Law Shaping Technology; Technology Shaping the Law', 27–28 March 2008, Glasgow Caledonian University (amended for publication).
2. Louis Brandeis in *Olmstead* v *United States* [1928] 277 U.S. 438, 48. S. Ct. 564, 72 L. Ed. 944.
3. Helmond, A., How many Blogs Are There? Is Someone Still Counting?', *The Blog Herald*, http://www.blogherald.com/2008/02/11/how-many-blogs-are-there-is-someone-still-counting/ (accessed March 2008)

Protecting 'privacy' through control of 'personal' data processing: A flawed approach

Karen McCullagh

Salford Law School, University of Salford, UK

The development of a frontier-free internal market and of the so-called 'information society' have resulted in an increase in the flow of personal data between EU member states. To remove potential obstacles to such transfers, data protection legislation was introduced. One of the underpinning principles of Directive 95/46/EC is the protection of privacy. Yet, the legislation does not provide a conclusive understanding of the terms 'privacy' or 'private' data. Rather, privacy protection is to be achieved through the regulation of the conditions under which personal data may be processed. An assessment of whether, 10 years after the enactment of the Data Protection Act 1998 (DPA 1998), a coherent understanding of the concept of personal data exists, necessitated an analysis of the decisions in *Durant* v. *FSA* ([2003] EWCA Civ 1746) and *CSA* v. *SIC* ([2008] 1 WLR 1550, [2008] UKHL 47). Furthermore, in order to examine the effectiveness of the legislation, this article examines whether the term 'personal' is synonymous with the term 'private' data and whether control over processing of personal information protects privacy. By drawing on interviews with privacy and data protection experts, and from the findings of a survey of bloggers, it will be shown that a review of the assumptions and concepts underpinning the legislation is necessary.

Introduction

As IT usage and processing capabilities evolve, regulators, privacy practitioners and citizens are increasingly questioning the suitability and adequacy of data protection legislation to allow the effective processing of personal data while simultaneously safeguarding the privacy of individuals. Indeed, the Office of the UK's Information Commissioner (ICO) commissioned research into how the EU Directive 95/46/EC should be updated, because

> We want to generate new thinking. European data protection law is increasingly seen as out of date, bureaucratic and excessively prescriptive. It is showing its age and is failing to meet new challenges to privacy, such as the transfer of personal details across international borders and the huge growth in personal information online.[1]

This article begins by exploring the relationship between privacy and data protection at EU and UK level. It will be demonstrated that the concepts of 'privacy' and 'private' data remain nebulous as they are not defined in the Directive. Instead, the Directive provides a definition of 'personal' data and stipulates the conditions under which such data may be processed. Thus, this research explores the meaning of the term 'personal' data by reviewing the cases of *Durant* v. *FSA*[2] and *CSA* v. *SIC*.[3] Also, the article assesses whether control over personal information protects privacy by drawing on interviews with privacy and data protection experts from a range of countries and disciplines. Furthermore, the views of potential data subjects are explored through a survey of bloggers, which reports their conceptions of the terms 'private' data. The article concludes that a review of data protection legislation is necessary, and that, in particular, the assumptions and concepts underpinning the term 'personal' and 'private' need to be revised.

Privacy in Directive 95/46/EC

The goal of privacy protection is expressly stated in the opening provisions EU Directive 95/46/EC, wherein Art. 1 states that the objective is:

> to protect the fundamental rights and freedoms of natural persons and in particular their right to *privacy*, with regard to the processing of personal data. (Emphasis added)

However, the term privacy is not defined in the Directive. Rather, the Directive seeks to achieve privacy protection through regulation of the processing of personal data. This is understandable because no adequate definition of privacy has ever been produced.[4]

Personal data defined

The Directive prohibits, subject to exhaustively listed exceptions, the collection and processing of personal data. In the DPD, personal data is defined in Art. 2 (a) as:

> Any information relating to an identified or identifiable natural person; an identifiable person is one who can be identified directly or indirectly, in particular by reference to an identification number or to one or more factors specific to his physical, psychological, mental, economic, cultural or social identity.

Whereas, personal data is defined in the Data Protection Act 1998, as:

> Data which relate to a living individual who can be identified:

(a) from those data, or
(b) from those data and other information which is in the possession of, or is likely to come into the possession of the data controller, and includes any expression of opinion about the individual and any indication of the intentions of the data controller or any other person in respect of the individual.

Korff[5] noted that the DPA 1998 makes a formal distinction between 'data' and 'information' but that in practice, it produced no material differences. The definitions in the Act and Directive are consistent in their use of the phrase 'relate to' but, under the Directive, consideration is first directed to whether the information relates to an identifiable individual and then whether it is processed. Whereas, the definition of personal data in the Act approaches the concept in the reverse order, as the Act focuses on the issue from a processing view first and then moves on to whether or not there is an identifiable individual. The Directive and Act also differ with respect to when an individual should be considered as 'identifiable'.

The term is wider under the DPA as it includes information that 'may' come into the possession of the controller. Korff argues that the phrase may mean that the definition of personal data in the Directive can be read as being 'relative', because potentially 'any data that can conceivably be linked to an individual (in whatever way, by whoever) [can] be regarded as personal'.[6] Booth et al.[7] observed that the way that the phrase 'relate to' is interpreted has major implications regarding what is or is not classed as personal data. If it is interpreted very narrowly, the term personal data could be restricted to data which is capable of identifying an individual, either by itself or in combination with other data. Identification, in this context, could be direct or indirect. In contradistinction, if the term 'relating to' is interpreted broadly it could conceivably include any data which may 'affect' the individual in some way, regardless of its capacity to identify. The consequences of a narrow interpretation of 'relating to' will be explored in an analysis of the Durant decision.

UK interpretation of 'personal' data

In the case of *Durant* v. *FSA*,[8] Mr Durant had lodged a complaint with the Financial Services Authority following a legal dispute with Barclays bank. The FSA dismissed his complaint. He then made a subject access request for information held manually and electronically by the FSA on his complaint. The FSA released the information held in computerised form, but refused to disclose the information held on manual files. Mr Durant applied to the Court under s 7(9) of the DPA 1998 for an order requiring the FSA to comply with the subject access request. The Court of Appeal was asked to decide: was the information held by the FSA relating to the investigation of Mr Durant's complaint 'personal' data under the Data Protection Act 1998? The definitional issue which arose concerned whether the data could be said to 'relate to' Mr Durant.[9]

Mr Auld LJ referred to Directive 95/46/EC and ruled that the statutory right of access under the DPA is designed to enable the data subject to:

> check whether the data controller's processing of it unlawfully infringes his privacy and, if so, to take such steps as the Act provides ... to protect it.[10]

From this the Court concluded that the relevant information is:

> information that affects [the data subject's] privacy, whether in his personal or family life, business or professional capacity.[11]

This interpretation of personal data means that not all identifying information will fall within the scope of 'personal' data. Rather, only information that is capable of adversely affecting the privacy of the data subject will be considered personal. In order to determine whether or not data 'relates to' the data subject, Auld LJ proposed two tests.The first test is:

> whether the information is *biographical* in a significant sense, that is, going beyond the recording of the putative data subject's involvement in a matter or an event that has no personal connotations, a life event in respect of which his privacy could not be said to be compromised.[12] (Emphasis added)

The second test is whether:

> the information has the putative *data subject as its focus* rather than some other person with whom he may have been involved or some transaction or event in which he may have

> figured or have had an interest, for example, . . . an investigation into the some other person's or body's conduct that he may have instigated.[13] (Emphasis added)

Buxton LJ agreed, stating that the potential effect of processing of particular data on an individual's privacy was the guiding principle. The Court also drew support for a narrow interpretation of the term personal data from the wording of the DPA 1998. Auld LJ asserted that the DPA's definition of personal data extends to expressions of opinion about an individual which would be otiose if the words 'relate to' were construed broadly. Thus, the Court of Appeal ruled that the information about Mr Durant's complaints to the FSA or about their investigation of his complaint were not 'personal data' as the data did not relate to Mr Durant in the requisite sense. Rather, the Court decided that the information sought by Mr Durant was information about his complaints, as opposed to data relating to him. Furthermore, the Court ruled that the mere fact that a document is retrievable by reference to the name of the data subject does not render the information personal data:

> Whether it does so in any particular instance depends on where it falls in a continuum of relevance or proximity to the data subject.[14]

Thus, simply because an individual's name appears on a document, the information contained in that document will not necessarily be personal data about the named individual. Rather, it is more likely that an individual's name will be 'personal data' where the name appears together with other information about the named individual such as address, telephone number[15] or information regarding his hobbies.[16]

This conception of the term personal data is very narrow. If this decision were to be followed, only information that is capable of adversely affecting the privacy of the data subject would be considered personal data. Subsequently the Art. 29 Working Group issued an opinion on the concept of personal data,[17] which contains a broader notion of personal data. Thereafter, the Office of the UK Information Commissioner issued a technical guidance note[18] to the effect that Durant is relevant to the question of whether data 'relates' to a living individual only in difficult cases where the information in question is not 'obviously about' someone. However, the ICO guidance note is not legally binding, as the Durant decision has not been overruled.

In the case of *CSA* v. *SIC*,[19] a researcher submitted a request under the Freedom of Information (Scotland) Act 2002 (or 'FOISA')[20] to the Common Services Agency (the 'CSA'),[21] for details of the recorded incidence of childhood leukaemia for certain years in a geographical area, broken down by census ward. The researcher wanted to explore a suspected risk to public health arising from the Ministry of Defence's operations, a decommissioned nuclear reactor and an operational nuclear processing facility. The CSA refused to disclose the information on the grounds that it was personal data, the disclosure of which would breach the data protection principles. On application to the Scottish Information Commissioner (the 'SIC'), the SIC ordered the CSA to disclose the information sought in an anonymised form using a technique called 'barnardisation' which perturbs the dataset in order to substantially reduce the risk that individual data subject could be identified from it. The case raised the importance of whether or not the barnardised information was 'personal data' within the meaning of the DPA 1998.

The Lords ruled that the barnardised data was information about the health of the children involved. It therefore obviously related to the children and there was therefore no need to turn to the Durant decision and its concepts of 'focus' and 'significant biographical data', to decide whether the definition of 'personal data' was satisfied.

The second issue which arose was whether any of the children could be identified from the barnardised information (either alone or taken together with other information in the possession, or likely to come into the possession, of the CSA). The Court unanimously ruled the fact that the CSA continued to hold 'other information' which would ultimately have allowed it to 'decode' the barnardised information to identify each of the children to whom it related, did not necessarily mean that the barnardised information was still personal data. However, several different rationales can be identified from the judgment.

Lord Hope took the view that data can be 'fully anonymised' in the hands of the data controller and thereby cease to be personal data, even where the data controller does have information which would theoretically allow it to unlock the identities of the subjects of that data, but did not explain exactly how, or, in what circumstances that anonymisation might be achieved. Lord Rodger thought that data would remain personal data in the hands of the data controller provided that the data controller could identify the subjects of that data using 'reasonable means'. However, the practical implications of that reasoning are not clear. In marked contrast, Baroness Hale focused instead on the proposed recipient of the data, and whether he or should could identify the subject(s) of that data from that data alone (given that he or she would not have access to any of the 'other information' in the hands of the disclosing data controller). This lack of unanimity appears to have arisen from the difficulty which their Lordships faced in reconciling the definition of 'personal data' in the DPA with the spirit of Directive 95/46/EC and in particular with Recital 26 of the Directive which states that 'the principles of protection shall not apply to data rendered anonymous in such a way that the data subject is no longer identifiable'. Indeed, Baroness Hale stated that '[while their Lordships would] all like the legal position to be that, if the risk of identification [of the children] can indeed be eliminated, the Agency is obliged to provide [the information requested]',[22] in line with the 'expectation in Recital 26', she had 'much more difficulty in spelling out [that conclusion] from the definition of "personal data" in section 1(1) of the Act'.[23] The foregoing analysis indicates that the attempt to protect privacy through regulation of processing of personal data is fraught with difficulties, due to the confusion surrounding the concept. The decision does not clarify how the 'identifiability' requirement should be interpreted and applied in future cases. Also, questions remain as to precisely what factors are to be taken into account in determining when data can be said to be 'fully anonymised' and as such, no longer personal data.

Relationship between 'personal' and 'private' data

Moreover, the absence of a concept of 'private' data in the Directive and DPA 1998 and the fact that privacy protection is to be achieved through the regulation of the conditions under which personal data may be processed, *prima facie* suggests that the terms 'personal' and 'private' are synonymous, or alternatively, that protection of personal data effectively protects privacy. Yet, there is a lack of research data the effectiveness of the model of privacy protection advocated in the Directive. This article seeks to remedy that deficiency by reporting the findings of interviews with privacy and data protection experts, and also the responses from a survey of bloggers.

Research method

To answer the questions posed, data was collected in two phases. First, semi-structured interviews[24] were conducted with forty privacy and data protection experts, namely: privacy commissioners, lawyers, corporate privacy officers, consultants, computer scientists and academics from sociology, politics, market research, statistics and law.[25] The second phase of the data collection process consisted of an online survey of bloggers from around the world.[26] Out of the total number (1314) of responses received, 1258 were selected for data analysis; the remainder of responses were incomplete and were disregarded. However, the resulting population of participants does not qualify as a random sample and, accordingly the results from this survey cannot be generalised to the entire blogging population.[27] Rather, the findings are representative of certain niches of the English-speaking blogging world.

Research findings

(1) Views of data protection and privacy experts

All respondents were familiar with the concept of personal data as they had knowledge of the EU Directive 95/46/EC or it had been implemented into their national legislation, but indicated difficulties in drawing the lines between 'personal' and 'not personal' data. Some discussed the fact that technological developments are causing difficulties, e.g. advances in genetics are leading to greater pressure to collect health data and, while this is often stored and processed in the form of 'coded' data, there is a lack of clarity whether such data should be considered personal data. Another example cited was transaction data/behavioural data on the internet, e.g. clickstream data can lead to a profile being created which may, or may not, be considered personal data. When asked whether the concepts of personal and private data are synonymous, a range of responses were recorded. They have been classified under four broad headings:

(i) *Private concept not legally recognised. Informally it is synonymous with personal data*

> I think in a legal sense – in a data protection sense, yes (the terms private and personal are synonymous). However, privacy protection and data protection are different, but in a colloquial sense they are synonymous. (Belgium)
>
> In our law the word 'private' isn't even used, so it doesn't have a legal meaning. The general population take them to mean the same thing. (Canada)

The experts drew a distinction between personal data that is protected in law and private data that is not legally recognised, but which in the mind of the general public, is a synonymous term. When asked to elaborate on the concept of private data, they stated:

(ii) *Private data is a subset of personal data that the individual wants to keep absolutely secret*

> Private data is the part of the personal data that the respondent does not want to make public. (Spain)

(iii) *Private data is a subset of personal data that the individual wants to control access to or reveal in limited circumstances*

> It is something not revealed to others, or only revealed to a select group. It is a concept close to confidentiality but without the legal connotations, e.g. disclosure to a family member/bank/personnel office e.g. my salary would be considered private. (New Zealand)
>
> Personal data is data relating to an individual . . . . Private data is something you want to keep to yourself or something that people need to seek your permission to give out. (Australia)

These responses imply that individuals will face choices regarding disclosure of information and that the individual providing the data should decide the nature and extent of disclosure. These responses reflect the informational control conception of privacy espoused by Westin, who defined privacy as the

> claim of individuals, groups, or institutions to determine for themselves when, how, and to what extent information about them is communicated to others.[28]

Similarly, in the German census case[29] the notion of 'informational self-determination' was advocated. The German Constitutional Court ruled that

> This basic right warrants in this respect the capacity of the individual to determine in principle the disclosure and use of his/her personal data. Limitations to this informational self-determination are allowed only in case of overriding public interest.[30]

However, while the experts identified private data as a subset of personal data that merits extra legal safeguards in order to protect privacy, they did not offer clearly delineated boundaries for this term, which could be of general application. Instead, the comments below illustrate that, in their experience, claims that information is 'private' arise on an *ex post facto* as opposed to *ab initio* basis.

(iv) *All personal data can be private, depending on contextual factors*

> They are not synonymous. Private, is an *ex post facto* term, used mainly to label those claims for non-disclosure that we've accepted on other contextual grounds. Whereas, the term personal, concerns information about which less contested claims are made, e.g. the personal fact that I'm bald and short-sighted is personal data but it is hardly a private fact. (UK)

> Personal data can become private. . . . Some pieces of data we don't want to go elsewhere are what we consider private – but it depends on the company, e.g. happy for A to know but not B to know. (UK)

> If data is generally personal, it may become private depending upon place, time and circumstances . . . in different circumstances people see the same data differently, therefore, it is very difficult to define this kind of data. For example, if we approach our bank manager for a loan then we will be willing to discuss our salary but, in other circumstances you won't tell someone your salary. (Finland)

The responses from the data protection and privacy experts embody the philosophical ideals of autonomy and dignity through 'informational self-determination'. The experts recognise that a data subject should have the right to a degree of control over information that identifies them or relates to them, since control over disclosure identifying information is necessary for the development of autonomous individuals. They further acknowledged that it is not possible to predict in advance what personal information will be claimed as private by a data subject, since such claims are usually made on an *ex post facto* basis, depending on contextual factors.

(2) Views of bloggers

In the survey, almost one-quarter (24.8%) of respondents said that they had posted personal information on their blog 'all the time'.[31] However, bloggers seem to reflect regularly on the content of posts when deciding whether or not to post personal information online. Most

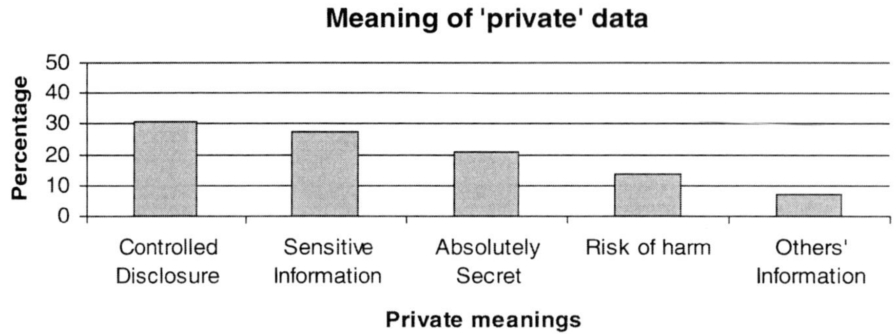

Figure 1. Graph illustrating meaning of 'private' data (source: Blog Survey 2006, $n = 101$).

respondents (65.6%) said they had considered some information 'too personal' or 'private' to write about on their blogs.[32] Respondents who stated that 'private' data did not mean the same as information which is 'too personal' (36.5%) to write about in their bogs were asked to explain what private information meant.

The largest percentage (30.7%) equated private with '*controlled disclosure*'. It is information which the individual wants to control access to, or disclose in limited circumstances. Below are some illustrative comments:

> Some information that I might want to discuss with only a select few .... Then I would make that entry a secure one, so that only those people belonging to that group could read and comment. It is not information that I consider public, but neither is it too personal to share.

> Private' information varies – there's stuff you'd share with friends, then only close friends, or nobody at all.

These responses mirror the responses of the experts and reflect the informational control conception of privacy, as they indicate that bloggers are aware that they constantly face choices about the nature and extent of information disclosures they make on their blog posts.

Private data was equated with either legally recognised or potential new categories of '*sensitive data*' by just over one-quarter (27.6%) of respondents, as illustrated by comments

> Private information is data about me as an individual such as biometrics, financial, political beliefs etc. Things which are too personal are to do with relationships with other people, etc.

> Private information, to me, describes data (financial information, phone number, etc.), whereas 'too personal' describes emotional information (how I felt about something my friend said last week).

These responses encapsulate the definition of privacy offered by Innes who stated that it is 'the state of possessing control over a realm of intimate decisions, which includes decisions about intimate access, intimate information and intimate actions'.[33] According to this view of privacy, not every disclosure of information about a person will amount to a loss of privacy; there will only be a loss when 'sensitive' or 'intimate' personal information is disclosed.[34] The responses indicate that bloggers are aware of such distinctions and actively limit disclosure of such information on their blogs.

It is information which the individual wants to keep '*absolutely secret*' was the meaning attributed to 'private' information by one fifth (20.8%) of respondents, as illustrated by comments:

> Private is information that I don't want to discuss with anyone.
>
> Information I would not trust other people with. It doesn't have to be 'personal' in the sense of intimate. It could be financial details, for instance.

A minority of bloggers (13.9%) equated 'private' data with the '*risk of harm*' arising from data uses:

> Private information, when it comes to an on-line environment, refers to any data which a third party having knowledge of could cause me actual harm, whether financial, or by restrictions of civil liberties. This therefore refers to my financial details, address and contact details (though to a lesser degree).
>
> Private information is information I don't want total strangers to have (e.g. home address), or that could be used to cause me a harm (monetary or otherwise, e.g. credit card and PIN numbers).

'*Information about others*' was the meaning attributed to private data by the lowest number of respondents (6.9%):

> This is information like the names of people I am writing about if they are not in the public arena or making them identifiable in some other way if I haven't asked.
>
> I don't write things that are too personal about my friends and family. I don't paraphrase them or post IM [Instant Messenger] conversations without running it by them first. I don't use other people's first names unless they have their own blog that they have given me permission to link to where they use their own first names.

These responses also indicate that bloggers are aware that the notion of privacy hinges on the concepts of control and consent regarding disclosure. Thus, each individual should decide for themselves the nature and extent of information which is disclosed. Also, there may be circumstances in which an individual does not have direct control over their personal information, but their privacy is nonetheless respected, e.g. a blogger does not post information about friends without express or implied consent. Indeed, the responses indicate that bloggers are aware that some information is shared in the context of a variety of relationships and that maintaining confidentiality and secrecy in respect of such information is a necessary requisite for healthy functioning relationships. These responses fall within the 'intimacy' conception of privacy espoused by Fried who, defined privacy as the 'control over knowledge about oneself'.[35] He based his definition of private information on intimate relationships by asserting that privacy should be valued because it is necessary to protect 'fundamental relations' of 'respect, love, friendship and trust'.[36]

Criticisms of approach in Directive 95/46/EC

The complexity surrounding the concepts of privacy, private and personal data is evidenced by the responses from experts and bloggers. The responses reveal that there are no consistently agreed meanings attached to any of the terms, and indeed, these terms are often used interchangeably and in an overlapping fashion. One reason for this is that the data protection principles are stated in broad, general terms, rather than in specific terms capable of precise legal delineation. However, Art. 22 of Directive 95/46/EC requires EU member states to provide a right to a judicial remedy for a breach of any of the rights guaranteed by the Directive. This means that UK Courts must necessarily confer some precise meaning on the general principles. The *Durant* decision illustrates the difficulties posed by this requirement. In that case the Court attempted to apply a purposive approach – asserting that because the purpose of the access right is to protect the privacy of the data subject, it is only information that is relevant to that purpose which can be subject to the access right. However, this approach is artificial and unhelpful, as it misconceives the role of personal data in determining the scope of privacy within data protection legislation. It also fails to recognise that data protection legislation serves other interests, e.g. data accuracy and data quality.

An alternative 'harm' based approach to privacy protection

The responses from the data protection and privacy experts embody the philosophical ideals of autonomy and dignity through 'informational self-determination'. The experts recognise that a data subject should have the right to a degree of control over information that identifies them or relates to them, since control over disclosure identifying information is necessary for the development of autonomous individuals. However, although control may in fact protect privacy in many circumstances, equating control with privacy is not always effective. For instance, individuals may be provided with control and subsequently decide to give up their privacy. Alternatively, once information is shared with another, e.g. in the course of a friendship or business transaction, an individual no longer has exclusive control over the disclosure of the information. Yet, the individual's privacy may (as a matter of good customer relations, or in the interests of sustaining a friendship), or may not, be protected in the absence of direct control over the information. Moreover, the responses by bloggers and experts acknowledge that it is not possible to predict in advance what personal information will be claimed as private by a data subject, since such claims are usually made on an *ex post facto* basis, depending on contextual factors. Accordingly, some of the experts were critical of the underlying approach of the Directive, claiming that this model of privacy protection which is based on collection limitation principles is outdated. They assert that it regulates at the wrong level and fails to balance competing interests properly. The Directive regulates the collection and processing of data, as opposed to regulating specific harmful uses of the data:

> There is a realisation that information is gathered, collected. It [data collection] is ubiquitous and [it is] impossible to chase wrongful collection; therefore, the focus has shifted towards a harm-based approach. (USA)

Accordingly, they contend the focus of regulatory activity should shift. It should centre on harm related to the misuse of personal information.

> Regulation of collection is a losing battle – instead ensure it is not used malevolently – information will always need to be collected, so you need to focus work on how it is used. (Australia)

Both bloggers and privacy experts recognised that personal data can be used or misused. The interchangeable and overlapping uses of the terms personal and private data by bloggers indicate that the focus of data protection legislation has erroneously been on the categorisation of data into personal or sensitive data, and the limitation of collection of such data, instead of the harm arising from data uses.

Conclusion

The foregoing analysis indicates that the decision in *Durant* v. *FSA* is at odds with the general principles of data protection. It attempts to limit the scope of personal data. While this approach is *prima facie* useful from privacy perspective, it fails to recognise that data protection legislation also serves other interests and that a broader interpretation of personal data is necessary to achieve these purposes. This failure undoubtedly reflects the notorious difficulties that have plagued attempts to give privacy a precise, analytically serviceable and universally accepted meaning. The failure to define 'private' data in data protection laws has a cost, in so far as it detracts from the capacity of those laws to offer prescriptive guidance. A further cost is that it perpetuates the vulnerability of the privacy concept to the criticisms that it is incapable of definition, has no independent, coherent meaning and should be subsumed by other concepts.

It is suggested that the time is ripe to review the provisions of the Directive, as the focus of the current legislative model is erroneously on the categorisation of data into personal and sensitive data, and the application of different levels of privacy protection to the different categories of data. The responses of the experts and blogggers indicate that, in the information society, the notion of privacy has changed. In this era, privacy is the absence of harmful use and application of information about an individual. As the UK Information Commissioner stated, the Directive 'out of date, bureaucratic and excessively prescriptive. It is showing its age and is failing to meet new challenges to privacy, such as . . . the huge growth in personal information online.' This paper echoes the Commissioner's call for a review of the legislation. In particular the interpretation of the concept of personal data should be reviewed. It is suggested that it should receive a 'broad' interpretation and the question of when information is 'identifiable' should be answered using a risk of re-identification approach. Also, the concepts of consent and control should be revisited. Further research is needed on the concept of consent. It may be worthwhile developing a test for implied consent in order to achieve a balance between privacy interests and the legitimate interests of others. Also, future legislation could focus on regulation of specific harmful uses of personal data and the availability of appropriate remedies.

Notes

1. Information Commissioner's Office (ICO), 'UK Privacy Watchdog Spearheads Debate on the Future of European Privacy Law', ICO, Wilmslow, Cheshire, 2008. Available at http://www.ico.gov.uk/upload/documents/pressreleases/2008/ico_leads_debate_070708.pdf (accessed February 25, 2009)
2. *Durant* v. *FSA* [2003] EWCA Crim 1746.
3. *CSA* v. *SIC* [2008] 1 WLR 1550, [2008] UKHL 47.
4. The issue has occupied the minds of scholars and jurists alike for decades. It is a common feature of any privacy analysis to start with a disclaimer about the inherent difficulty or impossibility of defining exactly what privacy is or, of dissecting the concept into its various components. While the definitions espoused by Judge Cooley, Samuel D. Warren and Louis D. Brandeis, Alan Westin have a certain intuitive appeal, none have become universally accepted.
5. D. Korff, 'Comparative Study of National Laws', EC Study on the Implementation of Data Protection Directive, 2002, http://ec.europa.eu/justice_home/fsj/privacy/docs/lawreport/consultation/univessex-comparativestudy_en.pdf
6. Ibid.

7. S. Booth, R. Jenkins, D. Moxon, N. Semmens, C. Spencer, M. Taylor and D. Townend, 'What are "Personal Data"? A Study Conducted for the UK Information Commissioner', 2004, http://www.ico.gov.uk/upload/documents/library/corporate/research_and_reports/final_report_21_06_04.pdf
8. *Durant* v. *FSA* [2003] EWCA Crim 1746.
9. Identifiabililty was not an issue because the information in the manual files essentially comprised letters of complaint written by Mr Durant and material generated in response to his complaint.
10. *Durant* v. *FSA* [2003] EWCA Crim 1746, [27].
11. Ibid., [28]
12. Ibid.
13. Ibid.
14. Ibid.
15. See European Court of Justice decision in *Bodil Lindqvist* v. *Kammaraklagaren* (2003) C-101/01, para. 27, as referred to in para. 28 of the Durant judgment.
16. See *Bodil Lindqvit* v *Kammaraklagaren* (2003) C-101/01, para 27, ECJ Judgment, http://eur-lex.europa.eu/LexuriServ.do?uri=CELEX:62001J0101:EN:HTML (accessed February 25, 2009).
17. Art. 29 Data Protection Working Party, 'Opinion 4/2007 on the Concept of Personal Data', 2007, http://ec.europa.eu/justice_home/fsj/privacy/docs/wpdocs/2007/wp136_en.pdf)
18. ICO, 'Data Protection Technical Guidance – Determining What is Personal', v1.0, 21 August 2007, http://www.ico.gov.uk/upload/documents/library/data_protection/detailed_specialist_guides/personal_data_flowchart_v1_with_preface001.pdf
19. *CSA* v. *SIC* [2008] 1 WLR 1550, [2008] UKHL 47.
20. The corresponding provisions of the Freedom of Information Act 2000 are in materially the same terms and the judgment is therefore of relevance throughout the UK.
21. A specialist health board in Scotland which collects statistical information from other health boards.
22. *CSA* v. *SIC* [2008] UKHL 47 [91].
23. Ibid., [92].
24. In the interviews semi-structured questions were used. The aim was to have a discussion with the respondent so that all the themes in the interview guide were covered. Some of the themes in the interview guide were too complex for a few of the participants. For instance, statistical methodologists were not comfortable when answering questions about the specific detail of the legislation in their country.
25. A respondent matrix was created using quota and snowball sampling. Snowballing is an effective technique for building up a reasonable sized sample, especially when used as part of a small-scale research project (M. Denscombe, *The Good Research Guide for Small Scale Social Research Projects* (Milton Keynes, UK: Open University Press, 1998).
26. The respondents were not randomly selected but were found through a variant of the snowball-sampling strategy. Announcements for the online survey were posted to mailing lists in three universities in the UK area as well as on a few high-traffic blogs. The viral nature of blogs meant that the links to the survey page quickly spread to many other blogs and YouTube.
27. It is the bloggers' subjective sense of privacy and liability that is revealed. This self-disclosure approach has three important implications: (1) There can be disparities between stated privacy attitudes and actions; (2) Participants' perceptions of their blogs might differ from those of outside observers and researchers; (3) accuracy is difficult to verify, e.g. no external validation was conducted.
28. A.F. Westin, *Privacy and Freedom* (New York: Atheneum Press, 1967), 7.
29. BVerfGe 65, 1. 'Volkszählungsurteil', 1983, http://www.datenschutz-berlin.de/gesetze/sonstige/volksz.htm
30. BVerfGE 65, 1. 'Volkszählung', 1983.
31. Only 2% of respondents said they had 'never' posted anything highly personal on their blogs.
32. It is important to note is that a consensus of definition does not exist regarding the terms private or personal. Indeed many used the terms interchangeably.
33. J.C. Innes, *Privacy, Intimacy, and Isolation* (New York: Oxford University Press, 1992), 140.
34. Ibid., 58.
35. C. Fried, 'Privacy', *Yale Law Journal* 77, no. 3 (1968): 483.
36. Ibid., 477.

Is it possible to define 'privacies' within the law? Reflections on the 'securitisation' debate and the interception of communications

Dan Ritchie

University of Cumbria, Carlisle, UK

This article originates from the author's ongoing research into whether common factors that define 'privacy' may be identified and theorised. The research focuses on privacy in relation to the interception of communications. The rapid development over the past three decades of new technologies of surveillance raises a number of important questions about what is perceived as the shifting relationship between the citizen and the state. With the Information Commissioner and others to claim that modern British society is a 'surveillance society', and that the privacy of citizens is being sacrificed on the altar of 'security'. However, it is not the case that a commonly accepted definition of privacy exists. The paper outlines the methodology to identify the contingents that are present in debates over privacy. First, it considers the difficulties in trying to define privacy since Warren and Brandeis', 'The Right to Privacy', essay famous, and argues that the term 'privacy' does not convey a purposeful meaning in terms of the interception of communications. Second, it identifies factors which allow privacy to be understood as a form of personal power. These factors point not only to whether information itself should be private to an individual but to the contexts in which the information is obtained. It is not information *per se* that is the key factor but its context. Finally, it is argued that it may be possible to isolate the factors that will produce a definition of privacy in relation to the interception of communications by looking at each set of circumstances and asking certain key questions.

Introduction

Many sites of social life are being reconfigured by new technologies of identification, monitoring, tracking, data analysis and control. We have seen the rapid growth of computerised databases for the purposes of gathering, storing and processing intelligence to be used by law-enforcement agencies, databases that have 'developed in the UK largely unnoticed' and without any significant public debate.[1] We have also witnessed the rapid development and use of biometric identification technologies in both daily life – witness the biometric fingerprinting of children in schools for example – and in the criminal justice system.[2] Add to these developments the blurring or decline of distinctions between external and internal security, policing and soldiering, and war and crime,[3] leading to the creation of international databases storing information on just about all aspects of individuals' movements, justified in the name of security, and it is argued that currently virtually all forms of policy are developed to facilitate governance through securitisation, a process in which 'an issue is framed as a security problem'.[4] Drawing so many individuals into the surveillance field is considered to be a dangerous reassertion and extension of state powers.[5] Bigo, for example, claims that 'Security is, conceptually, reduced to technologies of surveillance, extraction of information, coercion, acting against societal and state vulnerabilities, in brief to a kind of generalized "survival" against threats coming from different sectors, but security is disconnected from human, legal and social guarantees'.[6]

In these literatures there is an implicit assumption that these issues around surveillance and privacy are somehow new, or associated with new technologies. However, if we take an historical view, we see that privacy becomes a key feature of legal discourse in the eighteenth century Enlightenment, when debate about the proper relationship between the individual and the state forms a central problematic of secular philosophies. Since then, issues of privacy continue as a contentious dimension of the polity. From the 1990's to the time of writing, two developments have caused the notion of 'privacy' to become foregrounded in politics and law. First, the developments of 'new' communication technologies have expanded the possibilities for the surveillance of citizens. In particular, the widespread adoption of the Internet and mobile telephony among citizens has led to legislation to protect privacy, on the one hand (Data Protection Act), while on the other hand requiring providers of these services to store communications for scrutiny by law-enforcement and security services, thereby undermining the privacy of citizens. The development of biotechnology – storage of DNA in the police national database, for example – has added to unease about the power of the state in relation to citizen privacy. Second, following the attack on the USA on 11 September 2001, mechanisms of surveillance have increased leading to claims that 'securitisation' underpins and justifies a significant erosion of personal privacy.

All of these developments have led the UK Information Commissioner[7] and others to claim that modern British society is a 'surveillance society', an accusation investigated by the House of Commons Home Affairs Committee in 2007.[8]

One significant aspect of the issue, is the question of how to achieve a balance between the need of state organisations, such as law-enforcement and security services, to conduct effective investigations to fulfil their remit of protecting national security, on the one hand, and the interest of citizens to go about their day to day affairs without fear that their affairs are being unethically[9] monitored, on the other. In considering this question, the issue of privacy becomes of central importance. Privacy is arguably the factor that has defined pressure groups and legislation which reacts to technologies of surveillance and their implementations. The fundamental issue which strikes at the heart of debates regarding surveillance is a citizen's desire for privacy. In 2006, whilst conducting my doctoral research on the role of new technologies in the security vs freedom debate, with particular reference to the interception of communications, I was struck by the ubiquitousness of the term 'privacy', and the way it is invoked to criticise the use of technologies of surveillance. Yet, nowhere could I find any sustained discussion of the concept that provided focus on the interception of communications. So, I began to ask what exactly is privacy and exactly how does the desire for privacy shape legislation in the western world?

This paper sets out my exploration of these two questions. The discussion illustrates that the term 'privacy' is used in a variety of situations, each carrying different meanings. 'Privacy' is a word that, at times, is brandished all too freely. The overarching use of the word demonstrates the variety of situations where something personal to the citizen is perceived by them to have been violated. In contrast, my work investigates whether or not there is a definition of privacy that applies to surveillance in general, and whether such a definition can apply to the interception of communications as a mode of surveillance, or whether a more narrow definition is appropriate in this field for the purpose of theorising what privacy actually is in this context.

Privacy: just being left alone?

The *Oxford Dictionary of Law* merely defines privacy as 'the right to be left alone'.[10] This definition is invariably a product of the classical liberal ideal of a freedom from interference. Such definitions present the view that this is the dominant ideal to strive for when individuals wish to define their own sense of privacy, and leads to the consideration of only one ideological assumption of what privacy may be. However, when one turns to the legal and philosophical literature, there is little agreement on what defines privacy. Thus it is necessary to note at the outset that there is not one dominant ideal which is generally accepted. This was apparent when, in 1960, a publication by William Prosser sought to describe the new 'right to privacy' being upheld in the law of tort (informing debates concerning what privacy actually is, which have been ongoing in the USA for the last century). Prosser acknowledged that there was confusion and inconsistency in the development of the protection of privacy in the law, but found four different interests in privacy, which he described as 'four rather definite privacy rights'. These were:

1. Intrusion upon a person's seclusion or solitude, or into his private affairs.
2. Public disclosure of embarrassing private facts about an individual.
3. Publicity placing one in a false light in the public eye.
4. Appropriation of one's likeness for the advantage of another.[11]

As the time frame has evolved, so have the uses of the notion of privacy to create and enforce the rights of litigants. Privacy has been cited in a wide range of circumstances, from cases on abortion,[12] to the interception of communications,[13] with many other uses in between. Prosser himself drew on Warren and Brandeis's famous essay, 'The Right to Privacy' although Warren and Brandeis were concerned mainly with the second of the privacy rights identified by Prosser – public disclosure.[14] The difference between the two works was that Warren and Brandeis's essay advocated what should be protected, whereas Prosser was writing of the interpretation of the US courts of 4th Amendment cases over the 70 years since the appearance of the essay.

In considering the debates regarding surveillance, Prosser's first identification of privacy – intrusion upon a person's seclusion or solitude, or into their private affairs provides a useful starting point. First, we can consider overt surveillance (which is discussed here simply as a point of reference), ranging from CCTV on the streets and police video recording of demonstrations to the tracking of airline passengers. This is designed as a preventative method of policing. Second, there is covert surveillance, which encompasses the interception of communications, the use of intrusive listening devices (such as bugging equipment and long range microphones) and traffic analysis of data from electronic communications, which is designed to gather evidence and information. Here we can see the difficulty in defining a single notion of privacy which would be applicable to all forms of surveillance (in the first situation, the citizen is aware of the surveillance and in the second, they are not).

When considering surveillance, in order to go on to evaluate the concept of privacy more fully, an understanding needs to be established that privacy is not simply a place of tranquillity in which a persons' seclusion or solitude can be protected, expounded in the liberal view of privacy. This view may be described as a positive view of privacy. There is a sense of tranquillity and value in 'privacy', which grants its occupants a sphere to be free from the interference of others. Yet a utopian view discounts that 'privacy' also conveys a contrary, undesirable side. In the domestic sphere, by way of example, privacy can be used to hide events from others, such as repression and violence towards women and children in the home.[15] Privacy can therefore be employed as a smokescreen behind which unlawful and unethical activities can be hidden. In a wider context, it is all criminal and potentially threatening actions, for which the (largely employed) blanket notion, 'to be let alone', of 'privacy', is wholly inappropriate. If such a blanket notion of privacy was recognised by law, it would render detection of such activities almost impossible.

The implications of the communications market come into play here. In more practical terms, if we consider the millions of communications taking place daily, the work of Communications Service Providers (CSPs), would be made impossible in terms of guaranteeing quality of service to customers or fixing faults, if they could not conduct traffic analysis on their networks. Observation of traffic on data networks is vital for such work, yet reveals information of customers' behaviours. Indeed, such activities, which reveal information about consumer/customer habits, are rarely (if ever), viewed as an infringement of privacy. Customers derive benefits from CSPs monitoring traffic on their networks and recording data for itemised billing, although this data reveals much about customers' activities. For example, if we consider telephony we find that CSPs have records of which numbers were called, from where and for how long. In terms of internet usage, CSPs hold records of websites visited, the length of the visit, in addition to details of email correspondence. All these activities are accepted by telephone and internet users, suggesting that whether privacy is considered to be invaded can be considered more in terms of who takes the information and for what purpose, rather than the information itself.

The 'right to be let alone' *per se* simply does not apply in the majority of situations in the modern world of mass communications. Here I would suggest also that too much privacy in a social fabric can lead to dire consequences for the vulnerable. In addition to the example of domestic violence given above, one can think of elderly people who die in their home in the UK and their deaths go undetected until a complaint is made about the smell of rotting flesh emanating from their home, of children who die at the hands of their carers and of the phenomenon of elder abuse.[16] This list is not exhaustive, but the point is that a 'right to be left alone', taken literally, could have catastrophic consequences for the health, quality of life and possibly economies of any nation which followed such a principle in a literal sense. However, this notion of being left alone is deeply ingrained in our legal and political history, and I turn to this next.

Traditional legal philosophies of privacy

As shown in the previous section, the notion of privacy as a 'right to privacy' in a liberal *laissez faire* and a legal sense, can be understood traditionally to refer principally to the right not be intruded upon in one's home and not to have one's papers or affairs of business interfered with by those who have not been invited to do so.[17] This is a notion that developed during the latter part of the nineteenth and throughout the twentieth centuries when rapid social and technological changes prompted concerns with privacy and its infringement. It finds its roots in US legal philosophy, where systematic discussions of the notion of privacy often appear to begin with Warren and Brandeis' famous essay in which they claimed that:

> . . . the right to life has come to mean the right to enjoy life – the right to be let alone, the right to liberty secures the exercise of extensive civil privileges; and the term 'property' has grown to comprise every form of possession – intangible, as well as tangible.[18]

Their essay argued that the law as it stood (in the USA) and, in particular, the law of confidence, already protected the privacy of the individual. They focused largely, *inter alia*, on the press, and publicity brought about by new inventions, such as photography and newspapers, placing emphasis on the invasion of privacy brought about by the public dissemination of information relating to a person's private life. Warren and Brandeis argued that a number of existing cases could be used to support a free standing right to privacy in law. This would protect the extent to which a person's thoughts, sentiments and emotions could be shared with others.

The thrust of their argument was not that they were seeking to protect physical items or even intellectual property, but rather the 'inviolate personality'. This inviolate personality was linked with 'peace of mind', 'as a part of the more general right to the immunity of the person – the right to one's personality'.[19] Emphasis was placed by Warren and Brandeis that the privacy principle was present under the common law notion that 'one's home is one's castle', but that the advent of new technology made it important to recognise this protection under the defined notion of 'privacy'. This notion of privacy appears almost as a right of anonymity that is to be controlled by the individual.

However, of importance to us here, were the suggested limitations to privacy raised by Warren and Brandeis, which could be determined by way of analogy with the laws of slander and libel. The latter, for example, could not be used to prevent publication of information of public officials running for office. Hence a boundary was envisaged, in which the law could determine where a person could and could not have a 'right to privacy'. Thus the foundation was laid by Warren and Brandeis to the effect that privacy was control over the dissemination of information about oneself, albeit, limited in certain circumstances. Writing of emerging technologies in terms of media intrusion they stated:

> But where the value of the production is found not in the right to take the profits arising from publication, but in the peace of mind or the relief afforded by the ability to prevent any publication at all . . . .[20]

Thus the ability to prevent publication is control of the information and its flow by the individual. In such instances, privacy is argued to be a personal form of power of the citizen. This understanding is then taken up by theorists in the USA and becomes widespread throughout the twentieth century, so that Gross ventured that privacy is the 'condition under which there is control over acquaintance with one's personal affairs by one enjoying it'.[21] Here then privacy can also be interpreted as a freedom. It is the power of the holder that enables them to exercise their freedom. The power granted to the holder can operate in differing capacities, such as a power allowing for the freedom not to participate in the activities of others, or a freedom that can be lost, for example, when one is forced to listen to the sound from a busy road, or when one has to breathe polluted air.[22] The concept of privacy as freedom ventured by Den Haag[23] operates to demonstrate an element of what is invariably lost when this concept is considered in the context of directed and intrusive surveillance. In such instances the power to exercise a freedom not to participate is removed from the citizen if they wish to operate within the ordinary remit of society and the communications infrastructures of Western nations.

However, privacy as the intangible concept discussed above, at least in a historical sense, has been largely absent from the English common law. In terms of the legal implications of the technologies of surveillance, the concepts of privacy discussed so far are unsuitable to analyse what is lost or gained by individuals in terms of the interception of communications. The English legal view of privacy has traditionally attempted to rationalise whether the remedy exists only if it can in some way be viewed as a tangible commodity.

In English law, for privacy to be breached, there has historically been a requirement for some form of physical trespass.[24] Thus in legal terms, the intangible notion of privacy, that it could be linked with 'peace of mind', as advanced by Warren and Brandeis[25] cannot be purposeful for the seeking a definition of privacy if we were to consider English court interpretations alone. The common law doctrines advanced in cases such as *Entick* v. *Carrington* were based on the protection of property rights and did not evolve in the same manner in England as their codified equivalent did, into the 4th Amendment to the US Constitution. Yet, from the 1980s, arguments have been advanced in the English courts that there is a right to privacy[26] in its intangible sense. Although unsuccessful, the fact that such arguments have been entertained at all in English courts demonstrates that there is a notion that privacy is an intangible but, nevertheless, real commodity for the citizen.[27] The citizen who becomes aware that they have been the subject of intercepted communications still has a sense of violation in spite of the fact that no person physically entered their home, but what is it exactly that has been violated?

Informational privacy: dilemmas of democracy

To answer this question we need to revisit the concept of privacy as a power of the citizen, to consider how *informational privacy* as a power of the citizen becomes more apparent in postwar legal philosophy. Fried described privacy as 'the control we have about information about ourselves'.[28] Westin, who drew on a substantial body of work from anthropologists, sociologists and jurists, described the concept as 'the claim of individuals, groups, or institutions to determine for themselves when, how and to what extent information about themselves is communicated to others'.[29] This view of control of the flow of the information disseminated by others in a technologically evolving press was central to the theme of Warren and Brandeis's essay, as we have seen. In terms of technologies of surveillance it is axiomatic that such a claim or control is unlikely to be present for the subject of the surveillance. Control of information about oneself is invariably lost (or in fact, control was unlikely to ever have been present in the first place). Yet this in itself cannot always be said to be a violation of privacy, as surveillance takes many different forms. Can we say that a person walking down a street covered by closed circuit television (CCTV) has lost their privacy? The existence of CCTV may be interpreted as a threat towards those who do not wish to comply with such forms of surveillance. They have no say in how such information will be stored or communicated to others, but in one sense they have accepted the surveillance by not choosing to avoid that particular street.[30] That is, privacy relating to your movements can be maintained by walking down the unmonitored ally, where there is no protection (CCTV is envisaged here as protection from crime), or one can choose to walk down the well lit street with CCTV. The nature of the threat lies in the fact that areas in which CCTV is placed in operation usually see a dispersal of criminal activities to locations in which such surveillance is not yet present.[31]

This type of overt surveillance presents problems in establishing a definition of privacy that would be applicable to all forms of surveillance. First, there may be a perceived issue pertaining to personal safety relating to non-compliance. Second, there is the 'nothing to hide' syndrome. For example, in terms of CCTV, I venture that there may be an expectation on the citizen's behalf that unless they commit an offence, their presence will be ignored and the footage will be retained only with strict conditions affecting access.[32] In such an instance, the citizen has built in their own terms and conditions which avoid a loss of privacy (or that at least protects their 'inviolate personality' by allowing control over information relating to them). Yet what if the citizens' terms and conditions are not in place? Is consent then removed by the citizen, creating a perceived violation of privacy for that citizen?

There are further problems in considering consent as a protection from loss of privacy (if privacy is defined as 'the control we have about information about ourselves'). In terms of informational privacy, it must be considered that the citizen may have chosen to walk down a particular street precisely because it does have CCTV, for a feeling of personal safety. Hence, in the context of CCTV surveillance, we see privacy as a form of power or control over the information pertaining to the citizen, in that there may be a form or belief of control, regarding information about them. Hence a psychological condition pertaining to a feeling of control over privacy is created.

CCTV is however unique in that (in the main) it is an overt method of surveillance. Cameras are normally placed in locations where it is intended that they will be noticed. There are marked differences between overt surveillance (whose intended effect is deterrence as much as detection), as opposed to covert, intrusive and directed methods of surveillance, such the interception of communications.[33] In the covert arena of surveillance, can it be argued that a defined notion of privacy could encompass the power to control information about ourselves?

Miller's consideration of privacy conceptualises it as a form of power pertaining to information, describing it as 'the individual's ability to control the circulation of information relating to him'.[34] This definition provides a concept that cannot be said to be present in modes of surveillance. Once information is gathered and stored by a third party, control by the citizen is invariably lost. In terms of overt surveillance, it is arguably possible for the citizen to make contact with those who hold the information to seek clarification as to retention periods, storage arrangements; or even to make demands that the data is destroyed, (however futile these demands may prove to be). However, awareness of surveillance allows for a degree of empowerment (distinct from a power) over the information relating to the citizen. Although this empowerment may only be simply to ask questions to those who have surveyed them (and the answers may themselves make a citizen feel powerless) it can go further. Awareness allows for complaints to be made to politicians or the press. The highlighting of issues of public concern allows for debate in democratic societies, which in turn can have effects on the law.[35] Yet in terms of covert modes of surveillance, in the main, the citizen will be unaware that any information pertaining to them is in circulation or storage and, hence, there is no opportunity to attempt to gain control.

Contingents of privacy

What can we make of this so far? We have not yet arrived at a definition of privacy, but we can identify three main contingents. First, the contingent of a psychological state, in that when a person feels their privacy has been violated, they feel a form of psychological invasion or hurt. Second, that this psychological state is governed by the perception of the power to control what others may learn of the holder of the privacy and, third, that it encompasses the power to control the circulation of information that others have acquired. To develop further the definition of privacy, encompassing these three contingents, the following questions need to be addressed:

(1) In the circumstance considered, has the citizen lost or gained privacy?
(2) In the circumstance, should the citizen lose or gain privacy?
(3) Is the citizen aware in the circumstance that they have lost or gained privacy?
(4) Does the citizen approve of the loss or gain in privacy in the circumstance?

Question 4 holds the crux of the issue in terms of defining a personal feeling of privacy for the citizen. Individual approval or disapproval demonstrates the conceptual difficulties in reaching any definition of privacy. As Navarria states:

> Citizens are learning to comply with the requests and the soft-diktats of the new environment, and – in the name of protection or in search of a better quality of life – giving up their right to privacy by allowing government to collect and retain data about every aspect of their lives. From their experience as consumers, they regard this as perfectly normal. As subjects always connected to the system, they become permanently surveyable and controllable: indeed, they become data shared on a computer's database that is always easily accessible and retrievable. In the words of Gilles Deleuze, their position and identity is always known.[36]

Navarria helps to demonstrate that what may be considered as 'privacy' itself will always be dependent upon the circumstances of data collection. Consent is usually given in consumer situations, where a citizen signs up for a 'reward card' or equivalent and surrenders information on their personal habits or movements in return for goods or services. In a similar vein, this operates in democratic processes too. Citizens may elect governments and surrender privacy in return for security, yet in this scenario there is no opting out clause for those who do not wish to participate.

When considering the wide definitions of privacy in the literature, the authors who speak of privacy as a form of power over information allow for the above questions to be discussed separately. Hence, Miller and Fried's definitions allow consideration of the questions of whether the citizen has lost or gained control over information relating to them independently of the question of whether they should have lost such control. Both these questions are also independent of the questions of whether the citizen is aware of such a loss, or whether they approve or not. This allows for the consideration of claims to privacy against other important interests, such as those of national security and the prevention and detection of crime. Therefore it will be possible to distinguish the questions of whether a person has lost control, whether they should have lost control or whether they should have control in the given circumstances.

The single definitions of privacy discussed above do not allow for the same investigation. If privacy is simply described as a psychological state, it becomes impossible to discuss the four questions in the circumstances where a citizen has been subject to temporary communications intercepts without their knowledge. The psychological state of the citizen is unaffected by any loss of privacy in these circumstances. They are unaware of any surveillance, hence cannot suffer psychological harm. However, in terms of establishing a definition of privacy that is of relevance to the law in terms of the technologies of surveillance, an understanding of how privacy is interpreted by the law necessitates investigation of this concept.

Endnote

Readers of this paper will be aware (if not before, by now) that defining privacy is an area fraught with conceptual complexities and difficulties and that I have ventured down what some may describe as a 'fool's path'. Nevertheless, issues of privacy will not go away. Rather, as new technologies continue to emerge at a rapid rate (consider biometric identification systems based upon recognition of voice, body odour, ear shape, eye, keystroke pattern, brain pattern, face and veins, for example) debates over privacy will intensify. This paper is based on ongoing research and consequently a conclusion seems somewhat inappropriate. The continuation of the research will explore whether the factors addressed above have consistent threads in judicial dicta in case law regarding surveillance, in conjunction with further theorisations of privacy, in order to address the question of whether it really is possible to 'define privacies within the law'.

Notes

1. F. Donson, 'Data Bases – Positive Policing or Civil Liberties Nightmare?' in *Invading the Private. State Accountability and New Investigative Methods in Europe*, ed. S. Field and C. Pelner (Burlington, VT: Ashgate, 1998), 181.
2. M. Banner and J.E. Suk, 'Genomics in the UK: Mapping the Social Science Landscape', *Genomics, Society and Policy*, 2, no. 2 (2006): 1–27; Great Britain. Parliament (2007). Official Reports. Parliamentary Debates (Hansard) 23 July, http://www.parliament.the-stationery-office.com/pa/cm200607/cmhansrd/cm070723/debtext/70723-0018.htm (accessed January 12, 2008).
3. D. Bigo, 'Globalized (in)Security: The Field and the Ban-opticon', in *Illiberal Practices of Liberal Regimes: the (in)Security Games*, ed. D. Bigo and A. Tsoukala (Paris: l'Harmattan, 2006).
4. R. Higgott, 'US Foreign Policy and the "Securitization" of Economic Globalization', *International Politics*, 41 (2004): 148.
5. M.E. Beare, 'Fear-based Security: The Political Economy of "Threat"', Paper presented at the International Conference on 'Global Enforcement Regimes, Transnational Organized Crime, International Terrorism and Money Laundering',Transnational Institute (TNI), Amsterdam, 28–29 April 2005; Bigo, 'Globalized (in)Security'.
6. Bigo, 'Globalized (in)Security', 8.
7. Information Commissioner, Memorandum to the Education and Skills Select Committee Enquiry into 'Every Child Matters'. February 2005, ICO, Wilmslow, Cheshire. Available at http://www.informationcommissioner.gov.uk
8. House of Commons Home Affairs Committee, 'A Surveillance Society?', Fifth Report of Session 2007–2008, Volume I, HC 58-I, 19–21, 25–26, 32–38, *et passim*, 2008; Volume II, HC 58-II, Qs 6, 7, 15, 20, 24, 27, 31, *et passim*, 2008.
9. The term 'unethically' is used to surmise the situation of the state monitoring the communication of a citizens affairs' with disregard to a pressing need. Although not quite in line with George Orwell's *1984*, this situation is where communications may be monitored by state agencies regardless of whether suspicion of an offence exists.
10. E. Martin (ed.), *A Concise Dictionary of Law*, 2nd ed. (Oxford: Oxford University Press, 1991).
11. W.L. Prosser, 'Privacy', *California Law Review* 48 (1960): 383, 389.
12. *Roe* v. *Wade*, 401 U.S. 113 (1973).
13. *Malone* v. *Commissioner of Police of the Metropolis* [1979] 344 Ch.
14. S. Warren and L. Brandeis, 'The Right to Privacy', *Harvard Law Review* 4 (1890): 193. Available at http://www.abolish-alimony.org/content/privacy/Right-to-Privacy-Brandeis-Warren-1980.pdf (accessed February 24, 2009).
15. E. Pizzey, *Scream Quietly or the Neighbours Will Hear* (London: Penguin Books, 1983); C. MacKinnon, *Toward a Feminist Theory of the State* (Cambridge, MA: Harvard University Press, 1989).
16. L. Walker, 'Council Find Skeletal Remains in Flat', *Today's Chronical*, 13 July 2007. Available at http://icnewcastle.icnetwork.co.uk/chroniclelive/eveningchronicle/tm_headline=council-find-skeletal-remains-in-flat&method=full&objectid=19450306&siteid=50081-name_page.html (accessed July 19, 2007).

17. See, for example, *Entick* v. *Carrington* (1765) 19 ST 1030).
18. Warren and Brandeis, 'The Right to Privacy', 193.
19. Ibid., 200.
20. Ibid., 197.
21. Hyman Gross, 'Privacy and Autonomy', in *Nomos XIII: Privacy*, ed. J. Pennock and J. Chapman (New York: Atherton Press, 1971), 169.
22. E.V. den Haag, 'On Privacy', in *Nomos XIII: Privacy*, ed. J. Pennock and J. Chapman (New York: Atherton Press, 1971).
23. Ibid.
24. See for examples: *Entick* v. *Carrington*, *Howell's State Trials* 19 (1765): 1030; *Cooper* v. *Booth* (1785) 2 ESP 135; *Price* v. *Messenger* (1800) 2 Bos. & P. 158. For dishonest appropriation, see *Prince Albert* v. *Strange* (1848) 2 De G. & Sm. 652.
25. Warren and Brandeis, 'The Right to Privacy'.
26. In line with the views expressed by Warren and Brandeis, 'The Right to Privacy'.
27. *Malone* v. *Commissioner of Police of the Metropolis* [1979] 344 Ch at 369.
28. C. Fried, *An Anatomy of Values* (Cambridge, MA: Harvard University Press, 1970), 140.
29. A. Westin, *Privacy and Freedom* (New York: Atheneum, 1968), 7.
30. G. Marx, 'A Tack in the Shoe: Neutralizing and Resisting New Surveillance', *Journal of Social Issues* 59, no. 2 (2003): 369–390. Available at http://web.mit.edu/gtmarx/www/tack.html (accessed January 3, 2007)
31. P. Fussy, 'New Labour and New Surveillance: Theoretical and Political Ramifications of CCTV Implementation in the UK', *Surveillance and Society* 2, no. 2/3 (2004): 251–269. Available at http://www.surveillance-and-society.org/articles2(2)/newlabour.pdf (accessed February 7, 2007).
32. This is taken on assumptions of both respondents to questions regarding perceptions of surveillance and of the 50% public acceptance of an identity card scheme undertaken by ICM Research: ID Cards Survey Fieldwork: 8–9 November 2006. Available at http://www.icmresearch.co.uk/pdfs/2006_july_no2id_id_card_survey.pdf (accessed February 11, 2007).
33. B. Welsh and D. Farrington, 'Crime Prevention Effects of Closed Circuit Television: A Systematic Review', Home Office Research, Development and Statistics Directorate, 2002. Available at http://www.homeoffice.gov.uk/rds/pdfs2/hors252.pdf (accessed February 7, 2007).
34. A. Miller, *The Assault on Privacy* (Ann Arbor: University of Michigan Press, 1971), 25.
35. For example the governments changes to the 'Regulation of Investigatory Powers Bill' in the face of strong public criticism in 2002. Guardian Leader, *The Guardian*, 19 June 2002.
36. G. Navarria, 'E-government: who controls the controllers?', 2006, http://www.opendemocracy.net/media-edemocracy/egovernment_3254.jsp (accessed August 20, 2008).

Children's data protection vs marketing companies

Emmanuelle Bartoli

Cardiff Law School, UK

The opportunity that the Internet represents for children is undeniable. The increasing amount of children's personal data collected online raises an issue balance: how to protect children's privacy without impeding the development of children's online opportunities. Businesses collect children's personal data in order to profile and target them. Aware of the risks such practices represent for children's data protection, the US Congress has legislated the Child Online Privacy Protection Act (the so-called 'COPPA') which became effective in April 2000. In Europe, the collection and use of personal data is covered by the 1995/46 European Directive which has the fundamental aim of protecting individual privacy. The Directive does not, however, distinguish between data subjects who are adults and those who are children: it provides no specific protection for children's privacy.This paper considers the different approaches adopted in the USA and in Europe with regard to children's online data protection. In parallel, it appears that soft law is used as a new tool to regulate children's privacy. Particular attention will be paid to soft law adopted in the UK and in France.

Introduction

'Join now it's free', 'Don't have your account? Create one now!', 'Register now and get 100 extra points next time you play' – these phrases easily catch web users' eyes and enable many websites to collect customers' personal data. Children are very likely to have their personal data collected when surfing on websites, no matter whether those websites target them or not.

The presence of children online is increasing and children appear to be very skilful web users. The opportunity that the Internet represents for children is widely recognised. The European Union Commissioner responsible for Information Society and Media, Viviane Reding, very much aware of this phenomenon, has stated that although '[c]hildren have been very quick in making the most of online services such as social networking sites and mobile phones . . . many still underestimate the hidden risks of using these . . .'.[1]

One of these hidden risks may be the collection of personal data. Marketers use various methods to collect children's personal data. It goes from the promise to get access to free games to the possibility to earn virtual money which enables them to buy virtual clothes for their virtual pets! Collecting children's personal data may be a gold mine for online businesses who can profile children according to the details they provide with regard to their age, home town, gender, favourite cartoons, parents' occupation, etc. The information collected is used to target children with advertisements relevant to their interests, and to profile them as consumers.

Aware of the increasing risk of children's data being collected online and then used by e-businesses to target them, the American Congress has legislated to protect children's privacy online and adopted the Child Online Privacy Protection Act (the so-called 'COPPA'), which became effective in April 2000.[2]

In Europe, the collection and use of personal data is clearly framed by the 1995/46 European Directive[3] ('the Directive') which fundamental aim is to protect individual privacy. The Directive does not, however, distinguish between data subjects who are adults and those who are children: it provides no specific protection for children's privacy.

The question arises therefore as to know whether there is a need for specific 'hard' law legislation applicable to children's data protection in Europe.

This paper compares the COPPA provisions as applied to American businesses for the with the European policy as applied to children online data protection and considers the weakness and strength of each system. The place of children in the 'digital media culture'[4] needs to be first outlined.

Children and society

Children as marketing subjects

At the end of the nineteenth century, children became part of the merging culture of consumption. The child was considered as 'a symbol of consumer aspirations – a way of interesting parents in a product'.[5] Since the 1960s, the economic weight of children has increased.

Children are able to buy with the pocket money they receive and may as a result be qualified as consumers. In addition, children are often involved in the decisions their parents take when there are important things to buy. In consequence even general audience advertisements are likely to be meaningful to both parents and children.

The Children's Television Workshop in the USA constituted the first prime opportunity for marketers to start targeting children directly by TV advertisements. On the Internet, however, children can be targeted even more directly than on television. Marketers can advertise on websites targeting solely children and can send them e-mails directly on their own e-mail addresses. This way of marketing is all the more valuable since it is estimated that 93% of children aged 12–17 are online.[6] A study conducted in 2007 suggested that more than half of American children are expected to belong to a virtual world by 2011.[7] As a result of this growth many brands have invested in new child-friendly online services. In 2007 over £500 million has been invested in these new virtual worlds by venture capitalists.[8]

The commercial pressures resulting from these investments may lead online businesses to try to collect as much personal data as possible in order to target children with advertisements that match their profiles. It is little surprise, therefore that the Electronic Privacy Information Centre (EPIC) has spoken of 'phenomenal rate' of growth in the collection of data about children.

It is often argued that parents should play a greater role in the protection of children when surfing online and Michael Freeman has argued that 'children's privacy is largely controlled by parents'.[9] The generational digital divide between adults and children may however make this regulation problematic: it is, for instance, difficult to have parents managing their children's privacy when they are not themselves able to assess the risks encountered by their children when surfing on the Internet.

As a consequence of these difficulties it may well be argued that public bodies have a responsibility to intervene in order to develop (at the minimum) an awareness of the extent of the risks that the Internet poses for children's privacy, allied with proposals for appropriate safeguards.

The United Nations Convention on the Rights of the Child[10] ('the UN Convention') enshrines the principle that children are entitled to 'special protection'. Children are therefore considered as being entitled to rights different than those of adults.

Because children's decisions may be contrary to their own interests children's rights shall always be adopted in consideration of their 'best interests'.[11] Indeed, the child is not able to appreciate his or her own interests on his or her own and on top of that, it is not his or her interest at the present moment but at some later date, his or her interest as an adult at some undetermined future moment.[12] The fact that children are ready to give away their personal data in exchange for a present illustrates the fact that children tend to consider their immediate interest rather than their long term interest. Children are not mature enough to have the skills to defend themselves against the dangers that the Internet may present for privacy.

Aware of the increasing threat the Internet represents for children's personal data and of the need for children to benefit from specific protection, the US Congress began to consider the need for specific measures to protect them while online – whether learning or merely browsing, playing games, or participating in 'chat rooms'.

The US response to children's privacy concern

Aware of the fact that the presence of children online represents 'enormous opportunities for marketers to promote their products',[13] Congress noted the correlation between these opportunities and the ease with which marketers were able to collect a large amount of children's personal data.

Congress commissioned a survey of 212 sites that appeared to be directed at children under 16. The survey was specifically designed to assess the way data was obtained from children, i.e. whether parental consent was requested. The survey findings suggested that 89% of the websites studied collected personal information from children and of these only 12% notified parents of their information practices. In addition, it appeared that the majority of the websites disclosed information to third parties without obtaining prior parental approval.

The necessity for specific legislation regulating the collection of children's data online appeared obvious and in due COPPA was enacted by Congress on 21 October 1998 and became effective on 21 April 2000. In order to assess the effect that the implementation of COPPA had on practices relating to the collection, use and disclosure of information from children online, the behaviour of businesses and initiatives with regard to children's data collection, children's ability to obtain access to online information of their choice and the availability of websites directed at children, the Federal Trade Commission (FTC) organised a review of COPPA. The results were published in a report dated February 2007 ('the 2007 Report').[14]

The COPPA provisions: strengths and weaknesses

The provisions of COPPA are brief: the Act gives the FTC rule-making powers – aimed at prohibiting unfair and deceptive acts and practices in connection with the collection, use and disclosure of personal information from and about children online. The FTC published recommendations with regard to the implementation of the COPPA in November 1999.

The Act needs therefore to be read in conjunction with the rules and regulations that flesh it out.

COPPA applies to commercial websites and online services targeting children aged under 13 and to general websites that have actual knowledge that they may collect data from children aged under 13.

The relevance of the age limit may be put into question. How can websites know whether or not they are targeting children under the age of 13? The FTC has established criteria in order to determine whether a website targets children or not.

It advises that in order to foresee the 'overall character of a website' several issues shall be considered, including:

(1) the subject matter;
(2) the audio or visual content found on the site;
(3) the age of any models depicted on the site;
(4) the language used on the site;
(5) the presence of advertising on the site;
(6) other empirical evidence regarding the age of the actual or intended audience, such as whether the site uses animated characters or has other child-oriented features.

These criteria are considered to constitute effective and clear guidance for determining whether a website is directed at children. The FTC has decided that it was not necessary to further clarify the assessment criteria. However, it seems web actors are in favour of incorporating additional factors into those guidelines. One could for example think of including usability components that are used to attract and keep child readers' – particularly the colour and the interactivity of the website.

A further difficulty concerns the extent to which it is relevant to decide that an Act applies solely to children under 13. It may also be difficult to establish whether someone aged 15 is really more capable of deciding whether or not it is in his/her best interest to disclose personal data. 'Children's development [being] a process not a race',[15] makes it difficult to establish the precise age at which they can make an informed decision to provide businesses with their personal data and clearly a demarcation point at the 14th birthday is entirely arbitrary.

Websites not targeting children – the so-called general audience websites – having 'actual knowledge' that they are collecting personal data from a children also fall within the scope of COPPA. Many websites can easily fall into this category – for instance those collecting the date of birth of the users will have 'actual knowledge' of the fact that they are collecting data from children when web users will indicate they are under 18.

There is of course the problem of children who provide a false age. Technology does not exist to prevent children from visiting general audience websites. In fact, the 2007 Report reveals that an increasing number of general audience websites are calling for the provisions to be adapted to protect them from the increasing risk of children providing personal data to websites which are not directly targeting them. Indeed, general audiences' websites are not requested to obtain the verifiable parental consent. As a result they are not able to distinguish between web users who are adults and those who are children.

General audience websites reported that general sites have no way to know for certain the age of the people visiting their website. It appears that such websites would arguably need to obtain verifiable consent from or for all of its users to collect any personal information in order to comply with the proposed rules. Given that surveys proved that children tend to lie about their age in order to access general audience websites, it may be difficult to know for certain whether the web user who is logging on a given website is an adult whose collection of personal data is not subject to any restriction.

In consequence, in its 2007 Report the Commission proposed that websites should ask for age information in a manner that does not bias the answer, i.e. a website should not in general expressly state that children under the age of 13 are not permitted to access.

Operators to which the provisions apply are requested '(i) to provide notice on the website of what information is collected from children by the operator, how the operator uses such information, and the operator's disclosure practices for such information; and (ii) to obtain verifiable parental consent for the collection, use, or disclosure of personal information from children'.[16]

Website owners are required to state that children's personal data may be collected. Parents should in addition be informed of what the website owners intend to do with the information and whether or not they intend to disclose the children's personal information to third parties. For this purpose, website owners must display a 'clear and prominent' notice online of the site's information practices.

'Verifiable parental consent'[17] is one of the main contributions of the Act to the protection of children's privacy online. The problem, of course, is how to ensure that the consent provided is genuinely from a parent.

The two procedures proposed to establish the authenticity of the consent to the collection of the child personal data are: (1) the sending of an e-mail and (2) the provision of the parents' credit card details.

Children are however able to get this information quite easily. Technology as it stands does not yet provide an alternative verification process. Technology is in this context, therefore a significant limitation. The law itself is shaped by technology.

Websites owners are required to enable parents to review the data collected. The FTC requires that parents shall have the power to delete the data but not to alter it. Such a provision is aimed at protecting both children's right to privacy and autonomy. COPPA promotes the role of parents in preventing abusive data collection. However this may be in contradiction with the philosophy of the Internet where instant access is possible. Requiring parental consent before the collection of personal data (which may be needed to visit the website) may discourage children, such that they would abandon any visit to a websites that required such a data. This may have a direct effect on website audience and may result in economic losses to the website owners. Such a measure would have a preventive effect, i.e. websites may try to avoid proceeding to the collection of personal data. It appears that implementing the provisions relating to the deletion of children's data raises issues. Indeed there are numerous situations in which websites owner are ought to retain children's personal information. This is the case where relevant litigation is threatened or pending, where a law enforcement investigation is ongoing or where the information is necessary to detect or prevent unlawful activity. At present it appears that websites are complaining about having conflicting obligations. Therefore, there is a need to clarify for which purposes and to what extent should children's personal data be kept and not deleted.

The Act provides that websites must not condition children's access to certain games or parts of websites on the disclosure of personal data. This provision stems directly from research undertaken by the FTC in 1998 which revealed that many websites were requiring as a condition of gaining access to certain games or part of websites, the collection from the child of personal data. This provision is of particular importance because research indicates that children are willing to trade away personal information for speculative reasons – for instance in order to win a prize or to enter a contest. This suggests that many young people do not care about privacy.

In practice, it appears that web owners subject to COPPA have developed a number of innovative ways of offering interactive online experiences for children without collecting any personal information or collecting very little personal information, such as only an email address. This may be one of the explanations as to why businesses have not reported any excessive costs resulting from the implementation of COPPA.

Although it is often asserted that laws regulating the Internet may deter investors in online businesses, it results from the 2007 Report that broadly speaking the regulation imposed by COPPA does 'not appear to have adversely affected the number of websites directed to children',[18] and may conclude that children's online privacy is better protected since the adoption of the Act.

The assessment of the COPPA implementation showed that broadly speaking the COPPA provisions are being respected. Since the enactment of COPPA over ten enforcement actions have been taken by the FTC. While analysis of these cases is beyond the scope of this paper, it should be noted that the enforcement arm of COPPA is seen as crucial to its effectiveness and that companies found to be in breach of the COPPA regime have had very high civil penalties imposed and been required to delete all the information that they have collected in breach of COPPA.

The above review suggests that children's online privacy in the USA has been accorded a high standard of protection, albeit that there are some weaknesses. The question arises as to whether in Europe such a level of protection is available despite the fact that no equivalent 'hard' law has been adopted to protect children's online privacy.

The European privacy policy: no distinction between data subjects

The European Directive 95/46 on the 'Protection of Individuals with regard to the Processing of Personal Data' is the key piece of European legislation regulating the protection of personal data.[19] It has been widely (albeit recently) implemented by the member states.

The Directive requires that data is processed fairly and lawfully. This implies a high level of transparency in the process. Companies collecting and processing personal data must publish their data protection policy. Data must only be collected 'for specified, explicit and legitimate purposes'.[20] This requirement implies that before collecting personal data websites owners must clearly inform their users that data is being collected and must indicate the purpose of such collection. How, it might be asked, are children expected to understand the likely implications for them of providing their data? How can they judge whether the data collection process is in their best interests? To this extent the requirement to inform websites' users before collecting any personal data is not relevant as its stands if applied to children's personal data. It should at least be specified that web users are to inform their users in terms understandable by any class of age.

Article 6 of the Directive provides that data shall be kept up to date. Children's data may easily be outdated because their circumstances can change quite quickly and website owners could easily be found in breach of the Directive. To comply with such provisions, web owners targeting children will have to set up a process in order to make sure that the data collected and stored are up to date.

It results from Article 12 of the Directive that data subjects have a right of access to their data. In relation to children, the question is whether this access right is a right of the child or whether it is limited to the child's parents. In Europe, children have rights similar to adults. However, children are deprived of the right to exercise those rights. Parents have a right of access resulting from the fact that children cannot exercise their rights. It has to be noted that the result is roughly the same: parents have a right to control personal data that are collected from their children. This raises an issue that is beyond the scope of this paper but which still need to be taken into consideration: how to balance children's privacy and the needs for parents to control what their children do online.

The processing of personal data for the purposes of direct marketing is regulated by the Directive as well. Data subjects have the right to object on request 'to the processing of personal data which may be used for the purposes of "direct marketing"'. One of the aims of regulating children's data collection and use is to limit the amount of advertising mail (the so-called 'junk mail') children receive. Provisions of the Directive Article 14(b) does not provide – as it stands – an efficient protection for children against such junk mail. Indeed, how can one expect to have a child mature enough to address a request asking not to have his/her personal data used to receive unsolicited mail.

It results from the above that the Directives set up a high level of data protection for individuals. However, its provisions would need to take into consideration the difference of maturity between the individuals. European legislators, information commissioners and parents associations have called for the adoption of specific legislation top protect children's online privacy.

The sole significant European intiative to date results from the document issued by Article 29 Working Party on 18 February 2008.[21] This document provides a definition of children that appears to be slightly different from the one adopted by COPPA. In particular, Article 29 Working Party stressed that in most legal frameworks dealing with children's rights, a child is defined as someone under the age of consent (i.e. in the UK, 18). It refers to the specificity of children and their needs that 'education and responsibility are crucial tools in the protection of children's data'.

The Article 29 Working Party suggests therefore that when a child becomes sufficiently mature to make his or her own decisions, then website owners processing data must ensure that they have the child's permission as well as the child's representative's permission. The point is to determine how to assess a child's maturity.

Despite the lack of intervention from the EU, it should be noted that at national level, several specific Codes of Conduct and Recommendations have been adopted. The following section considers the soft law developments that have occurred in this respect in the UK and in France. Differences of implementation of the Directive in both countries could be studied. However, this would be beyond the scope of our paper.

The United Kingdom

Although the UK implemented the Directive 95/46 in 1998, it first enacted data protection legislation in 1984 following principles detailed in Guidelines issued by the OECD in 1980.

The influence of the UK during the drafting of the Directive was relatively limited because privacy was not considered to be a UK Governmental priority at that time. The implementation of the Directive became, however, a priority for the New Labour Government in 1997. The Directive has been strictly implemented into the British legal system. As yet no specific provisions relating to children's privacy have been adopted.

This does not however mean that British society is blind to the increasing risks that the Internet represents for children's data protection. 'Soft' law has, in this respect, overtaken the lack of intervention from the legislator.

The Direct Marketing Association's Code of Practice for Commercial Communications to Children Online[22] provides specific provisions relating to children's online privacy relating to children under the age of 14. In the same way as COPPA, the Code of Practice requires a verifiable parental consent before any children's personal data is collected and/or disclosed to third parties. Article 5.3 of the said Code of Practice provides that 'websites that are directed to children and that collect personal data from children must require a child to give their age before any other personal information is requested'. The efficiency of such measure may be limited given that children tend to give false ages in order to have access to websites that are not necessarily targeting them. The implemetation of such a provision would be efficient solely if additional provision were drawing up clear way for the age to be verified.

The Code requires that a notice is clearly displayed as to the rights of the data subjects, i.e. the child under 14. The privacy policy applicable to websites must be put in a notice understandable by a wide audience, including by children. Any websites, whether targeting children or not, are responsible for ensuring that they do not collect children's data. If they are aware that they are collecting such data they must comply with the provisions prescribed by the Code. This is the reason why websites must request the age of the web user before collecting any data.

The Model of Good Practices[23] encourages Internet service providers to limit the amount of children's personal information made available to other users. Providers of such services are also asked to offer information and advice in the form of clear security messages, and to warn children not to disclose contact details such as their phone numbers and home addresses.

Codes of practices constitute soft law regulations which are known for their greater flexibility as opposed to hard law legislation. Soft law being adopted by businesses actors such codes clearly demonstrates the concern of web actors with regard to the protection of children's privacy.

In spring 2008, the British Prime Minister called for a review on the general issue of children and the Internet, coinciding with the publication of a Government sponsored independent report on the subject, the much publicised Byron Review.[24] It is a pity that the report only refers briefly to the risks marketing profiling can represent for children's privacy. It is only reported that there is evidence that 'advertising is perceived by youngsters ... as an invasion of privacy and [that], according to one study, 95% of teenagers in the UK are concerned that personal information is being passed onto advertisers or other websites'.[25]

The report's author, Tanya Byron, emphasised the actually sensitive nature of children's privacy and their difficulty 'evaluating both the content and source of information while their brains are still developing the appropriate skills' and she concluded that it was 'clear that this kind of contact presents a potential risk to children'.[26] She advises that 'All sites signing up to a code for social networking providers should be required to set the privacy settings for under 18 users to the highest level by default. They might also be required to sign-up to a principle that privacy settings should reduce risk of under 18 users being contacted by strangers.'

One can deplore the fact that this report does not provide any clear recommendation as to how to prevent children's privacy from being infringed. It clearly calls for self regulation by industry but does not provide any clear guidelines.

France

In France, the Act '*Informatique et Libertés*', i.e. 'Computers, Files and Liberties' enacted on 6 January 1978 is the centrepiece of the French regulatory system with regard to data protection. This Act sets up the main rights and duties relating to processing of data protection without distinguishing between data subjects. Although France took its time to implement EU Directive 1995/46 into French law no specific provisions relating to children's privacy have been introduced.

However, the French Information Commissioner (the CNIL) has been actively involved in children's data protection issues for over 25 years. In 1983, for instance, the commision received a complaint from parents, concerned about the collection by a college of its pupils' personal data through the use of a questionnaire. CNIL held that personal data of this nature could not be collected without prior parental consent.

Subsequently, in 1985, the CNIL adopted a recommendation concerning the collection of children's data in schools and its position has been constant since then: parental consent should be obtained prior to the collection of children's personal data.

In 2001, the CNIL issued a report entitled 'Internet and the collection of children's personal data' ('the 2001 Report').[27] The 2001 Report stated that the collection from children of information relating to their circle of friends, as to their lifestyle and as to the socio-professional position of their parents was unconscionable and unfair. In France it is additionally a well-established principle that the collection of data relating to racial origin, political affiliation and religious views is prohibited without explicit parental consent.

In addition the 2001 Report prohibited the making of access to on-line games conditional on the communication of personal data. This recommendation is similar to that contained in COPPA. It results from the above that the recommendations enclosed in this 2001 Report are very similar to those contained in the COPPA.

However, while COPPA prohibits any kind of collection of children's personal data without parental prior consent, the 2001 Report concludes that website owners may collect, without prior parental consent, the e-mail address as well as the age of the children using their site for the sole purpose of sending a newsletter. Such recommendation seems to blur the rules concerning websites targeting children in Europe: indeed, the notion of 'what is a newsletter' could be the subject of a lengthy doctrinal discussion and clearly it may sometimes be difficult to decide on what constitutes the boundary between a newsletter and an advertisement.

There is however much to recommend the initiative of the French Information Commissioner – and the information programme that his Commission has developed, with web pages dedicated to children in order to explain to them how best to protect their privacy online. The French initiative therefore suggests there is much to be gained from educating both parents and children rather than by adopting specific rules which may impede the development of e-commerce without having any positive benefits for children.

Conclusion

On each side of the Atlantic, public authorities and web actors are aware of the risks that the Internet may pose for children's privacy: the US and European response to the problem is however markedly different. The US chose a legislative route that strictly limited the freedom of marketers' to collect children's personal data, and it did so at an early date – 10 years ago. Europe however has only shown concern about this issue recently. The COPPA provisions enable parents to control their children's personal data flow *a priori*. In Europe, the lack of specific legislation means that children have the same protection as their parents. However, children can only access their rights through their parents.

Once on the Internet children, in general, are left alone and in practice, their parents rarely check whether or not websites collecting data respect the European Directive on Data Protection. In Europe, the sole way parents can control the collection of data from their children is by exercising their children's rights to be informed. The control is therefore *a posteriori*. This represents a major weakness, because it is difficult to see how parents can in general know which websites their children have visited and, even if this is known it is difficult to see how in practice they could then request each website to provide them with the list of the personal data they have collected from their children.

In contrast, it is still too recent to assess the efficiency of the Codes of Practices and the Recommendations issued in Europe and as to how they compare to the COPPA regulatory regime.

In either case, however, it seems that both parents' and children's education will play a major role in the success of any children's data protection policy.

Notes

1. European Commission, IP/08/207, 'Let's listen to children: they know how to make the Internet a safer place!', Press release, Brussels, 12 February 2008.
2. Children's Online Privacy Protection Act of 1998, US Federal Law, 15 USC §6501–6506.
3. Directive 1995/46/EC on the protection of the individual with regard to the processing of personal data and on the free movement of such data, '(10) Whereas the object of the national laws on the processing of personal data is to protect fundamental rights and freedoms, notably the right to privacy, which is recognized both in Article 8 of the European Convention for the Protection of Human Rights and Fundamental Freedoms and in the general principles of Community law; whereas, for that reason, the approximation of those laws must not result in any lessening of the protection they afford but must, on the contrary, seek to ensure a high level of protection in the Community'.
4. Kathryn C. Montgomery, 'Children in the Digital Age', *The American Prospect*, no. 27 (July–August 1996): 69.
5. Stephen Kline, *Out of the Garden: Toys, TV and Children's Culture in the Age of Marketing* (London: Verso, 1993), 163.
6. Alexandra Rankin Macgill, 'Parent and Teenager Internet Use', *Pew Internet & American Life Project*, 24 October 2007, http://www.pewinternet.org/pdfs/PIP_Teen_Parents_data_memo_Oct2007.pdf (accessed July 2008).
7. Bobbie Johnson, 'Online Marketers Aim for the Kids', *The Guardian*, 17 October 2007, Technology, http://www.guardian.co.uk/technology/2007/oct/17/advertising (accessed July 2008).
8. Ibid.
9. Michael Freeman, 'The Convention: An English Perspective', in *Children's Rights – A Comparative Perspective*, ed. Michael Freeman (Brookfield: Dartmouth, 1996), 103.
10. 'Convention on the Rights of the Child', United Nations, Adopted and opened for signature, ratification and accession by General Assembly Resolution 44/25 of 20 November 1989.
11. Ibid., S.3.1: 'In all actions concerning children, whether undertaken by public or private social welfare institutions, courts of law, administrative authorities or legislative bodies, the best interests of the child shall be a primary consideration.'
12. Jean Carbonnier, *Droit civil – Tome 2, La Famille, Les Incapacités* (Paris: PUF coll. Thémis, 2004), 370.
13. Federal Trade Commission, 'Privacy: A Report to Congress', June 1998, www.ftc.gov/reports/privacy3/priv-23a.pdf (accessed July 2008).
14. Federal trade Commission, 'Implementing the Children's Online Privacy Protection Act – A Report to Congress', February 2007, http://www.ftc.gov/reports/coppa/07COPPA_Report_to_Congress.pdf (accessed July 2008).
15. Penelope Leach, *Children First – What Society Must Do – And is Not Doing for Children Today* (London: Penguin Books, 1995), 205.
16. Children's Online Privacy Protection Act of 1998, Section 1303 (b) (I) (A).
17. Ibid., (ii).
18. Ibid.
19. Ibid., 3
20. Ibid., 3.

21. Article 29, Data Protection Working Party, 'Working Document 1/2008 on the Protection of Children's Personal Data (General Guidelines and the Special Case of Schools)', 18 February 2008.
22. The Direct Marketing Association, 'The DMA Code of Practice for Commercial Communications to Children Online', http://www.myschoollunch.co.uk/Telford/files/general/DMA_Code.pdf (accessed July 2008).
23. Information Commissioner's Office, 'Good Practice Note – Collecting Personal Information using Websites', http://www.ico.gov.uk/upload/documents/library/data_protection/practical_application/collecting_personal_information_from_websites_v1.0.pdf (accessed July 2008).
24. Tanya Byron, 'Safer Children in a Digital World – The Report of the Byron Review', Department for Children, Schools and Families, and the Department for Culture, Media and Sport, 27 March 2008. http:www.dcsf.gov.uk/byronreview/pdfs/Final%20Report%20Bookmarked.pdf (accessed November, 1998).
25. Ibid., 58.
26. Ibid.
27. Commission Nationale Informatique et Libertés, 'Internet et la collecte des données personnelles auprès des mineurs', 12 June 2001.

The UK 2007–2008 data protection fiasco: Moving on from bad policy and bad law?

Joseph A. Cannataci[a] and Jeanne Pia Mifsud Bonnici[b]

[a]*Centre for Law, Information & Converging Technologies, University of Central Lancashire, Preston, UK;* [b]*Institute for Information Law, University of Amsterdam, The Netherlands*

A number of commentators were not surprised when the news broke in November 2007 that the personal data of 25 million UK citizens had been lost. This is because Information and Data Protection Commissioners around Europe had been meeting and comparing notes every year for a quarter of a century, during which period the lack of privacy culture in both public and private sector organisations had long been noted. This lack of privacy culture is exacerbated by data protection laws often setting up relatively toothless watchdogs. The UK was a classic example of the minimalist approach to data protection with the Commissioner being required to give prior notice of inspections. The UK Commissioner had long lamented that his organisation simply did not have the teeth to carry out inspections without warning. Following the November fiasco, the UK Commissioner received a commitment from Government that his powers would be increased but is this enough? This paper explores the limitations of law in such circumstances and especially how, even if the law is adequate, policy priorities or mistakes may be such so as to deny a data protection authority effective teeth through more bad law as well as inadequate funding for resources.

'Less is more' (Ludwig Mies Van der Rohe);

'The reports that have been published today show deplorable failures at both HMRC and MoD... Whilst these breaches have been highly publicised and involve big numbers, sadly they are not isolated cases' (Richard Thomas).

Any IT lawyers making the pilgrimage to Brno for an annual rendezvous with the Cyberspace conference[1] would do well to take a couple of hours off and make their way up the hill to the villa that Mies Van der Rohe designed for Fritz Tugendhat, built in 1930. There, a year after completion of his (now-reconstructed) German pavilion in Barcelona, 'Mies' was giving subtle expression to minimalist design in architecture. As you stand in the lounge looking out of the glass wall across the city you may also reflect on how popular 'minimalism' was becoming in the late twenties: while in architecture it had also found expression amongst other instances in Le Corbusier's *Villa Savoye* of 1929, in art the term was 'first used by David Burlyuk in the catalogue introduction for an exhibition of John Graham's paintings at the Dudensing Gallery in New York in

1929'[2] while in literature, just 2 years previously in 1927, *Hills like White Elephants* had seen its first publication in the collection of short stories, *Men without Women*, ushering in 40 years of Ernest Hemingway's literary mastery (and a whole new fashion) of doing 'more with less'.

If minimalism sometimes gives pleasure in art, architecture and literature, its transition to law-making is often less successful. For 'minimalist' in law can often be a euphemism for 'doing as little as we can get away with'. This paper does not afford us the space to indulge in a comparative analysis of minimalistic approaches to law but minimalism does serve as the starting point for our story. For in the late nineties there swept through some European data protection circles a 'minimalist wind'. Following the controversial birth of EU Directive 46/95 a handful of countries, whether established EU member states such as Sweden and the UK or aspiring 'accession countries' such as Malta, adopted a minimalist policy in their approach to data protection legislation. For our purposes here this minimalist policy will be defined as being 'the minimum possible for us to be said to comply with EU 46/95'. Unlike countries which took a tougher legislative stance (such as Italy and Greece) or the accession states in Central and Eastern Europe, some states which had had the good fortune of never suffering 50 years of communist surveillance and manipulation of information adopted a more 'relaxed' approach to data protection. Barely 10 years later, the first of these legislative chickens has come home to roost: 2007–2008 must surely win the accolade of *annus horribilis* for data protection in Britain. Before embarking on a closer examination of the events under survey, it is worth reflecting on some of the hallmarks of bad policy.

Policy 1 – toothless at law

The advocates of the 'minimalist' policy in the UK, presumably to avoid too much displeasure within industry or Whitehall, left the UK's Data Protection Commissioner virtually toothless and very much a 'minor office'. As will be explored in greater detail later, under UK law, until very recently, there was little in the form of real enforcement powers or deterrent.[3] Unlike many of his continental counter-parts, as a matter of UK government policy the Data Protection Commissioner was effectively barred from spot-checks of either the public or the private sectors. His officers could only inspect premises and records after giving advance warning and with the agreement of the civil servants or companies concerned.

Policy 2 – not important enough, so no direct funding by Parliament

It is ironic, and to an extent surprising, that the new incoming Labour administration of 1997 did not build upon its human rights credentials and extend policy priority to data protection. Whereas the new Labour Government did fulfil its electoral promise and bring about the enactment of the long overdue Human Rights Act, it failed to do the logical thing and treat data protection as being a rightful heir of the same standing. Thus, since the office of data protection was not considered to be important enough, the new Data Protection Act 1998 did not make the Office of Data Protection Commissioner one directly funded by Parliament. Missing the bus in 1998 was followed by another missed opportunity in 2000: when Freedom of Information (FoI) was added to the Data Protection Commission's duties under the 2000 FoI act, the Information Commissioner as he was now re-styled, remained (in relative terms) a second-class 'authority'. Whether this was the result of failure by their political masters to realise the true import of what was going on, or the persuasive powers of certain Whitehall mandarins in retaining control over administrative turf is something which is part of a history yet to be written but the result remained one which did not escape the notice of the UK Parliament's Constitutional Affairs Select Committee (CASC). The latter in 2007 found that:

> In our last Report on this subject we concluded that the relationship between the DCA [Department for Constitutional Affairs] and the ICO [Information Commissioner's Office] was not working as effectively as it might. We have not seen any improvement. We repeat our recommendation made in that Report that the Information Commissioner should become directly responsible to, and funded by Parliament.[4]

The incumbent Labour administration replied without justifying its position:

> The Government remains of the position that the present arrangements regarding the Information Commissioner are appropriate. They provide for independent decision making by the Commissioner while permitting proper scrutiny of resources.[5]

Policy 3 – not a priority area, so not enough funds

Having failed to endow the ICO with sufficient powers at law, government policy also left the ICO toothless in a more subtle but even more effective way: data protection was nowhere given priority as a matter of policy and thus insufficient resources were allocated for the ICO's office. Unlike education or the NHS, data protection was not a vote-winning priority and UK Government policy was clear if not overtly declared, i.e., to spend as little as possible on such matters. As late as December 2007 the Information Commissioner was lamenting that:

> ...his budget was insufficient and his powers too weak. The ICO total budget is £10 m compared to £890 m for Health and Safety or £143 m for the Food Standards agency. The £10 m comes from registration fees from data controllers – those deemed by the law to be liable not from the government.[6]

Whereas other 'authorities' are often directly accountable to Parliament and receive considerably larger allocations of public funding, the CASC in 2007 found that:

> We are not convinced that the funding of the ICO is sufficient to enable it to deliver an effective complaints resolution service. We question whether it is appropriate for the Ministry of Justice to set the funding levels for the independent regulator and thereby directly influence its capacity to investigate complaints. With regard to the proposed new charging regime, the cost–benefit analysis suggests that no significant additional resources would be provided to the ICO to enable it to manage the additional workload predicted in the Frontier Economics review. This suggests to us that the Government would be content to accept the consequentially slower complaints resolution process.[7]

In response to such criticism, just 1 month before the largest of the year's scandals broke in November 2007, the Government's policy of 'doing more with less' remained consistent, if not an altogether comprehensive reply to the CASC:

> The Ministry of Justice holds regular discussions with the Information Commissioner and the funding of the ICO is constantly under review. The Commissioner has made great improvements to the way his office operates and has received additional funding for the past 2

years. Along with all public authorities he must continue to deliver service improvements within his existing funding.

As the Government has decided not to proceed with changes to the fees regulations, there will be no additional workload for the ICO.[8]

Comparative positions at law in France, Italy, Spain, and Ireland

It is logical, indeed unquestionable, that if the UK public and private sectors lived within an enforcement regime where they could be raided and inspected by a Data Protection Authority without notice and if found in default they would risk a stiff penalty, then most controllers of personal data would be much more careful about the way they handled and stored such data. That this is not yet the situation in late 2008/early 2009 can only be the fault of the minimalist approach that the UK has taken to such matters in the past as a matter of policy. While this situation is set to be remedied by the amended Coroners and Justice Bill 2009 (see 'Epilogue?' in the final section of this paper) it has taken a long campaign by the ICO to make the powers-that-be see sense.

In a nutshell, at Christmas 2007,[9] the UK's Information Commissioner publicly stated that he wanted to receive that which he did not, as yet, have:

- 'a power for the Information Commissioner to inspect personal data and the circumstances surrounding its processing in order to assess whether or not any processing of the data is carried out in compliance with the [Data Protection] Act'.
- 'a power for the Information Commissioner to require a data controller to provide him with a report by a skilled person'.
- 'enhanced enforcement powers to enable the Information Commissioner to bring seriously unlawful processing to an immediate halt, to place formal undertakings on a statutory basis and to enable the Information Commissioner to take enforcement action to prevent breaches of the Act that are likely to occur'
- 'information notices that can be served on any person rather than just a data controller'.
- 'a penalty for knowingly or recklessly failing to comply with the data protection principles so as to create a substantial risk that damage or distress will be caused to any person'.[10]

In seeking these considerably increased powers, the ICO has reasonably invoked the following examples of powers that some of his European counterparts have enjoyed for years.[11]

Italy

The powers of Audit/Inspection of the Italian Data Protection Authority (DPA) arise from the Law on the protection of individuals and other subjects with regard to the processing of Personal Data Act – replaced by the Consolidation Act regarding the processing of personal data 8 May 1997/1 Jan 2004

- The DPA (in Italian 'Garante') targets organisations or sectors based on intelligence from complaints or by acting on their own initiative and according to their priorities.

If these paper inspections do not yield enough information, they can carry out on the spot inspections.

- These inspections can be 'dawn raids', but usually they give advance notice of an inspection, but do not say what they are looking for.
- They have a Memorandum of Understanding (MoU) with the financial police who can carry out inspections across Italy based on established questions and following the Garante's instructions. There is a special squad to deal with data protection cases and they have had training from the Garante and are familiar with the data protection law and requirements. This allows the Garante to cover the country. If it is a complex case there may be someone on site from the Garante as well.
- A report is done on site and signed by all present. The final decision on the case is published on the website.
- The DPA also uses name and shame tactics and can impose lower sanctions if the organisation has co-operated.
- In 2006 they carried out 350 inspections with 158 administrative breaches found and 11 cases referred to the judiciary.[12]

France

The powers of audit and inspection of the French DPA arise from Law 2004-801 of 6 August 2004, recently amended.

The French DPA can access all professional premises, request and copy all necessary documents, access all IT systems, and request transcriptions of data.

- They used to inform companies of inspections but this didn't work very well, so now most are on-the-spot inspections. They have to inform the local judge in case they are refused access to premises, in which case the judge can order the company to let them in.
- Non-compliance with report recommendations can lead to the threat of financial sanctions, or they can refer the case to the public prosecutor.
- In 2006 they carried out 127 inspections.[13]

Spain

The audit/inspection powers of the Spanish DPA are conferred by Spanish Law: Ley orgánica 15/1999 in force since 14 January 2000

- The Agencia Española de Protección de Datos (AEPD) have the power to inspect/audit without the consent of the data controller.
- Failure to collaborate in an inspection is a serious violation which may lead to a fine being imposed of up to €300,000.
- In the case of infringement of data protection law by public sector organisations fines are not imposed but public warnings are issued which may lead to disciplinary proceedings against individuals.
- Investigations/audits carried out in 2006.
- 1282 enforcement investigations started of which:
  - 281 led to penal sanctions legal proceedings,
  - 103 led to a public warning against public administration bodies.

Ireland

The Irish DPA has powers of audit/inspection conferred by law in terms of the Data Protection Act 1988, modified by Data Protection (Amendment) Act 2003.

- They have the power under Section 10 of their law to audit for practice and compliance with the Act. They don't tend to use this power. If they do, they contact the company and tell them they will audit on a particular date. The company has some leeway to change the date, but not much.
- Instead they use (and increasingly so) the power under Section 24 to be able to enter any premises at any time without notice. It is a power of entry and to copy information. They can turn up anywhere at any time and look at personal data processed or information relating to the processing. A failure by an organisation to cooperate is an offence and they are cautioned and possibly prosecuted. They do not take the police with them, it has not been needed so far, but they could if they wanted to.
- They are increasingly using this power with organisations involved in mobile marketing. Under the legislation that has enacted the e-privacy directive they have the power to prosecute any offences under that law and to impose fines of €3000 for every message sent or every failure to comply. The court can also order the deletion of a database and there is draft legislation at the moment to increase the fine to €5000; and a maximum of 10% of a company's turnover, or €4 million. Some large-scale prosecutions are expected.[14]

The previous examples have been cited to illustrate the point that the policy in these countries is clear: the protection of personal data is important enough to warrant our DPA being empowered to drop in to check whether your house is in order. That policy has been translated into law. While it is not impossible that there exists a strong element of under-reporting of cases of personal data losses in these countries, the increased vigilance empowered by law is likely to be one of the reasons why they may possibly have substantially fewer cases of such losses. Their law and their policy is for less lax than in the UK, the number of inspections and prosecutions are higher than in the UK and as a result their privacy culture may arguably be developing at a faster rate than in the UK. Yet, it has taken a year of highly publicised losses of personal data, 1 week after another since autumn 2007, and a plethora of reports for the UK authorities to spring into significant legislative action in January 2009 and, as will be seen later, even then the extent to which one risks having moved from one bad policy (and law) to another remains highly debatable.

From one loss of personal data to another... and another... *ad infinitum*

The catalogue of data protection fiascos during 2007–2008 is catastrophic in proportion and unfortunately shows no sign of abating. The facts of the main case as they unravelled in the autumn of 2007 in the UK are relatively well known and we shall here only go through them in outline, largely for the sake of international readership:

- 18 October – Junior official from Her Majesty's Revenue & Customs (HMRC) in Washington, Tyne and Wear, sends two CDs containing password-protected records to audit office in London through courier TNT, neither recorded nor registered.
- 24 October – When package fails to arrive, second one is sent by registered post and arrives safely.

- 3 November – Senior managers are told first package has been lost.
- 10 November – Prime Minister and other ministers are informed.
- 12 November – HMRC tell ministers CDs will probably be found.
- 14 November – When HMRC searches fail, Metropolitan Police are called in.
- 15 November – Richard Thomas, Information Commissioner, says remedial action must be taken before public is informed.
- 20 November – HMRC Chairman Paul Gray resigns; Chancellor Alistair Darling makes announcement to House of Commons. As a result it transpires that the two CDs contained the records of some 25 million people and that the personal data which have gone missing include:
  - National insurance number
  - Name, address and birth date
  - Partner's details
  - Names, sex and age of children
  - Bank/savings account details

This massive HMRC data loss of autumn 2007 was not an isolated incident. In the UK alone, reports of fresh data losses began to surface every week or two. At first we started documenting every case with the intention of including their analysis in this paper but the sheer volume and the rising number of cases meant that reasons of space would have precluded us from doing so and instead we represent some of our findings in Table 1. Twelve months after the HMRC case, the UK's Information Commissioner reported:

> I can reveal today that the number of data breaches reported to my office has soared to 277 since November 2007. There have been 28 breaches by central government; 75 within the NHS and other health bodies; with 80 reported in the private sector. We are currently investigating 30 of the most serious cases.[15]

Not all cases make it to the media but in Table 1 we have attempted to chart some of the more significant ones that we have been following since autumn 2007. These are by no means exhaustive and can only give a flavour of what is going on, yet the data speak volumes. Again and again, we read of personal data being lost and even a cursory glance at Table 1 will confirm that most of these losses did not occur as a result of intentional malicious attacks over the Internet but rather through negligent loss or ordinary theft of physical devices such as notebook computers, personal digital assistants (PDAs), USB data sticks and CDs. This is why it is difficult to avoid the sense that, with a data loss being reported on average once a week, the world and especially the UK seems to have lurched from one serious data loss to another. It has literally been a case of 10,000 records here, 600,000 there, a few million here... and the infamous 25 million 'over there'. In an effort to understand whether what was going on in the UK was an isolated phenomenon or whether it was representative of a wider picture our team has kept a watchful eye on reports world-wide that may have been reported in a number of languages. The results in Table 1 are organised into two sections, with 52 separate incidents identified in the UK, and the second section of the table surveying the international scene documenting 24 incidents in the USA, 3 in Germany, 3 in France, 2 in Australia, and 1 each in Canada, Chile and Italy. We have ascribed our own reference numbers to these incidents and hope to continue building on this research and eventually publish a more detailed analysis with more case names and identities when this is appropriate. At this stage, however, it is felt that Table 1 has a value in its own right to illustrate the magnitude of the problem as well as

Table 1. Personal data losses.

Name or JAC/ JMB ref.	Date of data loss	Means: remote or physical	Location	Data controller	Date reported and source	Date recovered	Number of data subjects affected	Any abuse traced
AF1	April 2008	Laptop	At McDonald's in London (close to Whitehall)	Army				
AF2	2004–2008	121 memory sticks		Armed Forces	July 2008			
AF3	October 2008	Missing hard drive belonging to contractor, EDS		Armed Forces/ Ministry of Defence	October 2008		The names, addresses, passport numbers, dates of birth and driving licence details of around 100,000 serving personnel across the Army, Royal Navy and RAF, plus their next-of-kin details +data on 600,000 potential services applicants and the names of their referees+possibly bank account details of personnel.	
BBC1	August 2008	Laptop and several memory sticks	From contractor's car	BBC	August 2008		Personal details of hundreds of children who had applied to take part in a TV show.	
CM1	June 2008	laptop	Salford	Cabinet Minister			Details of constituents.	
Def1	2004–2008	747 laptops 658 according to another article		Defence	July 2008	32 recovered		
DoT	2007			Department of Transport			Six occasions when the Department for Transport misplaced personal data, including three million records of driving-test candidates in May 2007.	

DWP1	October 2008	Memory stick – encrypted.	Cannock, Staffordshire, in pub car park. Loss by contractor employee.	Department of Works and Pensions	November 2008	3 days after loss (given to newspaper)	Number unknown
DWP2	October 2008	Papers	Train: Macclesfield – London Euston.	Work and Pensions Secretary Department of Works and Pensions.	October 2008	Fellow train passenger, few days later.	Information on one constituent.
DT1	May 2007	Hard drive	United States by contractor in Iowa.	Driving Standards Agency Pearson Driving Assessments (Contractor)	December 2007		App. details on three million candidates for UK driving test.
DT2	December 2007	Two discs	In post from Northern Ireland to Swansea.	Driver and Vehicle Licensing Agency			7685 Northern Ireland drivers' details.
DT3	December 2007	Confidential information sent to wrong persons.		DVLA			Around 100 drivers.
EY1	March 2006	Laptop	Miami	Ernst & Young BP			Details of 40,000 BP employees.
EY2	March 2006	Laptop	Miami	Ernst & Young Sun Microsystems			
EY3	March 2006	Laptop	Miami	Ernst & Young IBM			
EY4	March 2006	Laptop	Miami	Ernst & Young Cisco			
FO1	2007			Foreign Office			In five separate cases, the Foreign Office lost information affecting about 190 people.

(Continued)

Table 1. Continued.

Name or JAC/ JMB ref.	Date of data loss	Means: remote or physical	Location	Data controller	Date reported and source	Date recovered	Number of data subjects affected	Any abuse traced
GTC1	September 2008	Disc	On way to Birmingham from contractor – send by ParcelForce	General Teaching Council	26 September 2008		Information of 11,500 – including NI numbers and dates of birth but not financial data.	
HMRC1	18 October 2007	Two CDs	Between offices in Washington and London	HMRC	Reported to police 15 November 2007		App. 25 million	
HMRC2		Saliva samples	Heathrow Airport	HMRC	22 August 2008		12 saliva samples of suspected smugglers.	
HMRC3	September 2007	laptop		HMRC			Banking details of customers.	
HO1		Memory stick		Home Office & PA Consulting	21 August 2008		App. 10,000 prolific offender; 84,000 prisoners in England & Wales; 33,000 from police national computer	
HO2	July 2007	Hard drive	Contractor – EDS	Home Office	07 September 2008		Details of app. 5000 employees of the justice system/prison staff	
HO3	2007	Two CDs missing in the post		Home Office			Personal details of 3000 seasonal agricultural workers – including their passport numbers – when two CDs went missing in the post.	
Hos1	June 2008	Six laptops		Hospitals (which ones unknown)			20,000 patients' details.	
HP1		Memory Stick		Hertfordshire Police	Loss registered 5 March 2008		App. 165,000 pages of suspects' details from police automatic number plate recognition system.	

LC1	April 2007–April 2008	Data lost, stolen or 'inadvertently disclosed'.		Various London Councils		No specific numbers. In two separate incidents 4 months apart, workers at Kensington and Chelsea Borough Council took information on vulnerable children into bars, where it was stolen. And in October 2007, 375 student files were stolen from Havering Council.
MoD1	December 2005	Laptop	Edinburgh	MoD		App. 500
MoD2	October 2006	Laptop	Manchester	MoD		
MoD3	9 January 2008	Laptop	Birmingham	MoD	Reported to Ministers 11 January 2008	App. 600,000
MoD4	2007	68 laptops		MoD		
MoD5	2006	66 laptops		MoD		
MoD6	2005	50 laptops		MoD		
MoD7	2004	173 laptops		MoD		
MoD8	2004–2008	121 memory sticks		MoD	July 2008	
MoD9	9 October 2008	Computer drive	Hook, Hampshire		October 2008 by contractor EDS	Non-encrypted details of as many as 1.7 million people who had shown interest in joining the armed forces. In some cases includes bank details, passport, National Insurance and National Health Service numbers, driver's licence information and details of next of kin.

(*Continued*)

Table 1. Continued.

Name or JAC/ JMB ref.	Date of data loss	Means: remote or physical	Location	Data controller	Date reported and source	Date recovered	Number of data subjects affected	Any abuse traced
MoJ1	April 2007–April 2008			Ministry of Justice			Information affecting more than 45,000 people, in some cases revealing their criminal records and credit histories.	
MS1	May 2007	Laptop	Contractor	Marks & Spencer's			Details of 26,000 staff	
NCC1	July 2007	File wrongly placed on an insecure server, and subsequently uploaded to a computer address registered outside the country.		Newcastle City Council			Debit and credit card records of 54,000 people.	
NHS1	June/July 2008	Laptop		Colchester Hospital University NHS Foundation Trust			21,000 patient details.	
NHS2	December 2007	CDs		City & Hackney NHS			160,000 details of children (patients).	
NI1	2007						National Insurance numbers of 17,000 people.	
Sat1	2007	Laptop					Encrypted details of 17,000 SATs markers.	
SFS1		Laptop		Skipton Financial Services	ICO ruling 21 February 2008		Details of 14,000 customers.	

CLP1	30 December 2008	Memory stick with password attached.		Central Lancashire Primary Care Trust	January 2009		Personal details of more than 6000 prisoners (it included details of some prisoners' ailments, such as diabetes, asthma, mental health and sexual health, but not full medical history. The documents saved on it also include prisoner surnames, their age range, cell location, prison number and clinic appointment times.)
FD1	2007	Laptop		Nationwide		Fined £980,000 by FSA	Financial details of 11 million customers.
FD2	2007	Disc	Southampton	HSBC			370,000 customer details.
FD3	October 2007	Disc	Misplace by courier between Newcastle and Edinburgh.	HMRC			Details of 15,000 Standard Life customers.
FD4	2006	Laptop		Fidelity Investments			Details on 200,000 HP employees.
FD5	December 2007	Data unaccounted for.	During move.	Leeds Building Society			Salary and banking details of around 1000 employees.
International							
US1	May 2006	Laptop	Theft from home of employee.	US Department of Veteran Affairs		June 2006 Recovered	Details of 26.5 m veterans.
US2	2003–2006	Thefts of laptops, drives, unauthorised use of data by employees.			13 October 2006 in report of House Reform Committee.		19 US government agencies lost personal information 788 incidents.
US3	2003–2006	Laptops		Treasury Department IRS	13 October 2006 in report of House Reform Committee.		340 incidents.

(*Continued*)

Table 1. Continued.

Name or JAC/ JMB ref.	Date of data loss	Means: remote or physical	Location	Data controller	Date reported and source	Date recovered	Number of data subjects affected	Any abuse traced
US4	2003–2006	1,137 laptops lost since 2001.		Commerce Department Census Bureau.	13 October 2006 in report of House Reform Committee.		297 incidents of loss of data.	
US5	August 2006	Laptop	Fell off motorcycle driven by Navy recruiter.	Navy	13 October 2006 in report of House Reform Committee.		Details of 30,000 applicants.	
US6	2004	Disc	Lost in transit by commercial shipper.	Federal student-aid contractor.	13 October 2006 in report of House Reform Committee.		Details of 8290 borrowers.	
US7	2005	Hacker using malicious software.		National Nuclear Security Administration	13 October 2006 in report of House Reform Committee		Details of 1717 employees.	
US8	2005	Employees stole records.		Centers for Medicare and Medicais Services.	13 October 2006 in report of House Reform Committee.		Details of 1574 Medicare beneficiaries.	Identity theft.
US9	2005	Data tapes	Lost by card issuing charge cards company.	Interior department	13 October 2006 in report of House Reform Committee.		Details on 61,000 cardholders.	

US10	July 2006		Six Justice Department employees submitted computerised attendance reports containing Social Security numbers. The reports were downloaded 220 times and viewed 7772 times.	Justice Department	13 October 2006 in report of House Reform Committee.		Social security numbers.	
US11	2005	40 backup tapes	Lost by contractor Iron Mountain	Time Warner Inc.			Personal information of 600,000 current and former employees.	
US12	February 2005			Bank of America Corp.			Information on 1.2 million federal government charge cards.	
US13	2003 – 2005	Unauthorised access.		Reed Elsevier PLC ChoicePoint Inc.			59 incidents of data loss including social security and driver's license information.	
US14	2005	Theft of two computers.		San José Medical Group.			Details on 185,000 patients.	
US15	2005	Laptop	Theft	University of Berkeley		Laptop retrieved by police.	98,000 social security numbers.	Laptop put up for sale after being formatted but no proof of misuse of data.
US16	2005	Backup tape	While transferred between branches.	Ameritrade Holding			200,000 client records.	

(*Continued*)

Table 1. Continued.

Name or JAC/ JMB ref.	Date of data loss	Means: remote or physical	Location	Data controller	Date reported and source	Date recovered	Number of data subjects affected	Any abuse traced
US17	2005		While being sent to a credit reference agency.	Citigroup			Personal information including social security numbers of four million clients.	
US18	2005	Unauthorised access.		LexisNexis			Records of 32,000 customers.	
US19	2005	Unauthorised access.		Jackson Community College			8000 social security numbers.	
US20	September 2008	Stolen laptop from employee car (laptop left overnight in car).		HealthTexas Provider Network a subsidiary of Baylor Health Care System.	November 2008		7400 patients' records including Social Security Numbers (SSNs) and other personal information +100,000 personal records that do not include SSNs.	
US21	January 2008	Stolen laptop and storage device		Horizon Blue Cross Blue Shield of New Jersey and Georgetown University.		Security feature on stolen computer later erased data.	Sensitive data on 300,000 people.	
US22	March 2008	Stolen laptop		National Heart, Lung and Blood Institute			Sensitive data on about 2500 individuals had been stolen.	
US23	March 2008	Stolen laptop		Agilent Technologies Inc.			Confidential information on more than 50,000 current and former employees.	
US24	October 2008	Security breach		State Department			400 passport applicants including Social Security numbers	

Aus 1	2003–2008	Lost laptops (45% of all breaches); human error (42%); lost mobile phones or devices (30%); malicious actions by insiders (28%); the deliberate removal of paper records from organisations (26%); malware and hacking (24%).		Businesses in Australia (80% have experienced a data breach).		losing customer records (55% of all breaches), employee records (48%), intellectual property (43%), commercially sensitive information (35%), bank and credit card details (21%), and financial information (20%).
Aus 2	2008	Wrong email attachment (instead of dinner menu!).		Restaurant in Sydney		3499 credit card details.
Can1	2007	Unauthorised access to two local servers containing client data.		Winners		Credit card details of 45 million clients.
Ger1	15 March–20 June 2008	Error in password protection.		HSH, Germany	23 June 2008	Details of 500,000 Germans where available on Internet;
Ger2	October 2008	Leak of personal information to the Internet.	By a private contractor.	Axel Springer Company	October 2008	names, addresses, mobile phone numbers and bank account details of persons who placed classified ads on one of Axel Springer's newspapers.
Ger3	October 2008	Thieves hijacked data.		Deutsche Telekom		Sensitive data on millions of mobile phone customers.
It1	30 April 2008	Availability of tax records for 2005.		Italian Ministry of Finance		Tax records of 40 million Italian tax payers.
Chile1	May 2008	Hacking of systems.		Various government offices.		Records of six million persons.

(*Continued*)

Table 1. Continued.

Name or JAC/ JMB ref.	Date of data loss	Means: remote or physical	Location	Data controller	Date reported and source	Date recovered	Number of data subjects affected	Any abuse traced
Fr1	June 2007	Incorrect encryption of database.		French Ministry of Education			Student information left unencrypted and openly accessible in 'Base élèves 1er degré'.	
FR2	January 2006–June 2007	Misuse of personal information.	Passing on personal information (against payment) to unauthorised third parties.	French Police	14 March 2008 (Court case).		Personal information kept in police files.	
FR3	1998–2001	Unauthorised access and misuse of personal information.	Information passed on to former police officer formerly convicted of corrupt practices.	French police	26 May 2008 (Court case)		3000–3500 personal files.	

make readers reflect on the extent to which such incidents of loss of personal data are properly reported and recorded.

There are many caveats that we would make to readers of Table 1: our team scoured reports in English, French, Italian, Spanish and German but there are many losses and incidents that we may have missed out on, not least on account of linguistic competences. Moreover, some losses or revelations of personal data may be illegal but not necessarily accidental and may also reflect cultural or personal differences in attitudes to privacy. For example, during field-work in Poland, with assistance from a Polish colleague[16] we came across cases as varied as those of a doctor who made public personal data of 14-year-old girl who wanted to have an abortion,[17] Grono.net making public personal data of its users,[18] a person named Antoni Macierewicz making public the personal data of 200 officers and co-workers[19] and even a parish priest who apparently published the names of people who had paid (or not!) their dues to the church.[20]

While it is clear that media attention to losses of personal data appears to have shot up significantly in the UK since 2007, the same is not necessarily true of other countries. In a scenario where loss of personal data has suddenly become more news-worthy in the UK, it was relatively easy for a French sub-editor to include a caption like ‘L’Angleterre est championne... de la perte de données’.[21] Jibe or not, the number of UK cases documented in Table 1 is more than the rest of the world put together. We suspect that this is not necessarily representative of the true picture and that the loss of personal data is seriously under-reported in the media of many other jurisdictions. Indeed, the conclusion of the French article whose caption we reproduced earlier admitted as much:

> Is the situation better in France? That is scarcely probable, even if France is ‘a country where one never loses a portable computer...’ as Eric Domage, Research Manager, Security Products and Services at IDC, likes to remind people with more than a touch of irony. Our luck, and misfortune, must surely be that these losses are never made public. (Our translation)[22]

While under-reporting may be a factor in distorting the results, the only way to cut down significantly on the losses of personal data is to massively improve privacy culture within both the public and private sectors, whatever the country. To do so must be a matter of good policy which translates into good law. The extent to which this is taking place in reality is the focus of the next part of this paper.

Findings of 2008 reports – from data loss ‘entirely avoidable’ to requirement for ‘an invigorated and rigorous audit and compliance regime’

The official inquiries and reports undertaken and published in the UK during 2008 all confirm the impression that most, if not all, losses of personal data could have been avoided had, amongst other measures, the UK pursued a better (tighter, less lax) policy insofar as legally empowered audits and inspections are concerned.

The Burton Report

Sir Edmund Burton was asked to review the Ministry of Defence’s (MoD) protection of personal data in the wake of the theft (9 January 2008) of a Royal Navy (RN) recruiter’s laptop, which contained unencrypted personal records for more than 600,000 people (actually more than 600,000 personal records for recruits and potential recruits and around 400,000 next of kin and referee records).

His review found a number of data protection shortcomings that could have been foreseen and/or dealt with had a data protection inspection been carried out:

(1) outside MoD HQ and the Defence Staff (Health) area, there is very limited understanding of the Department's obligations under the Data Protection Act.[23]

(2) while the Department is custodian of tens of millions of data records,[24] there is no evidence (with the exception of the specialist personnel agencies) that these large data records are systematically reviewed and cleansed to meet the obligations of the Data Protection Act.[25] The Review lists a number of reasons why the Department has not carried out a full audit of its total personal data holdings and limited (and cleansed) the use of personal data. These reasons include:
   a The cost of the deletion is greater than the cost of storage.
   b Failure to consider the legal implications and risks accompanying user requirements for large quantities of data on removable storage devices. It is understood that the scale of personal data held on the RN/Royal Air Force Training Administration and Financial Management Information System (TAFMIS) laptops was attributable to the user requirement. There is no evidence that the legal implications and risks were considered, either by the user community, or by the contractor.
   c Data Protection Officers are not fulfilling their responsibilities.
   d Audit and compliance functions are not being exercised or overseen effectively at board level.
   e Data are replicated without due consideration. This can range from individuals saving duplicate copies of shared files within their own personal drives, to large scale data replication, e.g., the monthly transfer of data from Service Personnel and Veterans Agency (SPVA) to Defence Analytical Services Agency (DASA).[26]

(3) security procedures need to be reviewed and accompanied by 'an invigorated and rigorous audit and compliance regime'.[27]

(4) The loss of a laptop with more than 600,000 unencrypted personal records was in breach of a number of data protection principles. The Review identifies five principles that may have potentially been breached:
   a Personal data shall be processed fairly and lawfully.
   b Personal data shall be adequate, relevant and not excessive in relation to the purpose or purposes for which they are processed.
   c Personal data shall be accurate and, where necessary, kept up to date.
   d Personal data processed for any purpose or purposes shall not be kept for longer than is necessary for that purpose or those purposes.
   e Appropriate technical and organisation measures shall be taken against unauthorised or unlawful processing of personal data and against accidental loss or destruction of, or damage to, personal data.[28]

The IPCC and Poynter Reports

The massive HMRC case involving the loss of two CDs with 25 million records referred to previously in this paper was the subject of two reports: the IPCC Report – Independent Police Complaints Commission (IPCC) independent investigation report into loss of data relating to Child Benefit (June 2008); and the Poynter Report – Review of information security at HM Revenue and Customs Final Report by Kieran Poynter (June 2008). The Poynter Report has a wider remit that the IPCC Report. It was commissioned not only to investigate the loss of the two CDs containing personal information, but also to carry out a wider review of information security at HMRC. Insofar as identifying shortcomings that could have been avoided had a stronger policy empowering data protection inspections/audits been in place, there are no disparities between the reports.

A detailed evaluation of these reports is beyond the scope of this paper but for our purposes here it is worth noting what a tighter policy of data protection inspections and audits could have avoided:

(1) *Lack of ownership of data/failure to identify who was actually responsible for the personal information.* It is clear through reports that none of the departments involved took ownership and responsibility for data being transferred. The IPCC Report concludes that the issue of lack of clarity and consensus around data ownership appears to have been a contributory factor to the decision to supply the National Audit Office (NAO) with the entire Child Benefit records.[29] Poynter notes further:

> The lack of an appointed data guardian at the time of the incident was a significant contributory factor in the loss of the data. It is highly unlikely that the discs would have been permitted to leave HMRC premises in March without the authority of the data guardian, nor would a properly trained data guardian have permitted the use of internal post for the October transfer.[30]

(2) *Lack of awareness of guidelines on data sharing.* The IPCC Report reports that it is not clear whether HMRC staff were aware of any guidelines governing situations of data sharing. 'It does not appear that any steps were taken to seek any level of authority that may have been required for handing over such a large volume of highly sensitive data in a removable media format'.[31]

(3) *HMRC security policies unknown to staff.* Though HMRC has a Departmental Security Standards Manual[32] and an Information Disclosure Guidance Manual[33] detailing provision of information to the NAO, the IPCC found that 'in practice, most staff had a distinct lack of working knowledge about how these guidelines should be implemented in the workplace'.[34] Similarly, Poynter notes that the Departmental Security Standards Manual (DSSM) and Information Disclosure Guidance (IDG) policies lacked sufficient detail and strength to guide staff.[35] Importantly, the policies are inadequate when it comes to removable media and encryption policies (e.g., no requirement of encryption of information protectively marked as 'restricted').[36] HMRC was also still in the process of developing a risk management process arising from information assurance strategies driven by the Cabinet Office. (The draft risk management document had only been submitted through the approval process on 16 October 2007.)[37]

It is worth noting some of the key findings of Poynter's wider review:[38]

- information security, at the time of the incident, simply wasn't a management priority;
- HMRC did not and still does not possess documentation of its data flows at a level which would have allowed it to assess risk;
- the generic policies around information security that were issued from the centre were inadequate and tended not to be translated into Business Unit-specific

procedures – and no consistent assurance regime was in place to ensure that this translation was completed;
- the Security and Business Continuity (S&BC) function which was responsible for information security policies was weak in skills and experience and commanded no authority across the business;
- HMRC did not employ any information security professionals at the time of the incident; and
- staff received little or no training in information security.[39]

Poynter makes important recommendations regarding the Supervisory function of the ICO completely in line with the policies already adopted in other countries such as Italy, France Spain and Ireland illustrated previously.

> The recommendations made later in this report are consistent with banking practice on information security and we would ask government to think about what the equivalent regulatory regime to that operated by the Financial Services Authority ('FSA') should be for the public sector, and whether the ICO might fulfil the role of the FSA for the public sector.[40]

That the Government did think about it is clear and, within 6 months of the Poynter Report, it eventually produced the Coroners & Justice Bill 2009 containing proposals for reversing some of the bad policies of the past and granting the Information Commissioner powers of audit/inspection and introducing penalties more comparable to those available to a number of other EU data protection agencies. Whether the new Bill is a sufficiently positive reassurance that the UK has moved away from bad policy and bad law is a totally different matter, which is evaluated in the next and final section of this paper.

Epilogue? The Coroners & Justice Bill 2009 – 'conspiracy or cock-up?'[41]

A positive outcome of the data protection disasters of 2007 and 2008 has been the way that privacy and data protection have been put firmly in the public spotlight. At the end of October 2008, Richard Thomas put it thus:

> There must be a wake-up call each time there are headlines about unencrypted laptops which have gone missing, health or financial records found in the streets or memory sticks or hard drives which cannot be accounted for. But are there still too many people asleep at the helm?[42]

Barely had 2 months passed from when Thomas asked his question as to how many people are still asleep at the helm when, just after Christmas 2008, the Labour Government introduced the Coroners & Criminal Justice Bill which, it is reported, has led to The British Computer Society (BCS) writing to MPs asking them to kill the Bill, saying, 'It drives a coach and horses through the Data Protection Act'.[43]

The large and unwieldy Bill covers a number of diverse and unconnected areas of the Administration of Justice including Inquests, Murder, Infanticide and myriad other areas. David Howarth, the Lib. Dem. MP for Cambridge summed it up neatly:

> This is a very long Bill that, at a conservative estimate, contains 28 different topics for consideration. It amends 56 pieces of previous legislation and, even in the time that the Committee has been given, it will be difficult to consider all aspects of the Bill properly.[44]

Indeed, some IT lawyers would have spotted those sections like 49–56, which are clearly intended to bring the UK closer to ratifying the Cybercrime Convention, but Computer Crime was not to steal the show because, according to civil liberties group NO2ID:

> Hidden in the new Coroners and Justice Bill is one clause (cl.152) amending the Data Protection Act. It would allow ministers to make 'Information Sharing Orders', that can alter any Act of Parliament and cancel all rules of confidentiality in order to use information obtained for one purpose to be used for another. This single clause is as grave a threat to privacy as the entire ID Scheme. Combine it with the index to your life formed by the planned National Identity Register and everything recorded about you anywhere could be accessible to any official body. That is what we meant by 'the database state'. It is now a threat not a theory.[45]

The public furore that arose over Sections 152–154 was such that within less than 6 weeks from the Bill being introduced on 14 January 2009, one reads that:

> The Justice Secretary, Jack Straw, will make a U-turn over sweeping new powers which were to allow public bodies to swap the data they hold on individuals. In a clear sign the Government is worried about growing criticism that it is creating a 'Big Brother Britain', Mr Straw is to rewrite his Coroners and Justice Bill to build in new safeguards to protect the public. He will table several amendments to the measure when it reaches its report stage in the Commons next month.[46]

When the aforementioned report appeared on 24 February, things started happening thick and fast. Within 48 hours, the debate on the Bill at Committee stage focused on a number of amendments tabled to Clause 152, including one dealing with purpose:

> Clause 152, page 100, line 8, at end insert –
> '(1A) No information-sharing order may authorise data to be shared in any way that might result in the date being used for a purpose different from that for which its collection was originally authorised'.[47]

While the discussion of this amendment and others proceeded in a climate where it was known that the Government would be coming back with a number of significant amendments at Report stage, a day later, on 27 February 2009, a clearly defensive Jack Straw admitted that:

> Our record is not perfect but... Those who cast myself and my colleagues as Orwellian drones engaged in some awful conspiracy planned in Whitehall basements not only overlook all this government's achievements, they cheapen the important debate about getting the balance right so that a very important freedom, that to live without fear in an atmosphere of tolerance and respect, is nurtured and protected.[48]

We do not seek to cheapen any debate but cannot but note that Mr. Straw speaks much less about the other side of the balance, i.e. the freedom to live without interruption of one's right to private and family life, which his own Labour Government had introduced in Article 8 of the Human Rights Act of 1998. Nor do we seek to in any way overlook or undermine the achievements of the Labour Government, but even if we were to take Mr. Straw at his word and accept that this is not part of a conspiracy, does all the evidence point to yet another cock-up? Could it be possible that out of the hierarchy of lawyers in place to assist Mr. Straw draft the Bill, not one of them would have pointed out that, if implemented as drafted, Section 152 would obliterate the principle of 'purpose' which lies at the heart of data protection law internationally? If that is the case, (and it does strain the limits of credulity) then one must ask what poverty of privacy culture do the corridors of Whitehall still harbour? Is everybody there still asleep at the helm? If, on the other hand, the odd privacy lawyer here or there within Government did raise the alarm with the helmsman why were they over-ruled and who over-ruled them?

The main thrust of the concluding part of this paper is not the actual conclusion of the saga intrinsic to the progress of the Coroners & Justice Bill through the UK parliament, for when this paper went to press the proceedings had not yet been completed and that evaluation will have to await a follow-up paper to the analysis presented here. Our main interest here lies in what it tells us about the process and whether the UK has learnt anything or enough from the bad policies that produced bad laws in the past. The introduction of the Coroners & Justice Bill in January 2009 led to fierce opposition on a wide number of counts. What does this tell us about the nature of privacy culture within Whitehall if, on 16 February, the BCS was compelled to release the following devastating statement?

- The Bill runs counter to the intentions and provisions of the Data Protection Act (DPA) 1998; in particular by devaluing the principle of informed consent which lies at the heart of the DPA.
- The Bill severely curtails the independence of the Information Commissioner.
- It is doubtful whether it would stand scrutiny under the Human Rights Act 1998, Article 8.
- It has the potential to heighten the distrust citizens have of government and central initiatives, and thereby set back the efforts of Government and its agencies to provide faster, more cost-effective public services using IT.
- The Bill could have disastrous consequences in the hands of a less benevolent government.
- BCS has made representations to Her Majesty's Government and its agencies on several related topics over the last year or so, including the Data Sharing Review, the proposed National Identity database, the NHS Connecting for Health Questionnaire on the use of personal data for secondary purposes, and most recently the House of Lords Committee on 'Surveillance: the Citizen and the State'. The common theme of the responses, based on detailed consultation with members of the IT profession and others, is concern about the burgeoning power of the state *vis-à-vis* the citizen. The proposals conflict with the ethical codes practiced by several large professional groups, among which are clinicians and health informaticians. This issue is at the heart of the BMA [British Medical Association] response to the proposals which says 'it appears to permit an unprecedented sharing of confidential personal health data... This Bill strips patients and doctors of any rights in relation to the control of sensitive health information'. BCS agrees with this statement.[49]

Within 2 weeks, the vanguard of the Health sector followed up the BCS onslaught:

Eight healthcare organisations have called for medical records to be excluded from the data-sharing provisions of the Coroners and Justice Bill, in the latest stage of the campaign against them. The organisations, which include the British Medical Association, Royal College of Surgeons and Royal College of General Practitioners, have written to justice secretary Jack Straw to raise concerns about the plans, which would allow the sharing of personal data across Whitehall departments. The letter expresses 'grave concerns' about clause 152 of the Coroners and Justice Bill, which the signatories claim would grant the government

> unprecedented powers to access people's confidential medical records and share them with third parties. The letter adds: 'In our view the Bill will undermine the presumption of confidentiality, corrode trust in the doctor–patient relationship and could have a disastrous impact on both the health of individuals and the public'.[50]

Surely, these comments are not the hallmark of proposed legislation which reflects well thought-out, good policy intent on producing good law? We submit that even if the intentions were good, the way of introducing them was slipshod and that it is also bad policy to permit slipshod legal drafting. If everybody was 'not asleep at the helm', how was it possible for the UK legislator to produce in 2008–2009 a Bill, the drafting of which attracted the opposition of practically all the important actors on the stage? Perhaps the answer comes in at least two parts, which were provided by two of the MPs debating the Bill at Committee stage. Tim Boswell put it thus, reflecting implicitly on those civil servants and legislators who are not sufficiently immersed in privacy culture to be aware of the horrendous potential of what they may actually be proposing:

> The Government tend to take an on–off view of data sharing, as if everything has to be shared rather than just salient parts of the record, which may or may not be anonymised for the purpose for which they required to be shared?[51]

David Howarth was more interested in the malaise of sloppy drafting, as a matter of policy (albeit possibly unwritten, undiscussed and unadmitted and thus here referred to as a 'habit'):

> My underlying worry about the clause is that it has become a habit to draw up such statutory powers overbroadly. That is how the problems of detail are solved – not by thinking hard about them and being more specific. It seems that the tendency is to solve them by saying, 'We will grab the broadest possible power and leave the problems until later'. That is not good enough. Our duty as parliamentarians is to ensure that the powers are incapable of being used in an inappropriate way.[52]

The evidence, however, points to more than sloppy drafting. The UK's Ministry of Justice and the Home Office both have a number of lawyers and civil servants who are very familiar indeed with the second principle of the UK's Data Protection Act:

> Personal data shall be obtained only for one or more specified and lawful purposes, and shall not be further processed in any manner incompatible with that purpose or those purposes.[53]

This fundamental principle has been part of UK law for a quarter of a century, since the UK's first Data Protection Act of 1984 enacted to enable the UK to join the European Data Protection Club established in terms of the Council of Europe's 1981 Data Protection Convention.[54] Home Office and Justice Ministry lawyers and civil servants have been discussing it in London, Strasbourg and Brussels and otherwise imbibing it *ad nauseam* since at least 1984, yet they somehow let the UK Minister responsible, Mr. Straw, sponsor a Bill which radically and flagrantly contravenes this principle, putting him into an untenable position from which he had to undertake a dramatic U-turn within weeks. The incredulity which this arouses may be seen across the Web. As one post on a blog put it: 'Is this Government devious or just thick? It beggars belief that they haven't thought about the ramifications of this bill before getting so close to presenting it'.[55]

It is not as if the mistakes were not evident to even a first-year law student taking a basic module in IT law or that they had not been noticed within Parliament itself. The Research Paper dated 22 January 2009 produced by the House of Commons Library clearly found that:

> New section 50A includes a definition of sharing that explicitly overrides the second data protection principle: For the purposes of this Part a person shares information if the person… consults or uses the information for a purpose other than the purpose for which the information was obtained.[56]

And how it would have done so had Mr. Straw not had to make a U-turn, takes the prize for one of the most dangerous pieces of legal drafting the UK has seen in a long time:

> Clause 152 of the *Coroners and Justice Bill* would obviate the need for primary legislation to enable personal data sharing, providing instead a secondary legislation route. It inserts a new Part (5A) on information sharing in the DPA. In particular, a new section (50A) would enable Ministers to make 'information-sharing orders' enabling 'any person' to share information which consists of or includes personal data.[57]

Anybody familiar with 'purpose' (or *finalité* as the French would put it), the cardinal principle of European data protection law, would no doubt be amazed by the cheek of what the legal drafter was trying to pull off. Here was the UK according itself the right to break the obligations it had undertaken in terms of signing and ratifying the Council of Europe's 1981 Data Protection Convention *and* imposed upon it by EU Directive 46/95 *and* implied in its finally incorporating Art 8 of the European Convention on Human Rights into UK law in the 1998 Human Rights Act. This is such a serious matter that one is compelled to ask whether such flouting of established international and European law is now a matter of official UK policy? What would the UK's delegates to the Consultative Committee of the Data Protection Convention have to say when these inevitable questions came their way at their next meeting in Strasbourg?

More to the point, is this an official policy sanctioned at the very highest levels of Government? Is deliberately breaking Britain's international obligations a policy discussed and approved at Cabinet level or is it simply something that inept or Eurosceptic civil servants slipped unnoticed by their over-worked political masters? Well, it seems as if we shall probably not be allowed to know for, in another case, the same Jack Straw has overruled the Information Tribunal and set a precedent by refusing access to Cabinet minutes.[58]

It should be clarified that the UK Government is not the only culprit in perpetuating or promoting bad policy and thus producing bad law in the field of data protection (though it is ultimately responsible for what gets translated into law). Careful scrutiny of the Parliamentary proceedings would reveal that the business sector (through the Confederation of British Industry (CBI)) was lobbying quite hard to keep the Information Commissioner's improved powers of access restricted to the public sector and leave the private sector unaffected by new measures introduced to safeguard individual privacy:

> The Information Commissioner points out that the majority of complaints about violations of the principles of data protection are not directly against Departments or public authorities, but the rest of the economy in the private or voluntary sector. Amendments 105 and 106 would deal with that problem. (David Howarth, Cambridge Lib. Dem.)

I am acting in the spirit of finding out information rather than putting across a point of view. I usually expect the Opposition to be against interferences with private businesses, except on a warrant – as under existing law – and against imposing new burdens on businesses, yet the provision would put a new burden on them. Given that we have all received an e-mail from the CBI saying that it is strongly opposed to the amendment... (Mr. David Kidney, Stafford, Lab.)[59]

Happily for the interests of the citizen and the extended powers of the UK Information Commissioner, on this occasion at least the UK parliament appears possibly to have dodged an attempt by the vested interests of the private sector to implement a bad policy into law and the prevailing view to date seems to have been that of Michael Alun (Labour):

However, where a burden is needed in the public interest – to protect the public or individuals – it should apply fairly across the sectors. We should not imply that we can return to the old situation, in which it was clear that the public sector could be regulated and that there was no overlap with other sectors.[60]

This paper opened by examining the bad policies that spawned the bad laws that the same Mr. Straw ostensibly had set out to fix in the new Coroners & Justice Bill 2009. Like the Information Commissioner we can now make polite noises about finally dumping the bad laws of 10 and 25 years ago that resulted from the bad policies, but was there really a need to, in 2008–2009, draft things so clumsily and with such ineptitude that the gains made almost seem to be outweighed by the losses?

The data protection provisions of the Coroners and Justice Bill present a welcome but long-overdue opportunity to put rigorous safeguards in place and to address long-standing deficiencies in the Information Commissioner's powers, such as those you identified in last year's report on Data Protection and Human Rights. However, the Bill needs to be improved if it is to make the regulation of personal information more effective, and ultimately to help safeguard individuals' right to respect for their private life. Wider use of personal data must be balanced by the inspection and information gathering powers for the Information Commissioner's Office which will actually work in practice. The Bill's information-sharing provisions are too wide and the safeguards relatively weak. As it stands, we regret that the Bill will not give us powers to ensure that all those processing personal information do so in compliance with the principles of data protection. In particular, we must be able to serve an Assessment Notice on *any* data controller and there must be meaningful sanctions for ignoring a Notice.[61]

Thus, in the very same breath as introducing an imperfect Section 151 to finally give to the UK Information Commissioner what many other EU countries had given their data protection authorities from the very beginning 10 years previous and more, Mr. Straw saw fit to introduce the now-notorious Section 152. Mr. Straw's actions in introducing the Coroners & Justice Bill as drafted in January 2009 seriously contradict his claim that 'So long as we are in power it [the Human Rights Act] won't be watered down'.[62] As clearly indicated previously, his going through with Section 152 as drafted would have constituted a most serious watering down of the principle of finality of purpose, one of the most fundamental principles devised by Convention 108 and EU Directive 46/95 to implement Art 8 European Convention of Human Rights and Fundamental Freedoms (ECHR) in the Information Age. Indeed, in the same article, Mr. Straw is now having to admit error and trying to excuse his way out of this as follows:

I do not pretend we've got everything right. We haven't. Take the data-sharing measures proposed in the coroner's and justice bill. Their aim is good, but parliamentary scrutiny has thrown

> up justifiable concerns that the powers provided could be misused. It's not our intention but I agree, so we are acting to get a much better balance between data protection and access to services.

With all due respect, this just is not good enough. It should not take parliamentary scrutiny to tell you what anybody with the most basic knowledge of data protection and fundamental rights law could have told you in the first place. There are a number of lawyers and civil servants in the Ministry of Justice and in the Home Office with much more than a basic knowledge of both data protection and Human Rights law. Quite simply, if they did not tell Mr. Straw what was wrong about his bill, they were negligent or inept and if they did tell him or his Junior Minister about it then the buck stopped with him/them.

This is not an isolated incident but would appear to be only the latest of a series of examples of bad policy and bad law in the field of privacy and data protection within the UK:

> According to further reports in The Guardian, the Home Office has no plans to delete innocents' DNA profiles, going against a European Court of Human Rights ruling. In December 2008, the court ruled that the continuous retention of innocents' DNA samples is illegal. The Home Office was given three months to respond to the ruling, but allegedly it has 'no plans' to destroy samples of DNA.[63]

To borrow a sentence from David Howarth, insofar as bad policy and bad law is concerned one is tempted to say 'I am not sure whether it is a conspiracy, though I suspect that the right hon. Gentleman is right, but it has become a habit'.[64] There is no clear evidence that the UK has kicked the habit of bad policy and bad law but there is rather more evidence to suggest that, in the field of privacy and data protection if not elsewhere, the habit has become a dangerous addiction.

Notes

1. Organised by Masaryk University, http://www.cyberspace.muni.cz/english/index.php
2. See http://www.answers.com/topic/minimalism (accessed August 25, 2008).
3. Some new powers for the ICO to fine for breaches of the Data Protection Act were introduced in the Criminal Justice & Immigration Act 2008.
4. Government response to the Constitutional Affairs Select Committee Report, *Freedom of Information: Government's Proposals for Reform* (London: TSO, 2007), 10.
5. Ibid.
6. John Oates, 'Information Commissioner Calls For More Money and More Powers', in The Register, http://www.theregister.co.uk/2007/12/05/information_commissioner_evidence/ (accessed August 25, 2008).
7. Government response to the Constitutional Affairs Select Committee Report, *Freedom of Information: Government's Proposals for Reform* (London: TSO, 2007), 9.
8. Ibid.
9. Condensed from 'The Case for Amending the Data Protection Act 1998, v1 21, 12, 2007'.
10. Ibid.
11. Condensed from 'The Case for Amending the Data Protection Act 1998, v1 21, 12, 2007'.
12. Ibid., 18–23.
13. Ibid.
14. Ibid.
15. Richard Thomas, Speech to RSA Conference on Data Breeches, dated 29 October 2008, www.ico.gov.uk/upload/documents/pressreleases/2008/rsa_speech_oct08_final.pdf (accessed October 31, 2008).
16. We wish to acknowledge the assistance of Agnieszka Lewestam in bringing these incidents to our attention and providing translation.

17. http://fakty.interia.pl/polska/news/lekarka-ujawnila-dane-14-latki-w-ciazy,1128809 (accessed October 15, 2008).
18. http://www.wiadomosci24.pl/artykul/grono_net_informuje_o_bledzie_po_publikacjach_wiadomosci24_16867.html (accessed October 15, 2008).
19. http://serwisy.gazeta.pl/kraj/1,34397,4048349.html (accessed October 15, 2008).
20. http://miasta.gazeta.pl/rzeszow/1,34962,5638447,Proboszcz_upublicznial_nazwiska_darczyncow.html (accessed October 15, 2008).
21. 'England is Champion... At Losses of Personal Data', published just after the European Champions cup football tournament in a summer where the English team failed to qualify for the finals of Euro 2008, is the caption of an article authored by Christophe Elise on 25 August 2008, http://www.lesnouvelles.net/articles/divers/angleterre-championne-de-la-perte-de-donnees (accessed August 28, 2008).
22. 'La situation est-elle meilleure dans l'hexagone ? C'est peu probable, même si la France est "*un pays dans lequel on ne perd jamais un ordinateur portable...*" comme aime le rappeler – avec ironie – Eric Domage, Research Manager, Security Products & Services chez IDC. Notre chance, et malheur, n'est peut-être uniquement que de telles pertes ne sont jamais révélées au public' (Christophe Elise), http://www.lesnouvelles.net/articles/divers/ angleterre-championne-de-la-perte-de-donnees (accessed August 28, 2008).
23. Burton, Sir E., *Report into the Loss of MOD Personal Data*, compiled for the Permanent Under Secretary of the Ministry of Defence, 30 April 2008. Known hereafter as the Burton Report – Executive Summary par. 15, p. 3.
24. MOD holds some 60 million personal records in total (this includes duplicated records) – Burton Report – Executive Summary par. 38, p. 8.
25. Burton Report – Executive Summary par. 16, p. 3.
26. Burton Report – Part Two – MOD protection and management of personal data – par. 4, pp. 2–3.
27. Burton Report – Executive Summary par. 17, p. 3.
28. Burton Report – Part Two – MOD protection and management of personal data – par. 10, p. 6.
29. Independent Police Complaints Commission, *Independent Investigation Report into Loss of Data Relating to Child Benefit*, June 2008. Known hereafter as the IPCC Report par. 164, p. 36.
30. Poynter, K. *Review of Information Security at HM Revenue and Customs Final Report*, June 2008. Known hereafter as the Poynter Report par. VI.9, p. 38.
31. IPCC Report par. 169, p. 37.
32. IPCC Report par. 214, p. 47.
33. IPCC Report par. 215, p. 48.
34. IPCC Report par. 218, p. 48.
35. Poynter Report par. V.6, p. 33.
36. Poynter Report par. V.7, p. 34.
37. IPCC Report par. 223, p. 49.
38. Poynter Report par. VII.3, p. 43–44.
39. Poynter Report par. IX.2, p. 49.
40. Poynter Report par. XI.5. p. 56.
41. A number of commentators have considered the Coroners & Justice Bill from the increasingly classical 'conspiracy or cock-up?' perspective. For example: 'Vivienne Nathanson of the British Medical Association plumps for cock-up, not conspiracy. "Lazy future-proofing" is what she thinks is going on: the government is drafting powers widely because it is better to be safe than sorry', in 'Sorry, it's personal', *The Economist*, March 5, 2009, http://www.economist.com/world/britain/displaystory.cfm?story_id=13235015 (accessed March 6, 2009).
42. Richard Thomas, Speech to RSA Conference Europe on Data Breeches, dated October 29, 2008, www.ico.gov.uk/upload/documents/pressreleases/2008/rsa_speech_oct08_final.pdf (accessed October 31, 2008).
43. Ian Grant, 'BCS Urges MPs to Kill the Coroners & Justice Bill', *Computer Weekly*, February 24, 2009, http://www.computerweekly.com/Articles/ArticlePage.aspx?ArticleID=234974&Print
44. From the proceedings of the 1st sitting of the Committee on the Coroners & Justice Bill, February 3, 2009, p. 3, http://www.publications.parliament.uk/pa/cm200809/cmpublic/coroners/090203/am/90203s01.htm (accessed February 15, 2009).
45. Concealed Assault on Privacy, http://www.no2id.net/fpArchive.php (accessed March 2, 2009).

46. Andrew Grice, 'Straw Forced into Retreat Over Big Brother Data Sharing Plan', *The Independent*, February 24, 2009, http://license.icopyright.net/user/viewFreeUse.act? fuid=Mjg3Mjc2Nw%3D%3D
47. Amendments to Coroners & Justice Bill Thursday February 26, 2009. Available at http://www.publicationsparliament.uk/pa/cm200809/cmpublic/coroners/090226/am/90226s01.htm (accessed March 6, 2009).
48. Jack Straw, 'Our Record isn't Perfect. But Talk of a Police State is Daft', *The Guardian*, February 27, 2009.
49. Report summary as issued on the BC web-site and accessed on February 18, 2009, http://www.bcs.org/server.php?show=ConWebDoc.24509
50. Fiona Barr, 'Coroners Bill Protest Escalates', *E-Health Insider*, March 3, 2009, http://www.e-health-insider.com/news/4615/coroners_bill_protest_escalates (accessed March 4, 2009).
51. Tim Boswell MP Con during the tenth sitting of the Committee stage debate in the afternoon session of 26 February 2009 http://www.publications.parliament.uk/pa/cm200809/cmpublic/coroners/090226/pm/90226s01.htm (accessed March 6, 2009).
52. Ibid.
53. *Data Protection Act 1998*, Schedule 1, Part I.
54. Convention for the Protection of Individuals with regard to Automatic Processing of Personal Data, European Treaty Series No 108, Strasbourg 28 January 1981.
55. Reader's comment, posted March 4, 2009, http://e-health-insider.com/news/4615/?logout&r=/(accessed March 6, 2009).
56. Sally Almandras, Sally Broadbridge, Grahame Danby, and Pat Strickland, 'The Coroners & Justice Bill: Crime & Data Protection', Bill 9 of 2008–09, Research Paper 09/06, House of Commons Library, January 22, 2009, p. 108.
57. Ibid.
58. 'Jack Straw Blocks Release of Iraq Cabinet Minutes', *The Herald*, http://www.theherald.-co.uk/news/news/
display.var.2491436.0.Jack_Staw_blocks_release_of_Iraq_cabinet_minutes.php
59. Extract from the proceedings of the ninth sitting of the Committee, http://www.publications.parliament.uk/pa/cm200809/cmpublic/coroners/090226/am/90226s01.htm (accessed March 2, 2009).
60. Ibid.
61. Richard Thomas, in a letter to Andrew Dismore, Chair Joint Committee on Human Rights, dated February 27, 2009, http://e-health-insider.com/news/4615/?logout&r=/(accessed March 6, 2009).
62. Straw, 'Our Record isn't Perfect'.
63. Straw admits data sharing reforms, 27 February, 2009, http://www.publicservice.co.uk/news_story.asp?id=8731
64. From the debate in the House of Commons at Committee stage of the afternoon of Thursday February 26, 2009.

Is identity theft really theft?

Clare Sullivan

Law School, Ligertwood Building, University of Adelaide, Adelaide, South Australia and *International Graduate School of Business, City West Campus, University of South Australia, Adelaide, South Australia*

This article continues the examination of the emergent legal concept of identity now clearly evident in the UK as a result of the Identity Cards Act 2006 (UK) and its consequences. In 'Conceptualising Identity' (*International Review of Law, Computers and Technology* 2, no. 3 (2007): 237), the author asserted that identity is emerging as a distinct, new legal concept and considered the composition and legal function of the new concept. This article builds on that study and uses the emergent concept of identity, particularly token identity, to analyse the nature and consequences of identity theft. Identity theft is defined using the concept of identity now evident in the UK and the article examines misuse by a person of another individual's registered token identity for a transaction. The article considers whether an individual's identity is property that is capable of being the subject of theft, having regard to the nature and function of the emergent concept of identity.

Introduction

The earlier article entitled 'Conceptualising Identity' examined the new legal concept of identity now evident in the UK as a consequence of the *Identity Cards Act* 2006 (UK) ('Identity Cards Act') and the National Identity Scheme ('NIS').[1] In summary, the new concept consists of two components – database identity and token identity.

Database identity is all the information[2] recorded about an individual in the databases accessible under the NIS. Token identity is a subset of the information which comprises database identity. Token identity consists of name, gender, date and place of birth, date of death and 'identifying information',[3] i.e. signature, photograph and biometrics. The biometrics include a face scan, two iris scans and ten fingerprints.

Token identity does more than just identify. The token identity presented at the time of transaction, singles out an individual from the rest of the population and authorises the system to deal with that identity. Token identity is therefore the set of information that constitutes an individual's identity for transactional purposes[4] and it is the information which is most useful to an identity thief.

Use of another individual's registered token identity is made possible by the verification process whereby the required token identity information as presented, must match the record in the National Identity Register ('NIR') to enable the transaction. Not all the registered token identity information will necessarily be used to verify identity at the time of a transaction. The token identity information required will depend on the nature of the transaction and the requirements of the transacting entity. Usually name, gender, date and place of birth and one piece of the 'identifying information' will be required. Depending on the transaction, the 'identifying information' can be appearance in comparison with the photograph, handwritten signature and/or comparison of one or more biometrics. Routine transactions conducted in-person will usually require a match with the photograph, or a signature. Use of biometrics makes misuse more difficult (although not impossible) but biometrics will only be used for significant transactions.[5] Some transactions, most notably remote transactions conducted by telephone or using the internet, may not use any of the 'identifying information'. Answers to pre-designated questions may be used to check 'identity',[6] but their purpose is really to check that the token identity is in the right hands.

Misusing another individual's registered identity

Registration and the verification process under the NIS transforms the information which constitutes token identity, so that as a set, it becomes the individual's transactional identity. Misuse of an individual's registered token identity infringes that individual's ability to be recognised, and to transact, as a unique person. The use infringes his/her fundamental human right to identity, which includes the right of an individual to an accurate, fully functional token identity and to its exclusive use.

Unlike the individual pieces of information that comprise it, token identity has the essential characteristics of intangible property. Its misuse by another person not only infringes the individual's personal right to identity, it infringes the individual's proprietary rights in his/her registered identity, particularly in token identity.

When another person misuses an individual's registered token identity, he/she is using the set of information that constitutes the individual's transactional identity, as the perpetrator's own. The act is more than fraud. It is a misappropriation of the individual's transactional 'key'. The perpetrator is using the 'key' that enables the transaction and which is notionally connected to the individual through the 'identifying information', i.e. signature, photo, finger prints, face scan and iris scans, as recorded in the NIR. The perpetrator uses to his/her advantage, the implicit presumption that the person presenting the token identity is the individual to whom it is linked in the register. In doing so, the perpetrator acts dishonestly, but the essence of the crime is the misappropriation of another person's transactional identity, which infringes that person's rights in that his/her registered identity. This is a fine distinction, but an important one.

Under the NIS, identity is verified for the purposes of a transaction when the system matches the token identity as presented, with the information recorded in the NIR. The transaction is actually between the transacting entity and the token identity. Token identity is the legal person in the transaction, not the individual to whom it is connected in the register, nor the person who presents the token identity.

So, if B presents A's token identity as his/her own, A is the primary victim of the crime. The transacting entity C will seek to enforce that transaction as against A as the individual who is linked to that token identity by the 'identifying information' – a link which exits as a result of the scheme and the registration process. The evidential burden then falls on A to establish that he/she did not use the token identity for that transaction. Considering the nature of the wrong and the harm, the use by B of A's token identity is clearly more than just fraud, especially from A's perspective.

Is identity theft really theft?

This question has been given new currency in Australia because the Model Criminal Law Officers Committee in its Final Report on Identity Crime does not consider that an individual's identity can be the subject of theft:

> The phrase 'identity theft' is a misnomer, as identity theft does not actually deprive a person of their identity. The offence of theft or larceny traditionally involves an appropriation of the personal property of another with the intention to deprive him or her of that property permanently. Wrongfully accessing and using a person's personal information or forging proof of identity documents, without taking any physical document or thing, would not deprive the person of the ability to use that information.

The Committee instead conceptualised 'identity theft' as fraud or deceit and recommended that new Model Identity Crime offences to cover dealing in, or possessing, identification information with the intention of committing, or facilitating the commission of, an indictable offence.

The Committee's view is based on the long-held assumption that information is just information and that it can not be the subject of theft because its appropriation does not cause permanent deprivation. However, an individual's transactional identity under the NIS is more than just information. Registration under the scheme gives it the characteristics of property that is capable of being misappropriated.

Dishonest use by a perpetrator of an individual's token identity will not be noticed by the individual in the same way that an individual is likely to notice that his/her wallet or identity card is missing, for example. Initially, the misuse will not necessarily prevent the individual using his/her token identity for other transactions, but when misuse is suspected, the individual's use will be disrupted and the incident will be included as part of the information that makes up the individual's database identity.

The individual 'gets back' the token identity when his/her proprietary rights are restored, i.e. when another person is prevented from using it. The enduring nature of the information that constitutes token identity means that it cannot be restored to the individual without substantial impairment in its value. Another person is only prevented from using the token identity if the individual uses a new token identity, if there is a name change for example, or alternatively, if protection is provided by requiring a PIN or answers to additional questions at the time of a transaction. If a change of name is necessary as a consequence of the misappropriation, it illustrates the substantial impairment of the value of the original token identity. Similarly, the use of designated questions at the time of the transaction to provide additional protection, illustrates the impairment in integrity of the token identity. The impact of the appropriation is therefore fundamental and enduring and in that sense there is a substantial impairment of value from the perspective of the individual and the broader community.

While Alex Steel maintains that 'nothing of practical value is gained by extending theft to include intangible property; and that misuse of intangible property is best dealt with either by fraud or sui generis offences', dishonest use of an individual's token identity by another person is clearly more than fraud.[7] It is a misappropriation of the individual's transactional identity, not just dishonest use of identity information. Moreover, the criminal damage offence in the UK and computer offences under the Computer Misuse Act 1990 (UK) have limited application to the types of misuse which can be expected in the context of the NIS. Even the new offences in the Identity Cards Act do not apply to the dishonest use by another person of an individual's registered token identity.

Identity theft is theft

Section 1(1) of the Theft Act 1968 (UK) sets out the basic definition of theft which is generally followed in the Australian jurisdictions:

> A person is guilty of theft if he dishonestly appropriates property belonging to another with the intention of permanently depriving the other of it; and 'thief' and 'steal' shall be construed accordingly.

If a person uses the identity of another individual, or even just some parts of it, to obtain tangible property such as money, the elements of the theft offence are usually easily made out. However, the wrong and the harm arise when another person dishonestly uses an individual's token identity for a transaction. Dishonest use of an individual's transactional identity should be an offence; and the nature of that offence is essentially appropriation. When the elements of the offence are considered, it is clear that an individual's registered token identity is property that is capable of being stolen.

Token identity is property

Section 4(1) of the Theft Act defines 'property' as 'any property whether real or personal including things in action and other intangible property'. Section 5(1) states that:

> Property shall be regarded as belonging to any person having possession or control of it, or having in it any proprietary right or interest (not being an equitable interest arising only from an agreement to transfer or grant an interest).

When considered separately, the components of token identity do not have the characteristics of property, nor do they invariably identify an individual. An individual uses his/her name and date and place of birth for example but he/she does not own them. Even jurisdictions that protect some of the components, do not regard them as property, nor do they regard the individual as their owner. The right to publicity recognised in the USA for instance, protects the unauthorised use of a celebrity's name, image and even voice.[8] When considered separately these components can identify the individual because, as a consequence of the celebrity's public profile, the name, image or voice is distinctive. Nevertheless, the right is essentially personal, not proprietary.

On registration under the NIS, however, the information that makes up token identity takes on a different legal character. As a collective it assumes the essential characteristic of property, i.e. it becomes a 'thing' that is the subject of ownership rights, which are generally enforceable. It is capable of being controlled and of being misappropriated, and token identity is considered to 'belong' as defined in Section 5(1) of the Theft Act to the individual whose 'identifying information', primarily the biometrics, are recorded in the NIR. That individual has control of and proprietary rights in the registered identity.

Tony Honoré considers that ownership is determined by looking at the rights a person has to use the thing in the future.[9] He considers that the 'incident of residuarity' distinguishes possession from ownership, i.e. an owner has a superior right to possession and this reversionary interest characterises property. In other words, a person can possess something without owning it. Possession is a temporary right compared to the more enduring, reversionary right of ownership. While Honoré's comments apply to tangible rather than intangible property, the reasoning can be extrapolated to token identity. Given the nature of token identity and its relationship to the individual under the Scheme, the individual can be considered to have a residual right to his/her token identity. There is no difference in the fundamentals, except that token identity is intangible property.

Honoré's list specifies the right to possess the property, the right to use the property, the right to manage how the property is used, the right to income from the property, to security from interference with the right to the property and the right to transmit that right to successors.[10] Most of these rights are part of the broader right to database identity including token identity. All (with the possible theoretical exception of the right to possess, if the traditional interpretation is applied) are relevant to the relationship between an individual and his/her token identity, as is clear when the infringement of these rights is considered in relation to appropriation.

In all these respects, token identity is fundamentally different to the confidential information in the proof of an examination paper which was held in *Oxford* v. *Moss*[11] not to be intangible property that is capable of being stolen.[12] Token identity is also fundamentally different from the other more detailed information that makes up the rest of an individual's database identity. Like the examination paper in *Oxford* v. *Moss*,[13] the other Schedule 1 information is just information. Depending on the circumstances, unauthorised access to the other information, which makes up database identity, can be an offence under the Computer Misuse Act 1990 (UK), but it is not property that can be the subject of theft. Unlike the other information that makes up an individual's database identity, however, the nature of token identity, its functions under the scheme and its contingent connection to an individual, give token identity the characteristics of property that is capable of being stolen.

Alienability is often assumed to be a distinguishing feature. Indeed, in *National Provincial Bank* v. *Ainsworth*, Lord Wilberforce stated that property 'must be definable, identifiable by third parties, capable in its nature of assumption by third parties, and have some degree of permanence or stability'.[14] However, 'assumption by third parties' is not an essential feature as Kitto J of the High Court of Australia pointed out in *National Trustees Executors & Agency Co of Australasia Ltd* v. *FCT*: 'It may be said categorically that alienability is not an indispensable attribute of a right of property according to the general sense which the word 'property' bears in the law'.[15] Alienability is certainly not a feature of recently recognised concepts of property. The property rights recognised by the High Court of Australia in *Mabo No. 2* for example, do not include alienability.[16]

The NIS is based on the premise of 'one person – one identity', so there is necessarily a general duty on other members of society not to interfere with an individual's token identity, or its exclusive use by the individual, which is in line with Hans Kelsen's view that:

> The typical right to a thing (or real right) . . . is the property right. Traditional science of law defines it as the exclusive dominion of a person over a thing and thereby distinguishes this right from the right to claim, which is the basis only of personal legal relations. This distinction, so important for civil law, has an outspoken ideological character.
>
> Since the law as a social order regulates the behavior of individuals in their direct or indirect relations to other individuals, property too, can legally consist only in a certain relation between one individual and other individuals. The obligation of these other individuals not to disturb the first one in his disposition over a certain thing. What is described as the exclusive 'dominion' of an individual over a thing is the legally stipulated exclusion of all others from the disposition over this thing. The dominion of the one is legally merely the reflex of the exclusion of all others.[17]

Kelsen's views echo Charles Reich's views that protection of the private sphere derives its moral force from the liberal ideal of autonomy and particularly the protection of an individual's self-determination from interference.[18] Any interference with an individual's self-determination, impacts on the autonomy of society as a collective and on the values that underpin democracy. In this context, it is autonomy in the sense of being recognised as an individual and having transactional autonomy. Under the NIS, an individual must have 'exclusive dominion' over his/her registered token identity; and to maintain the integrity of the scheme, an individual's dominion over his/her registered token identity must be respected by others and protected from interference or disturbance.

Like Kelsen, Morris Cohen maintains that a 'property right is a relation not between an owner and a thing but between an owner and other individuals in reference to things. A right is always against one or more individuals'.[19] While that is undoubtedly true in relation to recognition of the property rights of an individual by others, there is also a relationship between the individual and the property. In *Yanner* v. *Eaton* the High Court considered this relationship and the importance of exclusivity and control:

> 'Property does not refer to a thing; it is a description of a legal relationship with a thing. It refers to a degree of power that is recognised in law as power permissibly exercised over the thing. The concept of "property" may be elusive. Usually it is treated as a "bundle of rights". But even this may have its limits as an analytical tool or accurate description, and it may be, as Professor Gray has said, that 'the ultimate fact about property is that it does not really exist: it is mere illusion.' Considering whether, or to what extent, there can be property in knowledge or information or property in human tissue may illustrate some of the difficulties in deciding what is meant by 'property' in a subject matter .... Nevertheless, as Professor Gray also says, 'An extensive frame of reference is created by the notion that "property" consists primarily in control over access. Much of our false thinking about property stems from the residual perception that "property" is itself a thing or resource rather than a legally endorsed concentration of power over things and resources.' ... Because 'property' is a comprehensive term it can be used to describe all or any of many different kinds of relationship between a person and a subject matter.[20]

The important consideration therefore, is the relationship. There is a relationship between the individual and his/her registered token identity that necessarily requires the control and exclusivity recognised as property in *Yanner* v. *Eaton*. There is also the broader relationship between the individual and others, whereby the relationship between an individual and his/her token identity is recognised and respected. Under both these approaches, and the bundle of rights approach; token identity is property.

Appropriating token identity

'Appropriation' is defined in Section 3(1) of the Theft Act which states that: 'Any assumption by a person of the rights of an owner amounts to an appropriation, and this includes, where he has come by the property (innocently or not) without stealing it, any later assumption of a right to it by keeping or dealing with it as owner'. Section 1(2) states that 'It is immaterial whether the appropriation is made with a view to gain, or is made for the thief's own benefit'.

Appropriation for the purposes of the law of theft requires that the thief acts as though he owns the property. In *R* v. *Morris* ('*Morris*') the House of Lords found that assumption of a single right of the owner can amount to appropriation.[21] Although Lord Roskill considered that a combination of acts by the defendant (as occurred in *Morris*) may amount to an appropriation, the subsequent decisions of the House of Lords in *R* v. *Gomez* ('*Gomez*') and *R* v. *Hinks* rejected that requirement and confirmed that assumption of any one of the rights of the owner is sufficient to constitute an appropriation.[22] As Alex

Steel observes 'This leaves appropriation as a very broad term which requires only the assumption of any one property right associated with the victim'.[23]

In the context of the NIS, an appropriation or dealing occurs when a person uses an individual's token identity as his/her own for transaction. When the perpetrator uses the token identity, he/she clearly assumes at least one of the ownership rights of the individual, specifically the right to exclusive use of the token identity. The assumption of that right is sufficient to constitute an appropriation within Sections 1 and 3 of the Theft Act but in using the individual's token identity, the perpetrator assumes most of the individual's ownership rights listed by Honoré.[24]

The perpetrator infringes the individual's right to security from interference with both the token identity and the individual's use of it, as well as the right to transmit that right to the individual's successors because the right to database identity including token identity, survives the individual's death and can be enforced by his/her executors and survivors. In using the token identity the perpetrator also infringes, then assumes, the individual's right to manage how his/her token identity is used. In dishonestly using the information that constitutes an individual's identity for a particular transaction, a perpetrator acts as though he/she owns that identity and assumes the proprietary rights that are exclusive to the individual.

Intention to permanently deprive the owner of his/her token identity

Section 6(1) of the Theft Act states that:

> A person appropriating property belonging to another without meaning the other to permanently to lose the thing itself is nevertheless to be regarded as having the intention of permanently depriving the other of it if his intention is to treat the thing as his own to dispose of regardless of the others rights; and a borrowing or lending of it may amount to so treating it if, but only if, the borrowing or lending is for a period and in circumstances making it equivalent to an outright taking or disposal.

In *R* v. *Lloyd* the court cited the opinion of Edmund Davies LJ in *R* v. *Warner* that 'Section 6 ... gives illustrations, as it were, of what can amount to the dishonest intention demanded by Section 1(1). But it is a misconception to interpret the section as watering down Section 1.' 'We should try to interpret the section in such a way as to ensure that nothing is construed as an intention to permanently deprive which would not prior to the 1968 Act have been so construed.'[25] However, JC Smith comments that 'before and since *Lloyd* courts have given the words of the section its wider ordinary meaning' (*sic*). Section 6(1) of the Theft Act was apparently intended to cover the situation in *R* v. *Hall* where the defendant took the owner's property and pretended that it was his own so he could sell it to the owner.[26] The defendant did not change the property in any way, nor did he remove it from the possession of the owner but he presented the property as his own.

Smith argues that the intention to use the property as one's own is not sufficient to amount to theft:

> It adds nothing to 'appropriates' since appropriation consists in an assumption of the right of the owner. The words, 'dispose of', are crucial and are, it is submitted, not used in a sense in which a general might 'dispose of' his forces but rather the meaning given by the *Shorter Oxford Dictionary*: 'To deal with definitely; to get rid of; to get done with, finish. To make over by way of sale or bargain, sell.'[27]

However, in *R* v. *Lavender* ('*Lavender*') in considering Section 6 of the Theft Act the court considered that the focus on the words 'to dispose of' and applying a dictionary definition to them was too narrow an approach and that the words 'if his intention is to treat the thing as his own to dispose of regardless of the other's rights' have to be read together. The court following what the statements of the Privy Council in *Chan Man-sin* v. *Regina*, considered that a disposal in the sense used in Section 6 includes dealing.[28]

In *Lavender* a tenant secretly took two doors from his landlord's premises to replace the damaged doors in his rented flat. The tenant's intention was to leave the doors in the flat after his lease terminated in about a year. Applying the second limb of Section 6, the court stated:

> So we think the question in the instant case is did the respondent intend to treat the doors as his own in dealing with the council regardless of their rights? The answer to this question must be yes. There can be no doubt that what the respondent did was regardless of the council's right. Those rights included the right not to have the doors at 25 Royce Road removed, and to require the tenant at 37 Royce Road to replace or pay for the damaged doors. In dealing with the doors regardless of those rights, when he consciously did, the respondent manifested an intention to treat them as his own.[29]

The common factor in *R* v. *Hall*, which is continued in *Lavender*, is that the defendant was considered to have stolen the property even though it was not removed from the possession of the owner and its nature was not altered by the offender's use.[30] Both cases involved tangible property but the basic principles also apply to intangible property like token identity. The crucial factor is that in each of these cases, the defendant exerted control over the property, and in doing so, usurped the owner's rights of control and exclusive use. Similarly, a person who dishonestly uses another person's token identity for a transaction exerts control over the token identity and thereby, usurps the owner's rights.

Dishonestly appropriating token identity

If the other elements of the offence are established, then it is a question of whether the misappropriation was dishonest. Edward Griew points out that 'dishonestly' 'has a negative function – as meaning 'otherwise than honestly' 'in much the same way as 'unlawful or 'without lawful excuse' is used.[31] Steel similarly observes that: 'In fact in England, whether an action amounts to theft will in practical terms depend on whether the person is dishonest'.[32]

The legislation does not define 'dishonesty' but in *R* v. *Feely* ('*Feely*') the Court of Appeal held that dishonesty does involve 'moral obloquy' and whether the accused is dishonest is a question of fact for the jury, applying 'current standards of ordinary decent people'.[33] This approach was modified by the Court of Appeal in *R* v. *Ghosh* ('*Ghosh*').[34] In *Ghosh* the Court of Appeal rejected the distinction between theft and conspiracy to defraud in relation to the test for dishonesty and emphasised that dishonesty refers to the knowledge and belief of the accused. The court doubted whether the court in *Feely* intended to establish an objective test and it reframed it as a two step test:

> In determining whether the prosecution has proved that the defendant was acting dishonestly, a jury must first of all decide whether according to the ordinary standards of reasonable and honest people what was done was dishonest. If it was not dishonest by those standards, that is the end of the matter and the prosecution fails.

If it was dishonest by those standards, then the jury must consider whether the defendant himself must have realised that what he was doing was by those standards dishonest. In most cases, where the actions are obviously dishonest by ordinary standards, there will be no doubt about it. It will be obvious that the defendant himself knew that he was acting dishonestly. It is dishonest for a defendant to act in a way which he knows ordinary people consider to be dishonest, even if he asserts or genuinely believes that he is morally justified in acting as he did.[35]

The belief of the defendant must be genuine. It need not be reasonable although that is a factor which is a relevant consideration in determining whether the belief is genuine. In the context of the NIS, use of an individual's registered token identity by another person will usually clearly be dishonest under this test.

Section 2(1) of the Theft Act sets out three situations in which appropriation of property is not to be regarded as dishonest, based on the defendant's belief. Under part (a) of Section 2(1), theft is not committed if a person appropriates the property believing that he/she has the legal right to deprive the owner of that property. Under part (b) if the accused believes that he/she has consent if the owner knew of the appropriation and circumstances, the use is not theft; and similarly the use is not theft under part (c) if the accused believes 'that the person to whom the property belongs cannot be discovered by taking reasonable steps'.

It is difficult to imagine how part (c) can apply to an appropriation of an individual's token identity by another person, but part (b) can apply when a friend or family member uses an individual's token identity of for a transaction. Part (b) is most likely to arise when control of an individual's token identity is assumed by another person, in the event of the individual's incapacitation due to injury, ill heath or old age. In these situations, the appropriation is not theft. However, the use by another person of an individual's token identity undermines the underlying assumptions of the Scheme so it should not generally be lawful, although the new offence provisions in the Identity Cards Act do not apply to this situation.

Of course, special arrangements are needed in the case of incapacity, but those arrangements should not include use of another person's token identity. It is possible for example, to design a system which links the token identity of specific people such as next of kin or a designated carer, with that of the individual, but which does not involve a person using another person's token identity, so as to uphold the presumption on which the scheme is founded.

Apart from use by family, friends, or a carer, the other most likely situation in the context of a national identity scheme, is where an individual is able to use another person's token identity as a result of system malfunction. At this time, it is difficult to visualise the circumstances of such a case, but it is conceivable that the appropriation may not clearly be within any of the exceptions in Section 2(1) of the Theft Act. In that event, the appropriation can still be held to be dishonest based on the defendant's genuinely held belief and the jury's assessment of that belief, applying the standards of ordinary people, so that 'dishonestly' operates as a safety net to prevent a possible miscarriage of justice.

Conclusion

Registration under the NIS transforms the components of token identity from information into a collective which assumes the basic characteristics of property and dishonest use of an individual's token identity fits surprisingly well within the requirements of the offence under Section 1 of the Theft Act.

Theft accurately describes the wrongdoing and differentiates it from other offences, especially fraud. Identity theft is fundamentally different to identity fraud in nature; and in terms of the wrong and the enduring harm it causes. Dishonest use of an individual's token identity by another person is a denial of the individual's right to the exclusive use of his/her transactional identity, and its use by another person fundamentally damages the integrity of the individual's token identity. To use Jeremy Horder's words, labelling the dishonest use by a person of another individual's transactional identity as theft 'captures the moral essence of the wrong in question, by reference to the best moral conception of that essence in society as it is today'.[36]

Notes

1. Clare Sullivan, 'Conceptualising Identity', *International Review of Law, Computers and Technology* 21, no. 3 (2007): 237.
2. In this paper 'information' includes 'data', unless otherwise indicated.
3. Schedule 1, Identity Cards Act.
4. 'Transaction' is used to describe any dealing, whether in person (i.e. face to face) or using remote communication (such as a telephone, the internet or a computer network), for which an individual is required to identify himself/herself. A transaction or dealing may be between an individual and a government department or agency or with a private sector entity, and can range from an enquiry to a contract. 'Transaction' does not include transactions and dealings of a non-business nature such as domestic and social interaction.
5. Biometrics will be required for relatively large financial transactions.
6. Questions can include address and mother's maiden name, for example.
7. Alex Steel, 'Intangible Property as Theft', *Sydney Law Review*; 30 (2008): 575.
8. The law in some European jurisdictions provides similar protection to persons who do not have a public profile but as a personal, not a proprietary right.
9. Tony Honoré, 'Ownership', in *Oxford Essays in Jurisprudence*, ed. A.G. Guest (Oxford, Oxford University Press, 1967), 113.<edn/publ 1960>
10. In examining the concept of ownership evident in most legal systems, Honoré found 11 elements consisting of nine rights, one duty and one liability, which are necessary for ownership of property. The duty is the duty to prevent harm. The liability is the liability to execution (see Honoré, Ownership).
11. *Oxford* v. *Moss*, 68 Criminal Appeal Reports 183. In this case a student dishonestly obtained the proof of an examination paper, read it and then returned it.
12. Although that decision was stated by the Court to turn on the question of whether information is property, rather than determining that question, the reasoning concentrates on whether information can be stolen. *Oxford* v. Moss (note 11 above) was really decided on the basis that the unauthorised reading of the proof of an exam paper by a student was not an appropriation of intangible property with intent to permanently deprive. In reading the proof, the student did not remove or change the information it contained (but arguably it did lessen its value as an assessment tool), so the defendant was not guilty of theft. Although not articulated by the Court, there is also a question a criminal conviction for theft was justified in these circumstances.
13. *Oxford* v. *Moss*, see note 11.
14. *National Provincial Bank* v. *Ainsworth* (1965) AC 1175.
15. *National Trustees Executors & Agency Co of Australasia Ltd* v. *FCT* (1954) 91CLR 540, 583.
16. *Mabo No. 2* (1992)175 CLR 1.
17. Hans Kelsen, *Pure Theory of Law*, trans. Max Knight (Berkeley: University of California Press, 1970), 131.
18. Ibid.; Charles Reich, 'The Individual Sector', *Yale Law Journal* 100, no. 128 (1991): 1409.
19. Kelsen, see note 17; Morris Cohen, 'Property and Sovereignty', *Cornell Law Quarterly* 13 (1927): 12.
20. *Yanner* v. *Eaton* (1999) 201 CLR 351, para 17–20.
21. *R* v. *Morris* (1984) AC 320. This interpretation has been criticised, particularly by A.T.H. Smith, as being an incorrect reading of Section 3(1). In Smith's view the right referred to in that section is 'a right "to it" i.e. the thing being stolen, which in context means the whole thing and all the rights in it'. Smith maintains that Section 3(1) and (2), which were relied upon by the Court in *Morris*, only show that 'the violation of a single right . . . might be sufficient to constitute an appropriation if it is accompanied by (as) an assumption of all the rights'(*sic*). See A.T.H. Smith, *Property Offences* (London: Sweet and Maxwell, 1994), 148, 149.

22. *R* v. *Gomez* (1993) AC 442; *R* v. *Hinks* (2001) AC 241
23. Steel, 'Intangible Property as Theft'.
24. Honoré, 'Ownership'.
25. *R* v. *Lloyd* (1985) QB 829; *R* v. *Warner* (1970) 55 Cr App R 93.
26. J.C. Smith, *The Law of Theft*, 8th ed. (London: Butterworths, 1997). 77, 80; *R* v. *Hall* (1849) 1 Den 381.
27. Smith, *The Law of Theft*.
28. *R* v. *Lavender* (1994) Crim LR 297; *Chan Man-sin* v. *Regina* (1998) 1 WLR 196.
29. *R* v. *Lavender*, see note 28.
30. *R* v. *Hall*, see note 26.
31. Edward Griew, *The Theft Acts*, 7th ed. (London: Sweet and Maxwell, 1995), 70.
32. Steele, 'Intangible Property as Theft'.
33. *R* v. *Feely* (1973) 1 QB 530, 538.
34. *R* v. *Ghosh* (1982) QB 1053, 1064.
35. Ibid.
36. Jeremy Horder, 'Re-thinking Non Fatal Offences Against the Person', *Oxford Journal of Legal Studies* 14, no. 3 (1994): 335, citing J.C. Smith and Brian Hogan, *Criminal Law*, 7th ed. (London: Butterworths, 1992), 350.

'Spam, spam, spam, spam . . . Lovely spam!' Why is Bluespam different?

Eleni Kosta, Peggy Valcke and David Stevens

Interdisciplinary Centre for Law & ICT (ICRI), Katholieke Universiteit Leuven, Belgium

The sending of unsolicited communications (commonly known as 'spam') is considered as a great intrusion into the privacy of the user of electronic communications services, and is therefore regulated in Article 13 of the ePrivacy directive. At the time of the adoption of the directive, the most common ways of spamming were via telephone, fax, electronic mail and SMS. Technological progress, however, has since created more types of spamming, one of which is Bluespam, i.e. the action of sending spam to Bluetooth-enabled devices, such as mobile phones, PDAs or laptop computers. Although, at first sight, it would seem that Bluespam should be considered as any other type of spam, and would therefore fall under the ambit of Article 13 of the ePrivacy directive, a closer look reveals that the answer is in fact not so obvious.

1. Introduction

Direct marketing has always been considered as a nuisance to consumers, and therefore already gained the attention of the Council of Europe back in 1985. At that time, direct marketing was defined as 'all activities which make it possible to offer goods or services or to transmit any other messages to a segment of the population by post, telephone or other direct means aimed at informing or soliciting a response from the data subject as well as any service ancillary thereto'.[1] At the beginning of the 1990s, unwanted electronic mail, usually in the form of advertisements for products and services, accompanied the advent of the Internet era. The sending of unsolicited communications via the Internet became commonly known as 'spam', which was also originally a trademark for canned ham by the firm Hormel. It is said to have taken its name from the *Monty Python* 'spam' skit, where the famous line 'Spam, spam, spam, spam . . . Lovely spam!' was repeatedly sung.

Increasing technological progress and the decreasing cost of transmitting messages has enabled the spread of unsolicited communications in new ways, such as via fax, SMS or MMS. These developments were taken into account by the European legislator during the drafting of the ePrivacy directive,[2] which regulates unsolicited communications under Article 13. A new term has appeared in the discussions on unsolicited communications: Bluespam. Bluespam is the action of sending spam to Bluetooth-enabled devices, such as mobile phones, PDAs or laptop computers. Although, at first sight, it would seem that Bluespam should be considered as any other type of spam, and would therefore fall under the ambit of Article 13 of the ePrivacy directive, a closer look reveals that the answer is in fact not so obvious.

2. Bluetooth as enabling technology for unsolicited communications?

Unsolicited communications, irrespective of the means via which they are sent, are considered to be a great intrusion into the privacy of the user. The European legislator indicated the significance he pays to this issue by including provisions for its regulation in various legislative instruments. Article 14(b) of the data protection directive,[3] and Article 7 of the e-commerce directive,[4] contained provisions on unsolicited commercial communications and direct marketing, and were succeeded by Article 13 of the ePrivacy directive.

As implied in recital 40 of the ePrivacy directive, at the time of its adoption, the most common ways of spamming were via telephone, fax, electronic mail and SMS. In general, the ePrivacy directive was aimed at the protection of the users of publicly available electronic communications services that are offered via public communications networks, regardless of the technologies used, seeking to implement the principle of technology neutrality into the regulation of data protection in the electronic communications sector (Rec. 4 ePrivacy dir.). However, questions arise regarding the applicability of the directive to several emerging technologies, such as Bluetooth and the legal problems that come up from their use in the field of electronic communications.

3. Bluespam as electronic mail

Article 13(1) of the ePrivacy directive stipulates that 'the use of automated calling systems without human intervention (automatic calling machines), facsimile machines (fax) or electronic mail for the purposes of direct marketing may only be allowed in respect of subscribers who have given their prior consent' (i.e. it stipulates an opt-in rule). Thus, the practice of sending electronic mail for the purposes of direct marketing, while disguising or concealing the identity of the sender on whose behalf the communication is made, or without giving a valid address to which the recipient may send a request that such communications cease, is prohibited. These provisions apply to subscribers who are natural persons, as explicitly mentioned in Article 13(5) of the ePrivacy directive. However, EU member states shall ensure that the legitimate rights of legal persons are also sufficiently protected. Paragraph 2 of the same Article, however, provides an exception from this rule for existing customers. More specifically, it sets out an opt-out system: if a person or a company receives electronic mail contact details from it own customers (whether they be natural or legal persons) in the context of the sale of a product or a service, then direct marketing for its own similar products or services is allowed unless the customer explicitly opts out.

Article 13 covers the use of automatic calling machines, fax or electronic mail for the purposes of direct marketing. As Bluespam does not entail the use of an automatic calling or fax machine, it is important to examine whether it falls under the definition of electronic mail. According to Article 2(h) of the ePrivacy directive, 'electronic mail' is defined as 'any text, voice, sound or image message sent over a public communications network, which can be stored on the network or in the recipient's terminal equipment until it is collected by the recipient'.

The UK Information Commissioner's Office (hereafter 'UK ICO') issued a guidance note entitled 'Guidance for subscribers on the Privacy and Electronic Communications (EC Directive) Regulations 2003' (PECR), where the sending of Bluetooth massages was mentioned. In the second version of the guidance note, it was explicitly mentioned that

'Marketing transmitted using "Bluetooth" technology, for example messages sent to all "Bluetooth" enabled handsets within a given radius, are also considered to be "electronic mail", as are WAP messages'.[5] Consequently, marketing messages sent using Bluetooth technology would have been subject to the PECR rules relating to the sending of unsolicited communications. However, the UK ICO amended its opinion in 2007, stating that Bluetooth is *not* covered by the aforementioned regulations, and that the legislative provisions relating to spam will not apply to Bluespam. Bluetooth messages are thus no longer mentioned in the Guidance for subscribers on the PECR as falling under the definition of electronic mail.[6]

This change in the opinion of the UK ICO illustrates the difficulty of the issue that needs to be examined. A Bluetooth message is definitely a text, voice, sound or image message. Crucial to the definition of electronic mail, however, is that the message is sent over a public communications network. The question whether this is the case for Bluetooth messages will, in this paper, be examined in the context of the general prerequisites for the applicability of the ePrivacy directive. As already mentioned above, the directive is aimed at protecting the personal data and the privacy of the users of publicly available electronic communications services that are offered via public communications networks. Therefore, we must consider three main issues:

(1) whether the sending of messages over Bluetooth is an *electronic communications service*,
(2) whether this service is offered using a *communications network* and
(3) whether the aforementioned service and network are *public*.

Electronic communications service and electronic communications network

The terms 'electronic communications network' and 'electronic communications service' are respectively defined in Article 2(a) and (c) of the framework directive,[7] while the term 'communication' is defined in Article 2(d) of the ePrivacy directive. Communication is defined as:

> any information exchanged or conveyed between a finite number of parties by means of a publicly available electronic communications service. This does not include any information conveyed as part of a broadcasting service to the public over an electronic communications network except to the extent that the information can be related to the identifiable subscriber or user receiving the information.

From the definition of communication, it becomes obvious that a communication should be seen in connection with an electronic communications service. However, it is important to point out that the concept of communication in the ePrivacy directive has a different meaning than the concept of electronic communications, as defined in the terms for electronic communications service and network in the Framework directive.[8] The definition of communication in the ePrivacy directive excludes information that is part of a broadcasting service and is intended for a potentially unlimited audience, save when the recipient can be identified, as for instance in the case of Video on Demand (Rec. 16 ePrivacy dir.).

An electronic communications service is defined in Article 2(a) of the framework directive as:

> a service normally provided for remuneration which consists wholly or mainly in the conveyance of signals on electronic communications networks, including telecommunications services and transmission services in networks used for broadcasting, but exclude services providing, or exercising editorial control over, content transmitted using electronic communications networks and services; it does not include information society services, as defined in

> Article 1 of Directive 98/34/EC, which do not consist wholly or mainly in the conveyance of signals on electronic communications networks.

Based on this definition of electronic communications service, the sending of any text, voice, sound or image message over Bluetooth should be considered as an electronic communications service, as it actually consists of the conveyance of signals, as required by the definition.

Furthermore, 'electronic communications network' means:

> transmission systems and, where applicable, switching or routing equipment and other resources which permit the conveyance of signals by wire, by radio, by optical or by other electromagnetic means, including satellite networks, fixed (circuit- and packet-switched, including Internet) and mobile terrestrial networks, electricity cable systems, to the extent that they are used for the purpose of transmitting signals, networks used for radio and television broadcasting, and cable television networks, irrespective of the type of information conveyed. [2(c) Framework directive]

The definition of 'electronic communications network' is very broad and covers a large scope of networks. In the case of Bluetooth, a network is created using a wireless Bluetooth connection, commonly known as *piconet*. In this type of network, one device provides the synchronisation reference and is known as the *master*. All other devices are known as *slaves*.[9] In simple words, Bluetooth technology enables the creation of an *ad hoc* network between the transmitting device and the Bluetooth enabled receiving device of the user.[10] Thus the network created falls under the aforementioned definition of an electronic communications network, as it permits the conveyance of signals.

More difficult to examine, however, is the third criterion, i.e. whether the electronic communications service and the network are public. No real definition of the term 'public' is included in the 2003 regulatory framework on electronic communications, and the term can be subject to various interpretations.[11] Article 2(d) of the Framework Directive defines a *public* communications network as 'an electronic communications network used wholly or mainly for the provision of publicly available electronic communications service'.

The concepts of a publicly available electronic communications service and a public communications network are closely interlinked. Defining a *public* communications network as one that is used wholly or mainly for the provision of *publicly available communications services* does not immediately provide much clarification for when a network is considered public or not. However, it becomes clear from the definition of public communications network that a publicly available electronic communications service implies the use of a public communications network.[12] Therefore, it is necessary to examine first whether the electronic communications network via which Bluetooth messages are offered is public.

The complicated discussion on definitions of electronic communications and services being public or private has not just taken place at a European level, but has also been transferred to the national legislation of the EU member states, via the transposition of the European legal framework on electronic communications of 2003. The UK did not manage to solve this very subtle issue. The terms 'public electronic communications network' and 'public communications service' are defined in Section 151 of the *Communications Act* 2003 as follows:

- 'public electronic communications network' means an electronic communications network provided wholly or mainly for the purpose of making electronic communications services available to members of the public;
- 'public electronic communications service' means any electronic communications service that is provided so as to be available for use by members of the public.

According to these definitions, it is important, for the qualification of an electronic communications network or service as being 'public', that they are *available to members of the public*. In neither definition, though, is there any further definition or clarification on what is meant by making the network or the use of the service available to the public.[13] Could it mean, for example, that the network or the service is available nationwide, thus making the criterion for its definition as public the geographical coverage it offers? The *Regulation of Investigatory Powers Act* 2000 (RIPA) defines a 'public telecommunications service' as 'any telecommunications service which is offered or provided to, or to a substantial section of, the public in any one or more parts of the United Kingdom' (Section 2(1) RIPA). So, the nationwide coverage of a network or the offering of a service is not the criterion for its classification as public, or at least it should not be the only one, as it will be illustrated in the following example. JANET (UK) is a non-profit association that, since 1994, has had responsibility for the management of the UK's higher education networking programme. Although the JANET network enables the universities and colleges it connects to provide Internet services to all of their staff and students, which is potentially a significant part of the UK population, the UK Office of Communications (OFCOM) characterises JANET as a private network. It appears that a significant factor in not classifying JANET as a public network is that individuals only gain access to JANET indirectly as part of the teaching and learning services they receive from the universities or colleges of which they are members, or by virtue of their engagement in research activities sponsored by these organisations.[14]

The aforementioned example implies that the characterisation of an electronic communications network or service as public depends on the conditions required to access them. Would, then, a network that allows every passerby to connect to it without registration qualify as public, regardless of its geographical range? Most likely, the answer would be positive. Would the answer, however, be the same when the owner of the network does not have the intention to offer it to any passerby? Would a network intended only for the residents of a hotel or for the customers of a specific shop be considered as private, even if no special prior authorisation needs to be obtained? Would the unsecured network of a non-technologically-savvy user qualify as public only because it is open to any passerby to connect to? And what about the networks where no real criteria need to be fulfilled in order to gain access to the network, but a prior notification is still needed? Does this make the network private, although it is in principle open to everybody?

The question whether an electronic communications network or service is public does not seem to have a simple solution. A lot of criteria can be listed in order to define whether or not a network or service should be considered as public. Such criteria could be quantitative, qualitative or a combination of both. For example, one could take into account whether the service or the network has been explicitly characterised as such by the relevant legislator, whether it is the provider's intention to offer the service to anyone who requests it, whether the service or the network is aimed at a specific group of people, is the breadth of the geographical area which is covered by the network or where the service is offered, whether standardised equipment is used, etc.[15] However, there is no consistent interpretation of the term throughout Europe, and the classification of a service or a network as public has thus become a great nuisance to companies and the industry.

In Belgium, the national legislation has excluded specific electronic communications networks and services from the obligation to notify the Belgian Institute for Postal Services and Telecommunications (BIPT). More specifically, notification is not required in the case of (i) the provision or reselling of electronic communications networks that do not cross the public domain, and (ii) the provision or reselling of electronic communications services or networks exclusively to a legal person, where the provider or reseller has a major participation (or to natural persons or legal persons), within the framework of an agreement in which electronic communications services or networks are offered purely as support for main activity, and on a secondary basis (Article 9, Sections 5, 6, Belgian Act on electronic communications). From these exceptions, it can be inferred that the Belgian legislator did not intend to consider electronic communications networks that do not cross the public domain, and services or networks where electronic communications services and networks are offered only on a secondary basis or as support to the main activity, as public. However, defining when an electronic communications network does not cross the public domain is again not clear, especially in the case of wireless networks.

The need for further clarification of the quite complicated definitions of public electronic communications and services has already been recognised by the Article 29 Working Party:

> the fact that provisions of the ePrivacy Directive only apply to provision of publicly available electronic communications services in public communication networks is regrettable because private networks are gaining an increasing importance in everyday life, with risks increasing accordingly .... Another development that calls for reconsideration of the scope of the Directive is the tendency of services to increasingly become a mixture of private and public ones. ... The Working Party notes that both definitions 'electronic communications services', and 'to provide an electronic communications network' are still not very clear and both terms should be explained in more details in order to allow for a clear and unambiguous interpretation by data controllers and users alike.[16]

The statement of the UK ICO that Bluetooth spam is no longer covered by PECR mentions that 'the Regulations only apply to messages over a public electronic communications network and we have concluded that Bluetooth messages are not in fact sent using such a network'.[17] The UK ICO argued that Bluetooth messages are conveyed over *ad hoc* peer-to-peer networks, called *piconets*, rather than over a public network.[18] From this statement, we can thus derive the *argumentum a contrario* that *ad hoc* networks are not considered as public networks. Regrettably, however, the UK ICO did not go into details regarding the criteria needed to classify a network as public or non-public.

Storage in the network or in the recipients terminal equipment

The definition of electronic mail in Article 2(h) of the ePrivacy directive requires that the 'message' can be stored in the network or in the recipient's terminal equipment until it is collected by the recipient. However, the transmission of a Bluetooth message requires a simultaneous communication between two Bluetooth enabled devices, and messages sent via Bluetooth cannot be stored on any network or in the recipient's terminal equipment until they are collected by the recipient (contrary to conventional electronic mail). Therefore, such messages cannot be considered as electronic mail, according to the definition of the ePrivacy directive.

Subscribers involved

Besides examining whether Bluetooth messages fall under the definition of electronic mail, it should be further examined if the rest of the criteria in Article 13 of the ePrivacy directive are fulfilled. As already mentioned above, Article 13 introduces an 'opt-in' system for the sending of electronic mail for the purpose of direct marketing and it prohibits the sending of electronic mail to 'subscribers'. The term 'subscriber' is defined in Article 2(k) of the Framework directive as 'any natural person or legal entity who or which is party to a contract with the provider of publicly available electronic communications services for the supply of such services'. According to this definition, the basic prerequisite for somebody to be classified as a subscriber is that the person has a contract with a provider of a publicly available electronic communications service, who will then actually offer the service. As already mentioned above, an *ad hoc* network, called a *piconet*, is created between the transmitting device, and the Bluetooth enabled receiving device of the user. Communication between the two neither requires a contract to be signed, nor a provider to be involved. Bluetooth messages are sent to anyone who passes close enough to the *master*, regardless of them being subscribers. In most cases, the user will have a contract with the company that provided the device, but this party does not play any role in the Bluetooth communication. Therefore, the recipient of a Bluetooth message does not qualify as a subscriber under the definition of the European Framework on Electronic Communications. The sending of Bluetooth messages for the purposes of direct marketing thus, it seems, does not need the prior consent of the user, as the provision of the directive requires that he also is a subscriber. The same argument was presented by the Dutch OPTA (the Independent Authority for Post and Telecommunications), when asked to express an unofficial opinion whether unsolicited commercial messages sent via Bluetooth fall under the ambit of anti-spam regulation.[19] The Dutch OPTA spoke of a potential *lacuna legis* that leaves such unsolicited messages out of the protective scope of the regulation against spam.

4. Regulating Bluetooth spam

The UK ICO decided that Bluetooth messages should not and would not be covered any more by the provisions of the PECR relating to the sending of unsolicited communications. Nevertheless, one cannot disregard the fact that unsolicited commercial Bluetooth messages are a great nuisance to consumers. At the beginning of 2007, the Dutch TV broadcaster SBS6 started a promotional campaign for the TV programme 'Stars Dance on Ice' by sending Bluetooth messages.[20] The messages were sent, via five bus stops in Amsterdam, to passersby and people waiting at the bus stops. According to the company *Bluetoothreclame*, 15,000 people consented to receiving the promotional video via Bluetooth, i.e. 15% of the people who received an invitation to accept the video because they had Bluetooth enabled.[21] However, a first message asking for consent to receive a commercial message is now no longer needed, as the 'opt-in' rule does not apply to Bluetooth spam. In both cases, it is beyond question that the nuisance to the user, who will have to reject an increasing number of commercial messages, is significant. Seeing that the danger of uncontrolled spamming via Bluetooth is at the gates, consumer organisations and privacy advocates urge marketers to consult industry guidelines on good marketing practices when it comes to the use of Bluetooth technology. Broadening of the scope of the regulatory provisions against spam in order to cover messages sent via Bluetooth, or specific legislation to regulate the issue, may also be needed in the near future.

As at June 2008, the European Regulatory Framework on Electronic Communications is under review and this would be a great opportunity to actually make some changes on issues that have proven to be problematic. The European Commission presented, on the 13 November 2007, a 'Proposal for a Directive amending ... Directive 2002/58/EC concerning the processing of personal data and the protection of privacy in the electronic communications sector ...'. Unfortunately, in its provisions, the proposal did not take into account the recommendations of the Article 29 Working Party to broaden the scope of the ePrivacy directive in order to cover private networks as well. The European Data Protection Supervisor (EDPS) expressed his dissatisfaction of this choice and 'regrets that the definition of services covered by the ePrivacy directive has not been broadened to include private networks'.[22]

However, the Committee on Civil Liberties, Justice and Home Affairs (LIBE) of the European Parliament adopted, on 26 June, an opinion on the Commission's proposal for the review of the ePrivacy directive.[23] LIBE proposed an amendment to Article 3 of the directive in order to broaden the scope of application of the ePrivacy directive in conformity with the proposals of the Article 29 Working Party and the EDPS. According to this proposal,

> [the] directive shall apply to the processing of personal data in connection with the provision of publicly available electronic communications services in public *and private* communications networks *and publicly accessible private networks* in the Community, including public *and private* communications networks *and publicly accessible private networks* supporting data collection and identification devices. [Emphasis added to illustrate the proposed amendments]

The LIBE amendment is aimed to expand the application of the ePrivacy directive to all networks, private and public, as well as to publicly accessible private networks. Expanding the application of the ePrivacy directive to all types of networks, private and public, would possibly solve problems regarding the classification of networks as being public or not. It would, however, cause a great deal of additional obligations for private networks, which was clearly not the original intention of the legislators. Furthermore, this LIBE amendment is not followed by similar amendments to the rest of the provisions of the ePrivacy directive, which in almost all cases still refer only to public electronic communications networks. The lack of clear definitions of public, private and publicly accessible private networks is therefore bound to increase the uncertainty regarding the classification of networks under these categories.

5. Conclusion

The aforementioned analysis illustrates that unsolicited commercial messages sent via Bluetooth cannot be covered by the anti-spam provisions of the ePrivacy directive, for a number of reasons. The messages are not sent to subscribers, as required by Article 13, they cannot be stored on any network or in the recipient's terminal equipment until they are collected by the recipient, and it is unclear whether they are even transmitted over a pubic communications network. Nevertheless, for a number of years, commercial messages sent via Bluetooth were considered as requiring the same protection with any other type of unsolicited commercial message. Therefore, the consent of the consumer needed to be obtained before the sending of the message. Although Bluetooth messages do not fall under the 'opt-in' rule that covers the sending of spam, it should be kept in mind that they do indeed greatly intrude into the privacy of consumers. Taking into account the limited storage capacities of most Bluetooth enabled devices, it can even be argued that the sending of unsolicited communications via Bluetooth can be of a far greater nuisance to the consumer than receiving multiple of e-mail spam messages in his e-mail inbox. Bearing this in mind, it is advisable that either the scope of the regulation on unsolicited communications be broadened in order to cover networks like Bluetooth, or that new regulations covering the sending of unsolicited Bluetooth messages be enacted.

Notes

1. Council of Europe, Recommendation No. R (85) 20 of the Committee of Ministers to EU member states on the protection of personal data used for the purposes of direct marketing.

2. Directive 2002/58/EC of the European Parliament and of the Council concerning the processing of personal data and the protection of privacy in the electronic communications sector (ePrivacy Directive), *Official Journal* L201, 37–47 (12 July 2002).
3. Directive 95/46/EC of the European Parliament and of the Council of 24 October 1995 on the protection of individuals with regard to the processing of personal data and on the free movement of such data, *Official Journal* L281, 31–50 (23 November 1995).
4. Directive 2000/31/EC of the European Parliament and of the Council of 8 June 2000 on certain legal aspects of information society services, in particular electronic commerce, in the Internal Market (Directive on electronic commerce), *Official Journal* L178, 01–16 (17 July 2000).
5. ICO, 'Guidance for subscribers on the Privacy and Electronic Communications (EC Directive) Regulations 2003' (2006, v2.0/December 2006).
6. ICO, 'Guidance for subscribers on the Privacy and Electronic Communications (EC Directive) Regulations 2003' (2007, v3.1/8 October 2007).
7. Directive 2002/21/EC of the European Parliament and of the Council on a common regulatory framework for electronic communications networks and services (Framework Directive), *Official Journal* L108, 33–50 (24 April 2002).
8. L. Asscher and S.A. Hoogcarspel, *Regulating Spam – A European Perspective After the Adoption of the E-Privacy Directive. Information Technology & Law Series* (The Hague: TMC Asser Press, 2006), 34.
9. Bluetooth SIG, 'Overview of Operations', http://www.bluetooth.com/Bluetooth/Technology/Works/Overview_of_Operation.htm. (accessed June 25, 2008).
10. R. Marchini and K. Tebbutt, 'Bluespam: Is it legal?', World Data Protection Report, BNA International, London, July 2007: 2.
11. C. Cuijpers, A. Roosendaal and B.-J. Koops, eds., 'The Legal Framework for Location-based Services in Europe', FIDIS-Project, Deliverable D11.5, 2007.
12. M. Gadzheva, 'Legal Issues in Wireless Building Automation: An EU perspective', *International Journal of Law and Information Technology* 16 (2008): 159–170.
13. R. Jay, *Data Protection – Law and Practice*, 2nd ed. (London: Sweet & Maxwell, 2003), 639.
14. Private Communication with Andrew Cormack, JANET.
15. S. Van der Hof, C. Cuijpers, M. Van Eechoud, S. Gijrath, M. Schellekens and M. De Vries, *Openbaarheid in het internettijdperk* (Den Haag: Sdu Uitgevers, 2006), 152–153.
16. Article 29 Working Party, 'Opinion 8/2006 on the Review of the Regulatory Framework for Electronic Communications and Services, With Focus on the ePrivacy Directive, WP 126', p. 3. Similar thoughts were included in Article 29 Working Party, 'Opinion on the Review of the Directive 2002/58/EC on Privacy and Electronic Communications' (ePrivacy Directive), WP 150.
17. ICO, 'Bluetooth Spam Not Covered by ICO Guidance', 11 October 2007, available online at http://www.ico.gov.uk/upload/documents/pressreleases/2007/bluetooth.pdf.
18. Personal communication with the UK ICO, e-mail, 13 June 2008.
19. Slashdot, 'Bluetooth Spam in Public Spaces', http://it.slashdot.org/article.pl?sid=07/01/28/2114253&from=rss. (accessed June 25, 2008).
20. Remco Tomeson, 'SBS6 zet Bluetooth in voor promotie ijsdansshiw, 17.01.2007', http://www.emerce.nl/nieuws.jsp?id=1835949. (accessed June 25, 2008).
21. Remco Tomeson, 'Bluetooth Marketing besorgt Opta hoofdbrekers, 26.01.2007', http://www.emerce.nl/nieuws.jsp?id=1845389. (accessed June 25, 2008).
22. European Data Protection Supervisor, 'Opinion on the Proposal for a Directive of the European Parliament and of the Council Amending, Among Others, Directive 2002/58/EC Concerning the Processing of Personal Data and the Protection of Privacy in the Electronic Communications Sector' (Directive on privacy and electronic communications), 10 April 2008.
23. European Parliament, Rapporteur Alexander Alvaro, 'Opinion of the Committee of Civil Liberties, Justice and Home Affairs for the Committee on the Internal Market and Consumer Protection on the Proposal for a Directive of the European Parliament and of the Council amending Directive 2002/22 on Universal Service and Users' Rights Relating to Electronic Communications Networks, Directive 2020/58/EC Concerning the Processing of Personal Data and the Protection of Privacy in the Electronic Communications Sector and Regulation (EC) No. 2006/2004 on Consumer Protection Cooperation', 26 June 2008, 2007/0248(COD).

Agents, Trojans and tags: The next generation of investigators

Wiebke Abel

AHRC/SCRIPT Law and Technology Centre, School of Law, University of Edinburgh, Old College, Edinburgh, UK

In a statement the Council of the European Union has recommended that member states should introduce clandestine remote searches of computers as a standard investigation method to combat cybercrime. At present, there is little analysis of the consequences such a development will have in the UK. The use of remote forensic software tools by law enforcement agencies has been, however, controversially discussed elsewhere and most notably in Germany where the Federal Constitutional Court had the opportunity to analyse the issue. This paper describes the use of this investigation method in Germany and analyses the reaction of the German and some other legal systems to give a first indication of the likely issues that its use in the UK will raise.

Introduction

In a statement the European Union (EU) council recommended that member states should undertake clandestine remote searches of computers of suspects, if provided for under national law.[1] This recommendation is part of a framework strategy developed to more effectively combat cybercrime and the increase in crimes committed using computer technology.

Police and secret services frequently face the question of to what extent traditional investigation methods are sufficient to deal with the challenges created by the networked world. The temporal and 'spatial' dimensions of cyberspace differ from the traditional crime scene, where time and space serve as non-negotiable boundaries. Hence, evidence acquisition and the surveillance of suspects in the digital world are different from these procedures in the real world and investigation methods and tools need to be adapted to keep pace with technological progress. However, these new investigation methods have to be in accordance with existing legislation and need to adhere to privacy laws and established evidence collection principles.

The remote search of computers raises several of these legal issues, and in countries that have introduced this method the legality of it has involved highly controversial discussions. The most prominent example for this is Germany, where in 2008 the Federal Constitutional Court had to decide on this matter.[2]

In the first part, the investigation method, remote searching, is introduced. In the second part of this article the legal problems surrounding this method are defined and regulatory approaches explored. The focus for this analysis is on Germany, which has introduced the most extensive legislation and case law regulating the use of this technology and therefore serves as the main case study for this article. A short comparison with the legal situation in the UK is undertaken.

Remote searching

The purpose of searching a computer remotely is to enable investigators to search the data stored on the hard disk and the working memory of a computer, to intercept the email traffic, and monitor web browsing habits and instant messaging.[3] To accomplish this, a specifically designed computer program, a 'remote forensic software' (RFS) tool is planted on the suspects' computer without raising his knowledge. This program is then able to copy all data stored on the computer and subsequently transfer it back to the investigating authority for evaluation. Such a program shares crucial features with well-known malware, in particular viruses and Trojans.[4] Both can be used to access and extract personal data from targets, and hence are equally suitable for data collection by police authorities. This is why the RFS tool facilitating remote searches is often referred to as 'Federal Trojan' in Germany. The advantage of using these technologies is that they can be installed clandestinely and without access to the suspect's house or physical premises. They are designed to be disguised as something harmless, when they actually include malicious or harmful code and therefore trick the suspect into installing them. Therefore, as with their criminal counterparts, police Trojans require the unwitting cooperation of the target.[5] This can happen through opening an email, for instance an email that purports to come from a *bona fide* state agency such as the local council or the Department for Pensions. For obvious reasons, police investigators would have little difficulty generating emails that cannot be distinguished from genuine information coming from other public authorities by spam filters and similar software – indeed; these public authorities may well be the source of the email which carries the Trojan as a payload on behalf of the police. It might not even be necessary to fake sender addresses and other identifying data embedded in an email.

Alternatively, the Trojan could be embedded in a website that the suspect is likely to visit, or could be part of software downloads from such websites. The police could set up for instance websites that look as if they contain material helpful for would-be terrorists, and infect the computers of visitors. The problem with this approach is that it would be highly indiscriminate, attacking every visitor, including accidental visitors following say a google link. It would be even more difficult to restrict the search to people named in a search warrant if this is the legal requirement. Alternatively, a combination of the two methods could be used, directing the suspect through an email to a website that requires log in, for instance a website that allows submission of tax returns – the suspect could be identified through his login information and he and only he then directed to an infected site that, apart from this infection, is identical to a genuine tax office website. All of these methods raise legal and political concerns which, however, go beyond the scope of this article. Apart from potentially undermining citizen's trust in e-governance, particular concerns are the role of Anti-malware providers, and whether or not they will collaborate with the police and disable their software for police controlled Trojans – especially if the police force is located in a different jurisdiction. If anti-malware products were disabled for police Trojans, the danger that they could fall into the wrong hands (a computer literate suspect might be able to take over the code planted on his machine for instance) and cause damage to third parties would increase exponentially, raising issues about police liability.

In Germany, the concept of granting police or secret services the power to remotely search a suspect's computer was officially introduced in 2006, when German Prosecution authorities suspected that information crucial to the investigation might be stored on the suspect's computer, and applied for a warrant to remotely search it.[6] The application was rejected and a subsequent appeal by the state prosecutor to the German Federal Court of Justice was equally unsuccessful.[7] However, the application and subsequent judgement triggered a public debate on the legality of remotely searching a suspect's computer.

The Federal Court avoided in its decision to discuss the substantive legal and constitutional issues that RFS tools raise. It did however indicate that remote searches are sufficiently different from existing surveillance methods and that they require explicit legislation to create a new police power. Neither an application under the laws regulating mail intercepts, nor under the laws regulating telephone surveillance, was deemed appropriate for this situation. For the Government, this meant that as a next step, it had to fast track enabling legislation to meet this requirement. Since most policing functions, including some antiterrorism functions, are a devolved matter under the German constitution, the discussion moved from the federal level to state level initiatives. As the first state, Nordrhein-Westfalen amended its 'law for the protection of the constitution' (Verfassungsschutzgesetz) on 20 December 2006[8] to enable the use of this new investigation method by the constitutional protection agency (Verfassungsschutz) of Nordrhein-Westfalen. Article 5 II of the Constitution Protection Act of Nordrhein-Westfalen (Verfassungsschutzgesetz Nordrhein-Westfalen – VSG NRW) was amended by adding paragraph 11. This paragraph permitted the secret observation and investigation of the Internet and in particular the clandestine interception of communication via the internet and the secret access of its IT systems. A constitutional complaint was filed against this amendment with the German Federal Constitutional Court (Bundesverfassungsgericht), challenging its constitutionality. The court declared in its judgement on 27 February 2008 that article 5 II paragraph 11 VSG NRW was in violation of the constitution and therefore unlawful.[9] However, the Federal Constitutional Court in its judgement did not generally declare the use of this investigation technology unconstitutional. Rather, it recognised in its judgement a new constitutional right in the confidentiality and integrity of information technology systems, a right that finds its limits only in the protection of other rights enumerated in the constitution, and thereby defined the scope and limits of the use of the 'Federal Trojan' or online search.

In the UK, courts have not so far had the opportunity to rule on the legality of RFS tools and the admissibility of evidence generated by the process. Remote searching of computers was officially introduced as an investigation method following the recommendation of the EU Council. The UK's Home Office adopted a plan that police officers and secret service agents are allowed to remotely and clandestinely search computers of suspects without a court warrant.[10] However, remote searching is not an entirely new investigation method in the UK. The method was quietly adopted in the UK when the relevant technology to remotely access computers became available and, according to the Association of Chief Police Officers, British police have been carrying out remote searches in the past and stated that 194 remote hacking operations were undertaken in 2007–2008.[11]

Legal problems

The use of RFS tools during crime investigations raises several legal issues. The abilities of this technology and its intended use can potentially violate privacy and data protection rights of affected persons, and challenge existing evidence principles. In the following, the most pressing legal threats are identified and how far these threats can be adequately addressed by existing legislation in Germany and the UK is analysed.

Classification problems – de lege lata

The first question the German courts had to answer was whether it was possible to subsume this new technique under established legal concepts. As described above, RFS tools are to be used by police and secret services to remotely and clandestinely access computers of suspect's to monitor the communication and search the documents stored on it.

In Germany, two existing investigation measures were proposed as possible 'matches': the search of premises and the interception of telecommunications. Both measures are regulated by and find their legal foundations in the German Criminal Procedural Code (Strafprozessordnung – StPO).

A search of premises of a suspect is governed by article 102 StPO. Under this law, a search of a flat or other premises, as well as a person and the person's belongings, is permissible if it is suspected that the search will lead to the discovery of evidence.[12] Generally, the search and confiscation of computers during investigations is permissible under article 102 StPO in conjunction with articles 110 and 94 ff StPO. Article 110 StPO allows the search of the suspect's documents and papers during an investigation. Under prevailing case law, this includes the search and confiscation of data storage devices and the data stored on them.[13] Articles 94 ff StPO regulate the confiscation of evidence relevant to the investigation. According to article 98b StPO, the confiscation of data stored on a computer is accomplished by copying the data, hence producing a duplicate of the original piece.[14]

At first glance, the online search of computers and laptops using RFS tools appears to be comparable to a search of premises. As personal property, the computer and the data stored on it can be searched if reasonable suspicion that the computer of the suspect holds information crucial to the investigation exists. Generally, it is irrelevant for the applicability of this law whether this is done remotely using an RFS tool, or locally in person. However, the difference is that searches using RFS tools are clandestine and undertaken without the knowledge of the suspect. Therefore, the question is in how far article 102 StPO would legitimate such an action. The regulations for the lawful performance of a search are laid down in articles 105 ff StPO. These articles define that the person affected by the search should attend the procedure, or if absent a representative should be there (article 106 StPO). Furthermore, a written notification about the search and a list of seized objects must be issued on request of the person affected by the action (article 107 StPO). This rule guarantees that the person is informed about the reason for the procedure and can verify the legitimacy of the search and consult a lawyer if necessary. These rules are mandatory laws and compliance with them is essential for the legitimacy of the search. Under no circumstances can a search purposely take place without witnesses to keep the suspect in the dark about the search.[15]

However, one of the main purposes of the online search of computers using RFS tools is that the suspect is unaware of the investigation and will also not be notified about it afterwards. This means that, although an online search of computers with RFS tools shares certain attributes with a search of premises, existing laws regulating the latter cannot be applied to the use of RFS tools. Note that the relevant articles of the law on criminal procedure regulate the conditions, under which a *prima facie* violation of a constitutional principle is permissible, the protection of one's home. This means that any deviation from these rules amounts to a violation of the constitution, not just a mere formal violation of a procedural law. It also means that mere amendments to the procedural law will not be sufficient.

The other possible analogy, the interception of telecommunications is regulated by article 100a StPO. This article allows monitoring and recording of the communication of a suspect without his knowledge in specific cases. Essential is that a flow of data between the suspect and a third party exists and that this data is the target of the interception. A traditional example of this is the data flow between two people talking to each other on the phone. A flow of data between the suspect and the ISP exists when the suspect goes online. This dataflow is used to transport the RFS to the suspect's computer and to transmit the collected data back to the investigating division. However, this dataflow is not the target of the investigation and is not intercepted.[16] It is purely a technical means utilised to transport the RFS tool and the data seized on the computer. Therefore, the legislation regulating the interception of telecommunications cannot be applied to the use of RFS tools.

For the police and government, this analysis, which in essence echoes that of the Federal court of Appeal,[17] created a dilemma of either restrict the operational utility of the new tool and make it more like a traditional search, with notification of the accused, or accept the finding and create new legal category of police investigative powers, and accept the inevitable delay (and possible constitutional challenges) to this new act.

By contrast in the UK, remote searching of computers has been legal since 1994. An amendment to the Computer Misuse Act 1990 made state hacking possible. However, such intrusive surveillance is closely regulated under the Regulation of Investigatory Powers Act 2000 (RIPA).

RIPA allows in Section II for covert directed surveillance of persons. Directed surveillance is defined as covert surveillance, which is undertaken for a specific investigation or operation that is likely to obtain private information about a person, and for the purpose of preventing or detecting a serious crime. The RFS tool searches the data stored on the computer and monitors the online activity of the suspect to gain information about a specific person to prevent crimes and acts of terrorism. The use of RFS tools is therefore governed by this Act.

Owing to the design of RFS tools, decisions about relevancy of data and suspect behaviour could entirely be made by the software itself, without direct influence or decision by a human officer. In which case, it remains to be seen whether these existing UK laws are sufficient to govern the use of RFS tools or if there will be a need for new legislation.[18]

Privacy and human rights violations

The purpose of using RFS tools is to monitor any activity of a suspect, and to copy all data and email traffic stored on the computer of the suspect. This allows investigators to gain, apart from relevant documents, access to passwords and encryption keys and an insight into the details of communication. This data collection process is automated and no human officer will actively decide what data is relevant and, more importantly, is highly sensible private data, such as medical and financial information or documents equivalent to diary entries. Also, information about innocent third parties can be found on the computer, in particular if the computer is also used for work purposes. Especially problematic is in this context that the search of the computer and seizure of data takes place without the knowledge of the suspect. All this could potentially violate privacy and human rights of the person affected by this search, and to the extent that the seized data forms part of the 'core' of private life, it may enjoy specific protection by the constitution and be generally shielded from investigative activities in some jurisdictions.[19] Hence the question is in how far the use of these tools complies with privacy and constitutional laws.

In Germany, the German Federal Constitutional Court established in its judgement about the amendment of the Constitution Protection Act of Nordrhein-Westfalen that a new constitutional right protects the use of ICT devices in confidentiality and integrity of information technology systems. It derived this right from the most basic human right the German constitution recognises, the protection of human dignity, a provision that had before served as basis for establishing a constitutional right in data protection.[20] This human right not only defines what is protected, but also how this right can be limited through state acts. Hence in Germany, if law enforcement agencies are using RFS tools, this must be done in accordance with the new human right to protect the privacy rights of the suspect. Therefore, a measure restricting this right is only proportionate where sufficient evidence exists that significant higher-ranking fundamental values, enumerated in the constitution, need be protected. Higher-ranking fundamental values are the life and integrity of other citizens, the foundations of the state and essential values of humanity. RFS tools can therefore only be used to prevent serious criminal cases, such as when acts of terror are suspected. Furthermore, any such measure is only permitted by a judge on a case-by-case basis to guarantee an objective and independent control prior to the execution, and on a constitutional legal basis. A further requirement is that any measure restricting the right in confidentiality and integrity of information technology systems does not violate the core area of the private conduct of life,[21] which includes, among other things, communication and information about inner feelings or deep relationships. The private conduct of life is an absolute fundamental right, which cannot be restricted (Art 1 I GG – right to human dignity). Since it will regularly be very difficult for the tool to differentiate between core area and non-core area data during the investigation process, the court states that adequate procedures have to be in place for the examination stage of the data. In particular, if core area data is detected, this data must be deleted immediately, and the use of this data by the state is prohibited. However, this raises the dilemma that the requirement to delete the collected core area data cannot make the violation of the absolute right to human dignity undone. Furthermore, the review of the data for core area data is in itself a very time consuming and labour intensive process. Even more problematic is that the German Federal Court judgement has established, as a requirement for the use of RFS tools by law enforcement authorities, that this selection process must be undertaken by an investigating judge, a state attorney, or a judicial officer.[22] As Frank, head of the German Judges Association point out, the German judicial system lacks the manpower to do this.[23]

In the UK the Human Rights Act does not contain similar provisions, and the balance between state interests in surveillance and privacy interest of citizens is in comparison more state friendly. However, according to RIPA, permission for a covert directed surveillance can only be granted if a senior officer determines that it is proportionate and necessary to prevent or detect a serious crime.[24] This means that a remote search of a computer cannot be permitted for just any minor crime. It is permissable only if the disadvantages for the affected person do not outweigh the gains of the measure and the gains are thought to be crucial for the course of the investigation.

These requirements are weakened however by the fact that no court warrant is required to authorise a remote searching of a computer and powers under RIPA have been used to put persons under surveillance for minor crimes in the past.[25] Also, the remote search of a computer is at least as intrusive as the physical search of a house, for which a magistrate's court warrant is required. It is therefore questionable whether this Act provides sufficient safeguarding of the potentially enormous infringement of privacy rights.

Use as evidence

While obtaining relevant data using RFS tools can be a difficult task in itself, making use of this data as evidence in court proceedings can be equally problematic. This is because the data that is collected by RFS tools is in digital form. Digital evidence, also referred to as electronic evidence or computer evidence is different from traditional, non-digital evidence and raises unique problems. Digital evidence can be defined as a 'representation of information using numbers, such as binary digits (bits)', which are not accessible to human senses.[26] This definition highlights one important difference between digital and non-digital evidence: humans cannot directly read much immediate digital evidence. It requires the assistance of a computer to do so. Furthermore, digital evidence can easily be altered and duplicated. These problems taking together show the greatest problem in computer forensics: how to ensure the authenticity of the data, when both the collection of the data and also its later presentation almost inevitably change it? While a weapon on a physical crime scene remains the same after collection by police and inspection by experts and jury, and can at any time in the proceedings be used as an objective comparator for the claims made by either side, digital evidence potentially changes every time it is open and viewed on a computer. In some sense, there is no 'enduring original' that can serve as objective comparator. The answer to this problem across a range of jurisdictions has been procedural in nature. By establishing best practice procedures for the collection of digital evidence, we can bring digital and physical crime scenes as closely together as possible, and ensure at least 'for all practical purposes' that the data given to the court is identical to the data generated by the suspect. As a result, digital evidence acquisition methods reflect the nature of the physical crime scene where time and space serve as boundaries.[27] Traditionally, when computers are searched during investigations to secure potentially relevant data, the computer or hard-drive is seized and taken off-line to guarantee that no changes occur and that the object will be in the same condition when the evidence is admitted as it was when the crime occurred. Once this is done the relevant data is secured. A bit-by-bit map of the suspicious computer is created and all investigations are carried out on this identical copy, leaving the original as a possible comparator for verification purposes. During this investigation, no active processes other than certified forensic tools are running on the computer.

By contrast, when authorities are using RFS tools to search computers and gain evidence, these computers are accessed remotely, remain in the control of the suspect and have to be connected to the Internet before, during and after the search to operate the tool. The mere fact that the RFS has been placed on the computer means the program interacts with other active programs running on the machine, changing the data in the process. This means that no physical source exists for later comparison with the admitted evidence. In other words, 'a live image (or copy) can only be verified against itself from the point when acquisition occurred, whereas images of "dead" machines can be verified against the original media'.[28] In addition to these inevitable technical alterations of data, intentional manipulation by the investigators is also possible. More problematically, data can be manipulated. For example, as Nikkel points out, 'IP and MAC addresses can be spoofed, various protocol headers can be faked, and the content transmitted can be fabricated. Network traffic can be intercepted and modified during transit'.[29] RFS tools betray their origin as malware. They are not primarily designed with evidence preservation in mind.[30]

These attributes raise a problem of authenticity of digital data and as a result, challenge the admissibility of digital evidence in court proceedings. So far, no court had to rule on the admissibility of remotely gathered digital evidence directly. However, we can identify some of the likely problems that will have to be addressed. In civil law systems, the investigating judge usually determines admissibility of evidence, with free restrictions placed on his discretion. In particular, evidence that is merely of low probative weight, or whose potential to be misleading outweighs its probative weight, will not normally be ruled inadmissible. It is therefore unlikely that the admissibility of remotely obtained digital evidence will be challenged on ground of its reliability.

By contrast, rules of evidence that have to accommodate trial by jury have traditionally placed a much more substantive burden on the reliability of evidence as an admissibility criterion. Digital evidence is no exception to this rule. Indeed, it was initially treated with a high degree of open hostility by the courts and explicit procedural safeguards were put in place to ensure its reliability. Until 2000, the admissibility of computer evidence was governed in England under provision section 69 of the Police and Criminal Evidence Act 1984. Under section 69, the burden of proof with respect to the reliability of computer evidence was with the party submitting the evidence. The provision assumed that computers are fallible and the party submitting the evidence had to prove that this was not the case for the computer system that had produced the evidence in question. Section 69 of the Police and Criminal Evidence Act 1984 would have been a major obstacle for the admissibility of evidence collected by RFS tools. Even though this specifically onerous section was repealed in 2000, it seems likely that a comparatively high level of judicial scepticism towards digital evidence will continue. The case of *R* v. *Aaron Caffrey* highlights in particular how difficult it might be to prove the reliability of RFS tools, such as a Trojan.[31] Caffrey was acquitted of a section 3(1) Computer Misuse Act 1990 offence of causing unauthorised modifications of computer material, allegedly having gained unauthorised administrator rights to Web services on the Port of Houston computer by using a known exploit within Microsoft software. He claimed in his defence that hackers had used a Trojan virus to gain control over his computer and launch programs to hack into the Port of Houston computer. Although no traces of a Trojan virus were found on his computer and it was therefore highly unlikely that hackers had gained control over his computer, he was acquitted of the crime on the basis that the possibility that a Trojan virus had been installed on the computer and had destroyed itself, leaving no traces, could not be excluded. Since RFS tools are nothing but Trojans used by the police, this shows how difficult it will be to prove that the RFS tool operated faultlessly during an investigation and, hence, that the evidence collected is reliable. If a person is acquitted because of the mere possibility that a Trojan infected his computer, *a fortiori* we would expect an acquittal if it is known that a Trojan, albeit under police control, was operative – first because the police Trojan itself might have compromised the crime scene, second because it proves that the suspect's computer was vulnerable to attacks in principle. If the police were able to gain access, it is highly likely that the computer was vulnerable and, indeed, that some malware will have exploited this vulnerability.

Cross-border searches

Using an RFS tool to search a computer or laptop can give rise to a further legal problem: the problem of knowingly or unknowingly undertaking the search in a different jurisdiction.[32] ICT devices are becoming smaller and are more frequently designed to be carried around and used while 'on the move'. Hence obviously, once an RFS tool is successfully implanted on a device, a suspect may carry the Trojan on a mobile device such as a laptop from one country to another and may also during the journey move into spaces governed in part by international law such as extraterritorial waters. This can cause several problems and in particular a problem with jurisdictional competence. Police searches of computers, just like the traditional search of a dwelling, are sovereign acts, intimately linked to the notion of the state and its territory. That the investigator is located in Germany does not change the fact that the remote device carries out investigative actions which are effective primarily outside the territory of the Federal Republic. Even within the EU, extraterritorial deployment of police officers for instance in the context of international football competitions, has met fierce resistance and required complex bi-national negotiations which reduced the foreign police force to mere observers without powers of arrest.[33] Without the consent of the country where the investigative action takes effect, such a search would be a violation of international law and, arguably, even a crime under public international law.

Assuming the consent of the nation on whose territory the investigative action takes place, a different set of legal issues arises. The consent may exist in the form of bilateral or multilateral treaties that describe in general terms the scope of any such concession. The interpretation of these treaties is governed by international public law. Alternatively, consent can be granted in the form of *ad-hoc*, one-off permissions, such as suggested by the EU council. In both cases, the permission can establish constraint on the operation of the Trojan that go beyond those that govern its use under national law. Also, in both cases a formal request through diplomatic channels will normally be required. Only exceptionally and only when a bilateral treaty is in place, can this request come directly from the investigative authority to its foreign counterpart.

Conclusion

The EU council with its decision to encourage the clandestine, remote access of personal computers by police and secret service agents has sent a clear message that this will become a standard investigation method in the future. This article has shown that RFS tools used by law enforcement agencies have, on the one hand, the potential of increasing the efficiency of investigative actions, but, on the other hand, also pose new threats to personal privacy and other core liberties, and challenge traditional evidence and regulatory concepts. If this is to become a standard investigation method in the future there is a great need for harmonised legislation that sufficiently protects privacy rights of citizens and therefore guarantees legal certainty, but also establishes how far the data collected by this technology is admissible as evidence in court. The German experience can only be a limited blueprint for the UK. The German Constitution requires the presence of the suspect in the search of his/her dwellings and this was one of the main obstacles for RFS tools, but this requirement does not exist in this form in the UK, nor is there an obvious analogy to the privacy jurisprudence of the German Constitutional court. On the contrary, the potential unreliability of the evidence is not an issue in the German context, but could potentially prevent an efficient use of the intelligence gathered by RFS tools as evidence in UK courts. The EU initiative to strengthen the use of RFS tools therefore seems to require more cross-border legal harmonisation than was anticipated, especially given the problem that the evidence might be collected outside the national boundaries of the investigating police force.

Notes

1. Council of the European Union, 'Council Conclusions on a Concerted Work Strategy and Practical Measures Against Cybercrime', 2987th Justice and Home Affairs Council meeting, 27–28 November 2008, available at http://www.ue2008.fr/webdav/site/PFUE/shared/import/1127_JAI/Conclusions/JHA_Council_conclusions_Cybercrime_EN.pdf
2. BVerfG, NJW 2008, 822.

3. D. Leppard, 'Police Set to Step up Hacking of Home PCs', *Timesonline*, 4 January 2009, available at http://www.timesonline.co.uk/tol/news/politics/article5439604.ece; K. Leipold, 'Die Online-Durchsuchung', *Neue Juristische Wochenschrift,* Spezial 4 (2007): 315.
4. U. Buermeyer, 'Die "Online-Durchsuchung" – Technischer Hintergrund des verdeckten hoheitlichen Zugriffs auf Computersysteme', *Onlinezeitschrft für Höshstrichterliche Rechtsprechung zum Strafrecht* 4 (2007): 154.
5. Ibid.
6. G. Hornung, 'Ermächtigungsgrundlage für die "Onlinedurchsuchung"?', *Datenschutz und Datensicherheit* 31 (2007): 575–580.
7. BGH, NJW 2007, 930.
8. *Gesetz-und Verordnungsblatt für das Land Nordrhein-Westfalen*, Jahrgang 2006, Seite 620 (GVBl NW 2006).
9. BVerfG, see note 2.
10. Leppard, 'Police Set to Step up'.
11. N. Morris, 'New Powers for Police to Hack your PC', *The Independent*, 5 January 2009, available at http://www.independent.co.uk/news/uk/home-news/new-powers-for-police-to-hack-your-pc-1225802.html
12. U. Hellmann, *Strafprozessrecht* (Heidelberg: Springer, 2005), 146.
13. BVerfG, NJW 2006, 976; BVerfG, NJW 2005, 1917; BGH, NStZ 2003, 670.
14. T. Böckenförde, *Die Ermittlung im Netz* (Tübingen: Mohr Siebeck, 2003).
15. BGH, see note 7.
16. The interception of email traffic data could be subsumed under this article if it is a live interception; hence a dataflow exists between the suspect and the recipient. Due to their design however, RFS tools are most likely to search emails stored on the computer of the suspect. Also, a live interception of email traffic is technically still very difficult, if not impossible (G. Hornung, 'Ein neues Grundrecht', *Computer und Recht* 5 (2008): 299).
17. BGH, see note 7.
18. B. Schafer, 'The Taming of the Sleuth-Problems and Potential of Autonomous Agents in Crime Investigation and Prosecution', *International Review of Law, Computers & Technology* 20, nos. 1&2 (2006): 63.
19. See for example in Germany, BVerfG, NJW 1990, 563.
20. BVerfG, see note 2.
21. German case law in the area developed subtle distinctions between a non-negotiable core of privacy and an 'outer layer' or privacy interest that can be balanced against other rights.
22. BVerfG, see note 2.
23. C. Frank, In 'Richter halten Kontrolle von heimlichen Online-Durchsuchungen für illusorisch', Heise 28.02.2008, available at http://www.heise.de/newsticker/Richter-halten-Kontrolle-von-heimlichen-Online-Durchsuchungen-fuer-illusorisch–/meldung/104238
24. A serious crime is defined as any offence attracting a jail sentence of three years or more.
25. See for example the case where a family was put under surveillance for 'suspected fraudulent school place applications' under provisions of RIPA, BBC, 'Council admits spying on family', April 2008, available at http://news.bbc.co.uk/1/hi/england/dorset/7341179.stm
26. E. Casey, *Digital Evidence and Computer Crimes* (London: Academic Press, 2004).
27. E.E. Kenneally, 'Confluence of Digital Evidence and the Law: On the Forensic Soundness of Live-Remote Digital Evidence Collection', *UCLA Journal of Law and Technology* 9, no. 2 (2005): 3.
28. Ibid.
29. B.J. Nikkel, 'Improving Evidence Acquisition from Live Network Sources', *Digital Investigation* 3 (2006): 89.
30. E. Casey and A. Stanley, 'Tool Review – Remote Forensic Preservation and Examination Tools', *Digital Examination* 1 (2004): 284.
31. E. George, 'UK Computer Misuse Act – The Trojan Virus Defence Regina v Aaron Caffrey, Southwark Crown Court, 17 October 2003', *Digital Investigation* 1, no. 2 (2004): 89.
32. For the purpose of this article the focus will be on the crossing of borders between nation states. For a detailed analysis of the problem of borders in relation to the use of RFS tools see W. Abel and B. Schafer, 'Big Browser Manning the Thin Blue Line – Computational Legal Theory Meets Law Enforcement', *Problema* 2 (2008): 51.
33. M. O'Neill, *Policing Football: Social Interaction and Negotiated Disorder* (Basingstoke: Palgrave Macmillan, 2005), 137.

Technology and the cultural appropriation of music

Richard Jones

School of Law, Liverpool John Moores University, John Foster Building, Liverpool, UK

Technology, particularly recording technology, has for more than a century threatened the copyrights of composers, publishers and performers. Users armed with this technology have been given the means to record, copy and distribute the works of others. The response of rights holders has been to advocate the reiteration and expansion of their copyrights. The increased copyright regimes while going someway to protect the rights of composers, publishers and performers has also swept material from the public domain, so making it unavailable to other artists and follow-on creators. This process is referred to by Lessig as the locking down and appropriation of culture, a process that some argue will lead to a lack of diversity and choice. The folk song *The Legend of Tom Dula* (*Dooley*) is one of the best known examples of this appropriation. This song had been freely available to generations of folk singers until it was captured in a recording. The recording was transcribed and copyright was claimed, the song was no longer in the public domain. Whereas technology provides the reason to expand copyright, information technology and particularly the internet has spurned a number of initiatives that may lead to the freeing of content. The open source movement has been very successful in freeing and generating content; this movement has itself led to other related initiatives. One of these, the Creative Commons, provides a broad based solution which through a series of alternative licensing contracts allows rights holders to lessen their control on their content making it more available for others to use. This paper considers the interplay of music, technology and intellectual property. It considers how developments in information technology can now be used to offset the expansion of copyright. After reviewing some of these developments, particularly the Creative Commons, and considering evidence now analysed from a European wide survey of musicians and publishers completed in 2008, the paper concludes that these fixes, rooted in intellectual property, unfortunately offer little by way of solution. However technological solutions not so closely tied to intellectual property may offer more appropriate and workable solutions.

1. The legend of Tom Dula

Tom Dula (pronounced Dooley) was hanged on 1 May 1868 for the murder of his fiancée Laura Foster. The lyrics of the song were written down soon after the hanging by a local poet Thomas C. Land and reflect the eternal triangle between the musician and ladies man Dula, Laura Foster and her cousin Ann Foster. Returning from the civil war Tom renewed his relationship with both ladies, even though Ann had during Tom's absence married James Milton. Accounts vary but what is clear is that Laura Foster's murdered body was found on a mountain side. Both Dula and Ann were charged but only Dula was tried.

Although legend has it that Tom composed the tune as he was waiting to be taken to the gallows, there is little evidence for this. Whatever the truth, the song continued to be sung by generations of folk singers. In the 1940s folk song collectors, Anne and Frank Warner recorded (collected) the song from a North Carolina folk singer, Frank Proffitt. Frank Warner took the song, arranged it and recorded it for Elektra Records in 1947; it appeared on his 1952 album *American Folk Songs and Ballads* (Elektra EKL-3).[1] The song was later published in John and Alan Lomax's book *Folk Songs USA*[2] with the credit 'words and melody adapted and arranged by Frank Warner'. In 1958 the song was recorded by the Kingston Trio, a recording later to be credited as beginning a folk revival. It was Warner's performance and arrangement from the 1952 album that was mistakenly used by the Kingston Trio as the basis for their recording. The resulting settlement of copyright infringement means that royalties from this recording continue to be paid to the heirs of Proffitt, Warner and Lomax. Collectors, recording technology and intellectual property rights were then to affect how folk songs and the culture surrounding folk songs were to develop.

2. Music, intellectual property, technology and culture

2.1. *Recording right*

The cultural impact of intellectual property has been stoked, and in part driven, by developments in technology. Copyright's origin in the Statute of Anne's preamble states 'An Act for the Encouragement of Learning, by Vesting the Copies of Printed Books in the Authors or Purchasers'. The Act, at first limited to printed materials, was introduced to deal with the challenges of the printing press, so beginning a close relationship between copyright and technology.

Music's oral nature changed because, through a series of recording technologies, songs became fixed. At first songs found their way into printed form, through the transcribing of performances by collectors, and then published either as collections or in journals. In 1899 the *Journal of the Folk-Song Society* was established by the Folk Song Society. The journal was instrumental in publishing songs collected during the feverish collection of folk songs in the early twentieth century. Printing captured the song and the lyrics, later recording technologies enabled the capture of the performance. The Pianola and the piano roll began a series of recording and playing technologies that progressed through to the disk, magnetic tape, vinyl disk and cassette tape (1963). Digital copying then became available with the CD (1982) and DVD (1996).

A song that previously was only in the head of a performer was now available, as well as its performance, in a range of mediums. The song now existed as a tune, lyrics, a sound recording and a performance. In the jostle for profits there was an inevitable conflict between manufacturers of recording and copying technologies and the rights holders. The first clash was over the piano roll. Since their introduction in 1898, there had developed a thriving black market in copied rolls. In *White-Smith Publishing Co.* v. *Apollo Co.* (1908) 209 U.S. 1. the US Supreme Court through Justice Day commenting on the legality of this said:

> a copy is that which comes so near to the original as to give every person seeing it the idea created by the original .... These musical tones are not a copy which appeals to the eye. In no sense can musical sounds which reach us through the sense of hearing be said to be copies.[3]

With the courts 'failing' to respond to the growth of technology and the subsequent attack on the rights holder of copying the matter was taken up by legislation. In the UK the Copyright Act 1911 provided record companies with the right to prevent the unauthorised copying (duplication) of their sound recordings. The case of *Gramophone Co. Ltd.* v. *Stephen Carwardine Co* (1934) additionally giving companies the exclusive right to control the public performances of their recordings. This protection has remained virtually unchanged through the Copyright Act 1956, Copyright Designs and Patents Act (CDPA) 1988 and the Copyright in the Information Society Directive (2001/29/EC). In the USA Federal copyright protection for sound recordings, as opposed to compositions, did not come into force until 1971 in the Sound Recording Amendment Act 1971 (US), amending the Copyright Act 1909 (US). Protection for recordings until 1971 was based upon a mixture of state law (sometimes erroneously called common law copyright), unfair competition and unjust enrichment.

Technology however continued to march on and provided users with ever more efficient copying mechanisms. The next battleground was to be cassette decks and blank cassette tapes. Again the industry responded by claiming lost sales, categorising the use of such tapes as theft and lobbying for legislative amendments. The result in the USA was that the Home Recording Act was presented before the US House of Representatives in 1985. The Act proposed a 'penny per minute' tax on audio cassette tapes. The bill failed to pass Congress and as a result no mechanism to redistribute the taxes has ever been developed. With no means to prevent copying and no mechanism by which to capitalise on the home recording market, the industry was forced to return to the courts.[4] Actions were first brought against the manufacturers of recording equipment arguing that the manufacture and sale of such equipment was an act facilitating copyright infringement. In *Sony Corporation of America* v. *Universal City Studios Inc* (1984) 464 U.S. 417 180 F.3d 1072 9th Cir. the court was asked to consider the legality of Sony's videocassette recorder (VCR), a machine that could videotape copyrighted television broadcasts. As a reproduction technology, the VCR could be used for a wide category of purposes, ranging from time-shifting for single playback to unauthorised collection of a programme library. After a number of conflicting lower court decisions the Supreme Court found in favour of the manufacturer Sony. Justice Stevens, delivering the majority judgment found that the VCR to be a 'staple article of commerce' that could be used for significant non-infringing use, i.e. non-commercial time-shifting of recording programmes for playback within the home. Accordingly, the sale of copying equipment, like the sale of other articles of commerce, does not constitute contributory infringement if the product is widely used for legitimate, unobjectionable purposes. Indeed, it need merely be capable of substantial non-infringement uses. The ruling was instrumental in encouraging the development of further technologies establishing that the potential for the misuse was not sufficient to prevent its production and sale, as long as it maintained a lawful purpose within the public interest.

While copying (and distribution of copies) using analogue technologies was costly, time consuming and led to degradation of quality, the nest technology, digital copying, had no such disadvantages.[5] The digitisation of recording and compression of songs twinned with the internet led to the rise of peer to peer systems with the consequent increase and rapidity of dissemination of music. Computerised sampling and personal computing allowed recording and mixing at a fraction of the cost of professional studios, removing the distinction between producers and consumers and enabling new forms of creativity such as hip hop. Reaction by rights holders, the Recording Industry Association of America (RIAA) and the British Phonographic Industry (BPI) was yet again to point to figures indicating that unit sales and profits had slumped.[6] Doubts have been expressed as to whether this was the case.[7] Nevertheless, rights holders succeeded in both developing and legitimating digital rights management systems (DRM) granting rights holders control over the distribution and use of their content.[8] In the United States the Digital Millennium Copyright Act (DMCA) 1998 prohibits the circumvention of access or copy controls in DRM systems, this being mirrored by Article 6 of the EU Directive on Copyright in the Information Society (2001/29/EC) and implemented in the UK in Sections 296ZA-296ZE of the CDPA 1988 added by the Copyright and Related Rights Regulations 2003 (SI 2003/2498).

DRM enables content owners to determine how their content is used by consumers, restricting personal use and limiting their fair use, raising concerns that rather than regaining the balance in copyright, it has instead shifted the balance in favour of the content owners, ushering in a cavalier attitude to consumer rights.

> In the content industry's view, consumers don't have rights; they have expectations. Consumers may not like DRM systems, but if 'legitimate' content is available only on this basis, they'll get used to it.[9]

2.1. *Performance rights*

While significantly enhanced rights were awarded to composers and publishers, less progress was made in relation to the rights of the performer and the protection of their performance rights. The vested interests of authors and collecting societies were for some time instrumental in holding back the granting of any substantive protection rights to the performer.[10]

In the UK the Dramatic and Musical Performers Protection Act 1925 prevented the unauthorised recording and subsequent dealing of a performance without consent. Somewhat stronger protection was subsequently introduced through the Dramatic and Musical Performers Protection Act 1958, the Performers Protection Act 1963 and the Performers Protection Act 1972. This stream of legislation was limited, offering only a limited availability of criminal sanctions and providing no civil actions as such. Performers stood helpless against bootleggers, some progress was made using Anton Piller orders (*Anton Piller* [1976] 1 All ER 779 in cases such as *Island Records* v. *Corkindale* [1978] F.S.R. 505), but it was left to the Whitford Committee to make a formal recommendation to allow a civil right of action to be made available. This recommendation was faithfully adopted in the CDPA ss 181–184 which gave a performer the right to control (and benefit from) the exploitation of their performance. The right has been substantially altered through a series of Directives and Regulations including the Rental and Related Rights Directive, Durative Directive 92/100/EEC, implemented by the Duration of Copyright and Rights in Performance Regulations 1995 and Copyright and Related Rights Regulations 1996, and the InfoSoc Directive 2000/31/EC. The result of this complex web of provisions is that the individual rights granted to performers under the 1988 Act are: a reproduction right, a distribution right and a rental and lending right. In addition there are rights against the copyright owner to an equitable remuneration should the performance be played in public or broadcast and a set of non-property rights in the performance.

The establishment of these rights took even longer in the USA where the Uruguay Round Agreements Act (1994) added section 2319A to title 18 of the United States Code. The provisions provide a range of criminal a sanctions concerning the unauthorised fixation of and trafficking in sound recordings and music videos of live musical performances. Civil actions also became available in 2004.

3. Folklore and intellectual property

The World Intellectual Property Organisation (WIPO) classifies folklore and folk music as a Traditional Cultural Expressions (TCE), the definition of which includes 'music, art, designs, names, signs and symbols, performances, architectural forms, handicrafts and narratives'.[11] Significant inroads have been made into the broadening of the protection of TCEs. The first effort to protect such knowledge was taken by the United Nations Educational, Scientific and Cultural Organization (UNESCO) in 1978. In 1985, WIPO and UNESCO produced 'Model Provisions for National Laws on the Expression of Folklore against Illicit Exploitation and Other Prejudicial Actions'. Five acts are defined as giving cause for action against TCEs – illegal exploitation, failure to acknowledge appropriate source for the material, failure to acquire the necessary authorisation, passing off an expression as deriving from a community and distorting an expression. These are embodied in 'Model Provisions' that may be incorporated into national statutes.

In 1989 the International Labour Organisation Convention No. 169 of 1989 concerning Indigenous and Tribal Peoples obliged states to 'respect the special importance for the cultures and spiritual values of the peoples concerned of their relationship with the land or territories or both' (article 13). The draft UN Declaration on Rights of Indigenous Peoples 1994 continued:

> Indigenous peoples are entitled to the recognition of the full ownership, control and protection of their cultural and intellectual property. They have the right to special measures to control, develop and protect their sciences, technologies and cultural manifestations, including human and other genetic resources, seeds, medicines, knowledge of the properties of fauna and flora, oral traditions, literatures, designs and visual and performing arts.

WIPO's direct and positive involvement in the issue of TCE continued and in 1998 its General Assembly established the Inter Governmental Committee on Intellectual Property and Genetic Resources, Traditional Knowledge and Folklore (IGC). The IGC's actions so far have focused on trying to understand the needs and expectations of traditional/local communities, ascertaining the adequacy of current methods for protecting TCEs and surveying proposals to enhance such protection. The strong position taken by the developing countries on the protection of TCE within the trade environment has led in another forum, the World Trade Organization (WTO), to its inclusion in the WTO Doha Ministerial Declaration in November 2001. Some years later in 2005 the WTO made permanent the Doha Declaration.[12] However a review of the effectiveness of the initiative shows a disappointing conclusion, and indeed negotiations were suspended due to lack of agreement in July 2006, although they have now been restarted within each of the strands.

3.1. Folk music

While many tunes that are part of the folk repertoire have a traceable author many folk tunes and lyrics do not and as such can be said to be part of folklore. Songs evolve through the folk process, which was described (although not so named) by Cecil Sharp in 1907 as involving 'three principles of *continuity*, *variation*, and *selection*'.[13] While songs can be recognised at different times and in different places they will exhibit subtle differences introduced by different artists. This process stands in contradistinction to the perceived creative process within copyright which is centred on the author providing original creative content. Conflicts between traditional musicians wedded to the folk process and intellectual property are therefore inevitable. Woody Guthrie, a prolific and influential folk singer, illustrates this with the following copyright notice that he inserted in his songbook.[14]

> This song is Copyrighted in U.S., under Seal of Copyright # 154085, for a period of 28 years, and anybody caught singin it without our permission, will be mighty good friends of ourn, cause we don't give a dern. Publish it. Write it. Sing it. Swing to it. Yodel it. We wrote it, that's all we wanted to do.

Guthrie, his songs and the folk process were subject of proceedings in *JibJab Media Inc* v. *Ludlow Music Inc* (2005). The case involved a Guthrie recording of a song called '*This Land is Your Land*'. Guthrie composed the lyrics to this song in 1940. Although a copyright registration for words and music was obtained in 1956 and renewed in 1984 it appears Guthrie first published the song in 1945, a copied broadsheet dated 1945 is in the Library of Congress. As no renewal of the copyright was applied for within the 28 year period the song entered into the public domain (17 U.S.C. 304(a)). In 2004 Ludlow Music initiated infringement proceedings against JibJab for infringement of 'melody, harmony, rhythm and structure' of the song. JibJab had created a web animation using the song parodying the US Presidential Election between George W. Bush and John Kerry. The case was barely off the ground when it was discovered, much to the embarrassment of Ludlow Inc., that Guthrie had in fact 'stolen', in the context of the 'folk process', the tune of the song from The Carter Family who had recorded the song in 1930 as '*When the World's on Fire*'. The fact that Guthrie's lyrics, first published in 1945 had not been renewed and the fact that Guthrie had not composed the tune led Ludlow to drop the action.

3.2. Folk music collectors

From the early twentieth century folk music, both in England and USA, has experienced several revivals. Movements of singers, dancers and members or organisers of folk clubs, worked to ensure that folk music remained alive. Prominent in these revivals have been the activities of the survivalists (or collectors): in England, Cecil Sharpe; in the USA, Anne and Frank Warner, and Alan and John Lomax. Sharpe's main imperative was to find, collect and transcribe the folk song that had 'survived' as a vestige of some earlier culture. The folk song was seen to have been passed on by the 'folk'. The folk had no conception of this process and in consequence made no creative contribution to the song. Similar motives could be ascribed to the Warner's and Lomax's. These survivalists created rather than discovered the concepts of 'the village', 'folk' and 'folk song'. Writers such as Boyes[15] and others[16] considered the concept of the folk song as 'surviving' as fundamentally flawed in that it ignored the creative role of the performers and their communities. Performers would, they argue, make new arrangements and mix lyrics and tunes. The result was the evolution and development of the song and its tradition.

While collectors can be credited in both introducing artists to wider audiences and sparking folk music revivals, their survivalist approach leaves them open to claims of underplaying the role of the artists and of some measure of self serving. Their role meant them becoming involved, either intentionally or unintentionally, in ownership and copyright issues surrounding the songs. Collectors approbated music from the public domain, with some collectors attempting to claim, for their own benefit, copyright through the activities of notation, arrangement and the making up of compilations. Frank Warner claimed copyright in his 'arrangement' of Tom Dula. While these activities and their relationship to copyright have already been considered by the author,[17] intellectual property, however, also impacts on folk music more generally.

4. Folk music and intellectual property

Folk music exists outside the sightline of the four major record labels.[18] Artists within this genre often have difficult relationships with the major labels. Folk musician Eliza Cathy described her time with Warner as 'ill fated'. The difficulty is in part due to the clash of cultures between on the one hand record labels behove to substantial intellectual property rights and a folklore culture emphasising continuity, selection and variation, on the other.

With folk music the author/composer is lost in the mists of time and subsequent performers are reluctant to lay any claim. The work may therefore be viewed as being orphaned, or more correctly in the case of folk music never owned. The large (and growing) pool of orphaned works has lead to a proposal in the Gowers Review[19] that will facilitate the creative reuse of orphaned copyrighted material by tapping into this currently unreachable pool of resource and removing a significant barrier towards copyright flexibility. According to estimations within the review, up to '98% of published work under copyright' is unavailable which results in a significant waste of both 'commercial and creative capital'.[20] Use of this material is avoided through fears of reprisal under copyright laws. Any procedures necessary to identify a work as orphaned would be potentially costly in terms of time and money, placing them predominantly within the reach of commercial enterprises only.

While attention has been focused on the integration and use of orphan works the danger is that attempts will be made to lay claim to such material. The courts in 2005 become appraised of claims by the recording industry over work where copyright was never registered (claimed) or has subsequently lapsed. This has involved the courts re-examining the murky waters of common law copyright, and review and reinterpret significant eighteenth century case law. This has resulted in a decision that will have profound effects on the relationship of copyright and music. US Federal copyright protection for sound recordings did not come into force until 1971. Recordings made before then, such as the recording of Tom Dula, would have had to have been protected under a mixture of unfair competition, misappropriation, unjust enrichment and state copyright, sometimes referred to as common law copyright. Common law copyright has been defined as a right of first publication and stands in contradiction to statutory copyright which is copyright after publication which arises through a special right created by statute. Conventionally the story of common law copyright is told as follows.[21] The Statute of Ann (1709) was considered to provide only a supplemental right to the already existing common law copyright. Common law copyright therefore survived in perpetuity the act of publication. This view was forcefully and successfully argued before the court in *Millar* v. *Taylor* (1769) 4 Burr 2303. However soon afterwards the great case of *Donaldson* v. *Beckett* (1774) 2 Bros. P.C. 129 held that the Statute of Ann was deemed to delimit the scope of these 'rights' after publication, any common law copyright was superseded and replaced by the statutory copyright. Any element of doubt as to the position of common law copyright was supposedly laid to rest in the case of *Jeffrey's* v. *Boosey* (1854), the court finding that common law copyright is replaced by statutory copyright.

Any concern that copyright would become too overarching and hence impinge upon creativity through exploitation could now be laid to rest; copyright would remain constrained within a statutory regime, kept with the limits decided upon by elected legislatures. Setting aside for the moment the fact that legislators in the 1990s and early twenty-first century have shown a distinct reluctance to stand up to the demands of the music industry for ever increasing intellectual property regimes, are we right to at least content ourselves in the knowledge that nearly 250 years after Donaldson we need have no fear of attempts by the record industry to look for further expansion of their rights through common law rights? Apparently not for contradictions within the understanding of the conventional analysis of common law copyright has left ajar a door through which the record industry has barged in *Capitol Records* v. *Naxos* (2005) 4 NY3d 540. Conflating the decisions in *Millar* and *Donaldson* has allowed some authors and now the court in *Capitol* to argue that a right known as common law copyright does exist. The absence of publication (or indeed the absence of a statutory right) can be relied upon to maintain control of material that would have normally been available within the public domain. Therefore when faced with a set of recordings made in the 1930s, to which no copyright is attached, the Court of Appeals in *Capitol Records* v. *Naxos* (2005) 4 NY3d 540 was able to imply the existence of a common law copyright in these recordings. As no statutory copyright was available in recording until 1972 common law copyright could be used to prevent the publication of the recording by a rival record label and in consequence these recordings would now remain locked in copyright until 2067. Under 17 U.S.C. § 301 (c), as amended by the Sonny Bono Copyright Term Extension Act (1998), state copyright will not be pre-empted by Federal copyright until 95 years after the recordings first became eligible for federal copyright in 1972. Not only would competitive labels be restrained but others who may wish to sample, broadcast or in any way build upon these recordings be so restrained until well into the second half of the twentyfirst century! The decision adds another layer of rights onto existing rights over music, particularly recordings which had been considered copyright free.

Intellectual property therefore approbates material from the public domain, stifling activity and creativity within the folk process. The Legend of Tom Dula is one, but not the only, example of this. The Open Source movement and in particular the Creative Commons initiative[22] argue for a reduction in the size of intellectual property protection, increasing and enhancing the public domain. To achieve this, the Creative Commons provides a broad based solution through a series of alternative licensing contracts that allow copyright holders to reserve and waive copyrights rights.[23] Some folk artists have found this a useful initiative. Roger McGuinn has posted songs on his site for free download enabling those songs to be shared, downloaded or simply performed.[24] In *Full Fat, Semi-skimmed No Milk Today – Creative Commons Licences and English Folk Music* using this framework the author considered how traditional music and the culture surrounding such music was being affected by the encroachment of intellectual property and whether salvation lies in the projects spurned by technology? The complete intellectual property regimes (or full fat in the context of the title) may have a negative effect on the development of the folk music tradition and increases in the scope of intellectual property are actively harming these traditions. Of the more liberal intellectual property licence regimes through the Open Source and the Creative Commons movements, these were the 'semi skimmed' regimes of our title, they are offered as a means of achieving flexibility within intellectual property regimes. Initially these seem tailor-made for traditional music – for example the Creative Commons 'Sharing Licence' contains the phrase: 'This licence allows others: To take a sample from your song and include it in their own'. Open Source and Creative Commons are licences designed to be used within an existing intellectual property regime, indeed the 'trick' of open source is to utilise the licensing provisions of copyright law to tie subsequent developers to the openness of the work. The schemes work and are dependant upon intellectual property regimes. We concluded that the Creative Commons and Open Source movements have a fundamental flaw; they have their roots in western intellectual property regimes based systems. Such systems while empowering some, dis-empower others:

> Folk culture is not merely the mechanical mixing and joining of tunes and lyrics, it is a set of values reflected in a set of processes where the music is refreshed, emphasising variation and selection but with little thought to individual rights.
>
> Herein lies the weakness of the Creative Commons system, the reluctance of folk music composers and performers to enforce copyright in their works. This then leaves these works vulnerable to the copyright claims of others .... Therefore whilst providing much welcomed flexibility to creators of 'original' (but not in its extended form) copyrightable works these licences focus on the sharing and distribution of new music and are therefore less useful in the protection and encouragement of folk music where reliance is placed more on adaptation and development that on the creation of the new. Thus even with the extensive use of such licences there inevitably continues to be, with the present extension to the copyright regimes, an erosion of amount of music available for free use.[25]

The conclusion seems to imply that folk music provides what may be an insurmountable challenge to any intellectual property regime: that the growth of intellectual property regimes provided threats to the very nature of processes such as those found in relation to folklore. Nothing has persuaded the present author that any of this has changed indeed, as intellectual property rights continue to expand at the behest of corporations, the threats have increased, but what is happening on the ground with folk musicians and music publishers?

5. What the musicians say

In testing the argument that the Creative Commons initiative provides the much needed flexibility for the encroachment of intellectual property a number of approaches were considered. Google provide two online tools. Google Trends is a tool that allows the number of searches against a particular word, phrase, or combination of words to be graphed over time. Although this has benefits in seeing how many Google users have searched against phrases such as 'folk music' or 'creative commons' it does not provide exact figures on the numbers of search results, instead presenting search statistics in a relative manner to other results. Google Zeitgeist follows a similar theme to Trends but it differs in providing information on the most popular searches over time and by geographic region. Despite both Google tools providing an interesting insight into the types of searches that Google users have performed, they turned out to be unable to provide adequate quantative data. Attention was turned to the statistical information made available on the Creative Commons website. Again this information proved to be inadequate, being outdated and only providing a breakdown on the types of licences that have been issued and not the nature of the content being licensed (this is understandable because of difficulties in categorising content). Specific searches were then considered but were deemed unsuitable, given the extensive subjective interpretation and judgement involved and the subjective nature of the search process and search terms.

Ultimately it was decided that the most effective form of research would be a survey for folk musicians. The design permitted specific statistics to be harvested while still providing artists with the ability to leave valuable comments and responses. The survey design provided a mixture of both quantative and interview results and was distributed using the internet, through forums and folk websites as well as via the authors own website http://ipmusicresearch.com. The survey itself was created using Bristol Online Surveys (BOS), which is an online survey application that provides report generation and real-time analysis of survey results. These features enabled the author to continually analyse the responses to enable trends to be identified prior to the completion of the survey period. The design of the survey enabled statistical information to be gathered while at the same time enabling participants to comment on each question instead of simply selecting from available responses.

The first group of questions were around the artist's repertoire of traditional music including to the extent to which they relied on traditional music, their use of their own or the arrangements of others. The second set of questions sought to elucidate the artiste's view of the role of intellectual property and folk music. The third set of questions sought to see the extent to which technology, particularly the internet and in particular the Creative Commons initiative had been embraced. The final set of questions addressed in a more open question form how the folk community believe that their culture and music should be preserved and protected.

Responses to the first set of questions showed that while the majority of respondents used traditional songs within their repertoire, over 80% would use their own arrangement of the song. Despite this there was a distinct reluctance to protect their arrangements in any way with 62% making no effort to register their work in any form and over 60% happy to allow their arrangement to be used freely by other musicians. As to the role of intellectual property only 23% of the artists responding to the survey saw intellectual property having any place in traditional music and arrangements of traditional music. Typical of the artists who responded was Paul Clifford who in an interview said:

> . . . intellectual property seems like a term made to once again give ownership to something that isn't ours, like land, and resources, in the true colonial spirit . . . ask a native American–Canadian what they feel about intellectual property. What really gets me is cultural appropriation. Is Paul Simon a thief or was he deeply inspired with a culture?

Others commented:

> It's not ok for the specific restrictions [in copyright] to prevent the taking and adapting and developing existing songs . . . .

As expected, and found in other research, folk musicians and intellectual property are a potent mix. Yet this should not be taken as a rejection of intellectual property, many respondents commented on the importance of intellectual property in rewarding and protecting innovation in the composition of new songs. Rather the application of intellectual property within the sphere of traditional (common music and arrangements and as a restriction within the folk process) was seen as unhelpful. The attitude to technology was rather more positive. The survey did reveal willingness in the folk community to embrace the internet. Almost 70% of those participating in the survey saw the internet as a positive medium to distribute music, with only 4% seeing the internet as a tool for exploitation. While the majority embraced the internet, the Creative Commons initiative has not made major inroads. Only 28% who were aware of the Creative Commons and even of these the majority admitted to knowing little about the nature of the initiative with only 18% (of the 28%) having ever considered using a Creative Commons licence. Typical was the response from Woven Wheat Whispers,[26] an internet based folk music distribution service:

> We and our artists don't really trust the Creative Commons licence as a robust tool . . . . The Creative Commons is really a 'gentlemen's agreement' which is fine until a mass commercial exploitation happens. We have proper contracts and terms with our artists and explain them fully prior to working together.

6. Conclusion – technology as the problem and the solution?

The expansion of intellectual property rights, prompted by developments in technology, has been justified on the utilitarian argument that enhanced rights are needed to reward rights owners, thereby encouraging innovation and development. There is little evidence that intellectual property encourages innovation, indeed stronger and ever more expansive copyright requires new authors to licence an increasing amount of copyright material, raising the cost of new works and/or reducing their number, so discouraging innovation. Further extending the length or scope of copyright does little to encourage the production of marginal ideas. In 2006 it was argued by EMI and Phonographic Performance Limited (a collecting society for performers) before the Gowers Review[27] that an extension of the copyright term (and a consequential revival of copyright in past performances) for performers' rights, was required as an incentive to the creative process. It is difficult to see the strength in this argument given that performers' economic rights, at least in their modern form, did not exist until their introduction in the UK in 1996 (Copyright and Related Rights Regulations 1996) and even later in the USA. There appeared to be no impediment to development before these dates. Gowers was equally sceptical and rejected the claim.

The ballad of Tom Dula, which had been passed down through generations of folk singers, is now encircled in intellectual property rights. Frank Proffitt's 1940s performance and Frank Warner's 1952 performance both predate effective performance copyright but the recording of both may now be caught within the questionable area of common law copyright. The recording now captured through technology has been approbated with intellectual property preventing later singers continuing the evolutionary process so necessary within the folk process. While it is not the author's intention to deprive performers of their rights of their own commercial recordings, Proffitt's performance was not a commercial performance. It was given in the context of the preservation of a folk song to collectors. Although Proffitt was grateful for his royalty cheque, the payment was as a consequence of locking away a tune he had learnt from earlier generations of singers. Further what value has been added to justify rights being attributed to this singer and collector? Is it appropriate that Warner's arrangement and Lomax's reproduction would both be covered by copyright? The result is that provided both were renewed in the year preceding the 28th anniversary of publication copyright will continue for 95 years starting at the publication date (17 U.S.C. 304(a)), that is 2047 and 2052.

The ballad has been ill served by intellectual property regimes, the many and varied versions of the Ballard of Tom Dula current in the early twentieth century stand in stark contrast to the stagnation of the ballad since it was fixed and encircled within copyright. There has been little innovation or development. Lonnie Donegan's version of the song varies little from the Kingston Trio's. Only in the 1964 version by Doc Watson is there any evidence of any innovation or extension or development of the song. The fact that the original ballad (whatever that may be) is still within the public domain and available for use is of little comfort to the current generation of artists and musicians who are fearful of approaching the ballad for fear of impinging one of the many and varied copyrights that encircle it. This ballad is indicative of the wider record industry which while trumpeting wide ranging rights for musicians and performers offers little by way of variety, diversity or choice. The fallout is particularly damaging with minority musical genres where enhanced rights have driven to the heart of how these genres evolve and develop. Nor have initiatives from users such as the Creative Commons provided a solution. Minority music genres must both embrace the technology but also lobby for more positive pluralistic systems that reinforce the idea of these traditionals, systems that are preferable to a system that is merely protecting what rights holders have and not stifling variety, diversity and choice. Our attention has been distracted and we have lost sight of the fact that copyright should be justified on the basis of the interests of society and not just the rights holder. One need go no further than the Statute of Anne to remind ourselves that the first Copyright Act was primarily about the advancement of learning through the granting of copy rights. The questions, should always be what do we want from our knowledge systems and how can we adopt the architecture of such systems to achieve this.

There are significant challenges when considering folk music and other TCEs operating outside intellectual property rights regimes. Solutions must accommodate the many and varied objectives of TCEs, preservation, protection and promotion. Despite national examples it remains a significantly controversial topic with regard to determining specifically how such systems should provide protection. To this end three general approaches have been developed. The first focuses on protecting them through their recognition as a form of cultural heritage. The second allows the establishment of the rights under an umbrella of a collective human right. The third approach, adopted by both the WTO and WIPO, investigates the use of *sui generis* rights often as a variant of intellectual property rights; at present only a small number of nations provide this form of protection.

Whichever approach is adopted, technology divorced from intellectual property parameters, may provide some assistance in the preservation and protection of TCEs through the use of databases. Databases where TCEs can be collected, registered, stored and protected. Then releasing the information into the public domain as prior art, preventing its subsequent approbation into intellectual property regimes. Unfortunately the use of databases introduces a number of new challenges most notably that many communities that do require protection do not wish to place their TCEs into the public domain; in some instances customary laws within communities may actually prevent such disclosure. However in those communities in which it is permissible public databases release information as prior art into the public domain and thereby prevent patents from being obtained. This approach to protecting TCEs still permits its use, but prevents it from being monopolised.

An international consensus is emerging from the WIPO and the Convention on Biological Diversity (CBD) that requires full participation from indigenous and local communities on any laws, rules and policies concerning TCE's; access to resources is available through free prior informed consent of the respective communities; and that indigenous and local communities have rights to determine benefit sharing, with the use of the TCEs only taking place in light of mutually agreed terms between the involved parties.

Within such an approach groups and communities would through some 'appropriate' system be encouraged to register their knowledge, songs and folklore. The challenge is in devising appropriate systems that are accessible to all communities. While there would be challenges to the use of such systems with developing countries' communities that may be remote from such technology, traditional and folk artists within the developed countries would have access to such database systems. Artists would have access to the internet and the resources that it provides, enabling them to register and copy traditional music online, but how would such a system work? The process would involve some mechanism of registration whereby recognition can be given as to what tune is traditional and what is not. Within the folk community, there is already a tacit recognition of what a traditional song is and what is not. This needs to be formalised.[28] Songs placed within this database, or databases, would be known therefore to be formally within the public domain, thereby preventing them being corralled into copyright.

This mechanism would not however be the complete picture, for ultimately, the protection afforded to traditional music and other TCEs may not be able to be standardised within one regime and focus may need to be made on a range of solutions working together within a multifaceted pluralistic regime. A mix of customary/traditional rules that would prevent approbation of songs into the private sphere, intellectual property rights, common-law concepts (such as 'undue enrichment') to reward the genuinely new, and legal and contractual agreements to aid exploitation could be used to provide the necessary protection for creativity. This mix would enable the folk process to continue, allowing and encouraging '*continuity*, *variation*, and *selection*'.

With social dependency on digital technologies increasing, it is important that technology offers not only potential to create new possibilities, but also the means and opportunities for preserving those already in existence. For a number of reasons technology is continually touching deeper into previously untapped cultural resources, and as TCEs equally follow this trend the emphasis on identifying the most appropriate form of protection becomes increasingly important. Choosing how to best protect such works in a digital world is the crucial challenge, and one that society, scholars and legislators need to continue to debate.

Acknowledgement

I would like to thank my research assistance Roksana Moore for her help in the preparation of this article.

Notes

1. Original performances of the song by Proffitt recorded by the Warners were placed on the compilation *The Warner Collection*, Vol. II. *Nothing Seems Better to Me: The Music of Frank Proffitt and North Carolina* (Appleseed Recording, 2000).
2. J.A. Lomax and A. Lomax, *Folk Song: USA*, ed. A. Lomax, C. Seeger and R. Crawford Seeger (New York: Duell, Sloan and Pearce, 1947).
3. M. Landau, 'Publication, Musical Compositions, and the Copyright Act of 1909: Still Crazy After All These Years', *Vanderbilt Law School Vanderbilt Journal of Entertainment Law & Practice* no. 28 (2000): 47.
4. B. Haring and D. Chuck, *Beyond the Charts: MP3 and the Digital Music Revolution* (Los Angeles: Off the Charts, 2000), 29.
5. The record industry is part of the music industry which includes not only the recording industry but also the publishing industry, music and event merchandising, concerts, touring events industry and live entertainment. The record industry is dominated by a small number of global players; the four major record labels are Sony/BMG, EMI Group, Warner Group and Universal.
6. RIAA 2005 Year End Statistics, http://www.riaa.com/News/newsletter/pdf/2005yrEnd Stats.pdf (accessed March 9, 2007); BPI Commercial Piracy Figures 2005, http://www.bpi.co.uk/pdf/Comm_Pir_FIgures_2005.pdf (accessed March 9, 2007).
7. F. Oberholzer-Gee and K. Strumpf, 'The Effect of File Sharing on Record Sales – An Empirical Analysis', June 2005, p. 36. Available at http://www.unc.edu/~cigar/papers/FileSharing_June2005_final.pdf
8. T. Gillespie, *Wired Shut Copyright and the Shape of Digital Culture* (Cambridge, MA: MIT Press, 2007).
9. P. Samuelson, 'Digital Rights Management and Fair Use by Design', *Communications of ACM* 46, no. 4 (2003): 43.
10. Report of the Copyright Committee (Gregory Report), Cmnd.8662 (1952) paras 165–176.
11. WIPO, Traditional Cultural Expressions (Folklore), http://www.wipo.int/tk/en/folklore/ (accessed June 12, 2008).
12. WTO, Ministerial Declaration on Doha Work Programme, 18 December 2005, http://www.wto.org/english/thewto_e/minist_e/min05_e/final_text_e.htm (accessed June 15, 2008).

13. C. Sharpe, *English Folk Song: Some Conclusions* (London: Simpkin; Novello, 1907), 16. Italics in original.
14. Songs of Woody Guthrie, http://www.geocities.com/Nashville/3448/guthrie/html (accessed March 5, 2008).
15. G. Boyes, *The Imagined Village: Culture, Ideology, and the English Folk Revival* (Manchester: Manchester University Press, 1993).
16. D. Harker, *Fakesong: The Manufacture of British 'Folksong', 1700 to the Present Day* (Milton Keynes, UK: Open University Press, 1985).
17. R. Jones and E. Cameron, 'Full Fat, Semi-skimmed No Milk Today – Creative Commons Licences and English Folk Music', *International Review of Law, Computers and Technology* 19, no. 3 (2005): 264–270.
18. The four major record labels are Sony/BMG, EMI Group, Warner Group and Universal. The number of music labels dropped from five to four when Sony Music Entertainment and BMG Entertainment merged in 2004.
19. Gowers Review of Intellectual Property (2006), available at http://www.hm-treasury.gov.uk/gowers_review_index.htm, 4 (accessed August 3, 2007).
20. Ibid., 40.
21. For a detailed analysis of the history of copyright with in the context of these cases, see R. Deazley, *On the Origins of the Right to Copy: Charting the Movement of Copyright Law in Eighteenth-Century Britain (1695–1775)* (Oxford: Hart, 2004); and R. Deazley, *Rethinking Copyright* (Cheltenham, UK: Edward Elgar, 2006).
22. L. Lessig, *Free Culture: How Big Media Uses Technology and Law to Lock Down Culture and Control Creativity* (New York: Penguin, 2004).
23. Creative Commons. Legal concepts, http://creativecommons.org/about/legal/ (accessed May 3, 2008). The Creative Commons is a movement based on the Open Source principles.
24. D.J. Spooky and Roger McGuinn interviews, available at http://creativecommons.org/audio/djspooky-mcguinn (accessed February 15, 2007).
25. WIPO, note 12, 270.
26. Wave Wheat Whispers, http://www.wovenwheatwhispers.co.uk/ (accessed February 15, 2007). Site now closed.
27. Gowers Review, note 19.
28. For example there exists a number of databases of traditional songs – see for example Folkinfo, http://www.folkinfo.org/songs/ (accessed June 2, 2008).

Decentralised P2P technology: Can the unruly be ruled?

Hasina Haque

Flat 162, 35 Pinkston Drive, Glasgow, G21 1YQ, UK

Decentralised Peer to Peer (P2P) technology has added a significant challenge to the copyright domain. To address the problem the US court has added a third theory; namely inducement theory into the genre of secondary infringement. The aim of the article is to examine the prospect of implementing inducement theory into the UK context. However, after examining the current scenario this paper suggests that instead of adding a new theory into the domain of secondary infringement, the challenge of decentralised P2P technology should be addressed by way of device protection.

The problem

The astonishing growth of decentralised P2P (Peer to Peer) technology has added yet another challenge to the secondary liability regime of copyright. In this new context the most imminent concern before the court remains how to regulate and respond to the infringement caused by this new technology. A classic example of decentralised P2P technology is *MGM Studios Inc.* v. *Grokster Ltd* (2005). In this landmark case the court encountered an appalling situation in experiencing that the current liability regime of secondary infringement is not operating in the new context. The phenomenon resulted from the advent of distinct features of decentralised P2P technology where every aspect of the architecture namely; the storage of material, the exchange of material and the location of information tool are entirely decentralised as opposed to the centralised P2P architecture; its predecessor; *A&M Records Inc.* v. *Napster Inc.* (2001) is a good example of centralised P2P technology as its location of information was managed through a central database/server over which Napster had full control. In fact, centralised P2P architecture posed a subtle challenge or no challenge at all to the courts as the courts could apply the traditional liability regime; namely, the contributory and vicarious liability without any difficulty owing to the presence of certain features, i.e. the central server and ongoing control. The same however, is not true for the decentralised P2P technology. Since, decentralised P2P technology does not offer any central server it inevitably does not leave the scope of exercising any control over the server. Essentially, in the absence of any central server and ongoing control traditional liability regime of secondary infringement ceases to work. Consequently, the non-application of traditional doctrines forced the courts in devising a new category of secondary infringement, namely the inducement theory. This is a third theory added to the genre of secondary infringement, whereupon those who induce others to infringe copyright may be liable for that infringement. In the *Grokster* case it was held that inducement occurs where a defendant distributes a device with the object of promoting its use to infringe copyright, as shown by clear expression or other affirmative steps taken to foster infringement. The focus of the inducement theory in essence is focus on behaviour rather than functionality and in this respect this theory differs from Sony.

Why was the theory needed?

In the USA, secondary liability for copyright infringement remains anchored in the common law doctrines of contributory and vicarious infringement. A contributory infringer is one who, with knowledge or the infringing activity, causes or materially contributes to the infringing conduct of another. A vicarious infringer is one who is liable for the copyright infringement committed by another where he is in a supervisory relationship to the primary infringer and receives some financial benefit from the infringement. Thus, the elements necessary in establishing liability under the common law doctrines for contributory liability are; knowledge plus material contribution; for vicarious liability; control plus authority plus financial benefit. However, the advent of digital technologies and novel network architectures has posed new legal problems and practical threats to the status quo of copyright mechanism. The new technologies have made the traditional liability regime of secondary liability entirely inoperable as they do not satisfy the necessary elements required by any of these liability regimes. The issue did not come to light until the district court in the *Grokster* case found that the respondents in Grokster and Stream Cast networks fell outside the existing law relating to secondary liability and the law needed urgent revision. The problem posed by these technologies cannot be undermined. In January 2008 IFPI report revealed that there are somewhere between 8.7 million and 10 million people simultaneously sharing files at any one time. Tens of billions of illegal files were swapped in 2007. The ratio of unlicensed tracks downloaded to legal tracks sold is about 20:1.

Significance of inducement theory

The significance of inducement theory is that it is a significant addition to the genre of secondary infringement. The primary aim of the theory is to address the infringement caused by decentralised P2P technology that has the actual intention to induce infringement. The theory has important ramifications too in shaping the scope of copyright; determining the extent of copyright holders' rights over new technology that has the actual intention in inducing infringement and also for those who manufacture, distribute, facilitate, promote these technologies. In fact, the theory has expanded the scope of secondary liability for copyright infringement as it defined the scope of copyright more broadly than it had previously been understood in the technological context.

Additionally, this theory has brought numerous challenges and changes. One significant transformation brought by this theory is that it has replaced the traditional knowledge element with intent. Not only that, the theory requires the court to look into the clear, purposeful, culpable expression or conduct rather than looking into the actual/constructive knowledge. Moreover, instead of looking into the traditional elements required by the secondary infringement such as contribution, control, authority and financial benefit the court would look into the intent to encourage infringement, taking affirmative steps and active encouragement.

Framework of inducement theory

Under the inducement theory inducement occurs where the defendant distributes a device with the object of promoting its use to infringe copyright as shown by clear expression or other affirmative steps taken to foster infringement. Under this rule, liability by inducement requires evidence of the following elements: (1) intent to bring about infringement; (2) distribution of a device suitable for infringing use; and (3) actual infringement by the recipients of the device. In sum, the inducement rule premises liability on purposeful, culpable expression and conduct. The new element required for inducement, which was not included in any of the existing categories of secondary liability, is intent.

Measuring intent under the inducement theory in Grokster and Streamcast

Under the inducement theory, evidence of intent is gathered by tracking (1) communication, (2) distribution of the device, (3) avoidance of adopting non-infringing measures, and finally (4) revenue model:

(1) *Communication*: The court held that Grokster and Streamcast demonstrated a clear intent by communicating an inducing message to the users of a known source of demand for copyright infringement by way of advertisement. This was established by showing that both of the companies deliberately targeted Napster users and assisted the users to infringe and thus filled the gap left by the demise of Napster.[1]
(2) *Distribution*: Both of the companies (Grokster and Streamcast) distributed a device that is suitable for overwhelming infringing use and ensured that the technology deployed is capable of infringing use.
(3) *Avoidance of adopting non-infringing measures*: The court held that neither of the companies (Grokster and Streamcast) adopted any step to develop or filter tools that would eliminate infringing activity taking place in their network.
(4) *Revenue model*: The court was satisfied about the fact that the business model of the two companies was heavily reliant on infringement with approximately 90 per cent of all use infringing.

Arguments surrounding measuring intent

Adopting filtering steps as a measure in determining intent has been criticised by scholars. This is because a question remains regarding the effectiveness of filtering technology in differentiating between infringing and non-infringing files on the scale required.[2] Moreover, their view that eliminating infringing use is a very tall order remains. Others are concerned with the resultant impact of measuring intent; as they fear developers of new technologies that are capable of non-infringing use may also be required to undertake action to filter out infringing behaviour.[3] This they fear in turn will give rise to chaos as the general duty to develop filtering tools will shift the cost of enforcement to technology designers rather than leaving it for negotiation between the parties. Adopting the business model as another criterion of measuring intent was also criticised by scholars. BitTorrent's technology, which is based on a mere algorithm, successfully managed in hiding its intent in the business model as a mere algorithm does not admit intent.

Decentralised P2P technology – UK position – the current framework

Secondary infringement

Secondary liability for copyright infringement is the term used to describe the liability that applies to someone other than a primary infringer of copyright: a primary infringer being someone who exercises any of the exclusive rights of a copyright owner without the proper authorisation. English law also recognises the theories of contributory and vicarious liability which come under the heading of secondary infringement. Sections 22–26 of the CDPA (Copyright, Designs and Patents Act) (1988) deal with secondary infringement. Under the current UK copyright framework vicarious liability is covered by the 'authorisation' theory. Moreover, the scope of the 'authorisation' theory was determined in the landmark case *CBS Songs Ltd* v. *Amstrad Consumer Electronics Plc* (1988). The House of Lords considered whether Amstrad, the distributor of a double-speed twin-tape recorder, had 'authorized' the purchaser of the model to copy a record in which copyright subsisted and by so doing infringed the exclusive right of the copyright owner as conferred by s. 1(1) of the Copyright Act of 1956. Their Lordships agreed with the definition that: 'to "authorise" means to grant or purport to grant to a third person the right to do an act complained of, whether the intention is that the grantee shall do the act on his own account, or only on account of the grantor' and held that 'Amstrad did not sanction, approve or countenance an infringing use of their model'. It has been observed that 'authorisation' theory is not applicable on the decentralised 'P2P' technology because of the lack of control/supervision mechanism in it.[4] Moreover, it is worth mentioning that, so far, in the UK, no major case of secondary liability for copyright infringement by a P2P technology either centralised or decentralised has appeared before the court[5] though police have arrested six people for uploading pre-release music files via the defunct BitTorrent tracker OiNK.cd.[6]

So what action to be adopted for decentralised P2P architecture?

This article purports that the challenge posed by decentralised P2P technology should be addressed by way of device protection instead of adding a new theory into the genre of secondary infringement. This is because this article disagrees with intent based liability regime and alternatively seeks to suggest a liability regime that is premised on the behaviour and the functionality of the technology, the reason for such recommendation being that an intent based liability regime is not free from criticism. Numerous concerns have been voiced regarding the viability of intent based liability regime. The theory has been roundly criticised for its lack of practical applicability, its future viability as a deterrent of file sharing technologies post *Grokster*. The concern became more relevant when inducement theory failed to address the BitTorrent architecture properly. Thus, concern has been expressed that inducement theory is not likely to succeed for the technologies beyond Grokster. Not only that, concern has also been expressed that inducement theory has introduced a higher standard of liability regime.[7] This is due to the fact that the standard of intent necessitates arguably a higher standard of knowledge whereas simple awareness may satisfy this requirement.

The primary reason of implementing the inducement theory in the UK would be to fill the gap that has been left by the 'control' element of the authorisation theory. However, one view is that 'intent' should not replace 'control' or in other words 'intent' should not act as a substitute for 'control'.[8] Concern has been expressed that the unclear scope of the inducement theory may stifle innovation because developers of new technologies may find it difficult to predict the scope of their liability and may remain excessively cautious. Thus, the risk of liability may chill investment in new technologies. The consequential impact could be damaging as it will largely broaden the liability regime as the expanded scrutiny of intent makes it difficult for developers of copying and distribution technologies to predict their potential liability. Moreover, one most commonly expressed concern is that it lacked setting in any clear liability regime as it has extended the copyright holders right over the new technology that has infringing use.

Another argument against the intent based liability regime is it will unduly broaden the current liability regime of secondary infringement set by *CBS Songs Ltd* v. *Amstrad Consumer Electronics Plc* (1988). Already repercussions are taking place. It has been reported that as soon as the Grokster case was finalised; the chief executive of the Lime Group decided to no longer distribute Lime Wire as it appeared too difficult to meet the implied standards of the inducement theory.[9] In fact, historically intent played very little role in finding liability until the advent of the peer to peer file sharing cases.

Having said so, it is not to say that the device protection approach is free from criticism or challenge. Because the device protection approach targets the manufacturer of the device it becomes daunting to prove that a manufacturer designs a device primarily for the purpose of facilitating infringements. This is because of the fact that a device that is widely used for infringing purposes might also have a commercially significant non-infringing use. For example, BitTorrent, which is equally a file sharing service similar to Grokster, managed to demonstrate sufficient non-infringing uses even under the more stringent standard favoured by Justice Ginsburg.[10] Similarly, decentralised P2P technology has many advantages to offer. The architecture of the decentralised P2P technology offers removal of intermediaries and provides advantages including efficiency, security and political freedom. By demonstrating all these features decentralised P2P architecture will not only qualify for 'significant non-infringing use' but also would be able to demonstrate 'transformative use'. In *Campbell* v. *Acuff Rose* (1994), the term 'transformative use' was meant to introduce something new, with a further purpose or different character, altering the first with a new expression, meaning or message.

What needs to be done?

This article recommends the adoption of a narrow device protection approach. This can be achieved by targeting devices that have facilitating behaviour and enable mass infringement. This approach would address both the functionality and the behaviour of the device. So far, what has been discerned is that the intent based liability regime (inducement theory) only emphasises behaviour. It can be argued that targeting solely the behaviour of the device and leaving aside largely the functionality undermines the potential danger that can be caused by the device. The first case that took the functionality of the device into consideration was *Sony Corporation of America* v. *Universal City Studios Inc.* (1984). In *Sony*, the Supreme Court dealt with the then-novel issue of contributory copyright infringement by vendors and manufacturers of so-called dual-use devices that are capable of being used for both infringing and non-infringing purposes. The owners of copyrighted television programmes sued Sony and several vendors of its videotape recorders for their customers' infringing uses. The Court created a safe harbour by borrowing 'staple-article of commerce' doctrine from the patent domain. While analysing this, the Court reasoned that 'the sale of copying equipment, like the sale of other articles of commerce, does not constitute contributory infringement if the product is widely used for legitimate, unobjectionable purposes. Similarly, the functionality of a device also received considerable attention in *Campbell* v. *Acuff Rose* (1994). In *Campbell*, while determining fair use, the Court held that in finding fair use, the device should offer some 'transformative' character – suggesting that the device should provide something new, with a further purpose or different character, altering the first with a new expression, meaning or message.

The current UK copyright legislation, CDPA (1988), proscribes devices that have infringing purposes. In the UK CDPA (1988) for the first time introduced the concept of 'infringing article'.[11] Section 24 of CDPA (1988) deals with 'Infringing article'. However, this section does not apply to photocopiers or dual tape recorders and is rather implemented to address copiers that make copies of specific works.[12] Moreover, it has been held that mere distribution of a product that has infringing purposes does not give rise to any liability in the UK.[13] A similar decision was also delivered in *CBS Songs Ltd* v. *Amstrad Consumer Electronics Plc* (1988) and in *CBS Inc* v. *Ames Records & Tapes Ltd* (1982). In *CBS Inc.* v. *Ames* (1982) it was held that in the absence of authorisation, the mere act of facilitation was not an infringement. In fact, the most relevant current provision on device protection in the online environment is contained in section 296ZB, CDPA (1988). This section makes it an offence to facilitate or enable the circumvention of an effective technological measure. Any person who performs any of the following activities relating to a device, product or component, which is primarily designed, produced or adapted for the purpose of enabling or facilitating the circumvention of an effective technological measure is liable:

a. for making for sale or hire;
b. for importing otherwise than for private or domestic use;
c. for selling or letting for hire, offering or exposing for sale or hire, advertising for sale, possessing or distributing in the course of business; or
d. distributing otherwise than in the course of business so as to affect the copyright owner prejudicially.

The problem with the foregoing provision, however, is that it is designed to address the circumvention of technological measures that are attached to the device. This paper aims to suggest that there remains a clear need of adopting a device protection provision divorced from circumvention. The aim of the proposed provision would be to address the article/device that facilitates infringement on a mass scale. This can be achieved by addressing the behaviour as well as the functionality of the device. 'Behaviour' corresponds to encourage, facilitate and assist to infringe. Similarly, functionality means possessing the characteristic and architecture to infringe on a mass scale. The ACTA (Anti Counterfeiting Trade Agreement) committee has been considering the measures that need to be adopted to deter online piracy posed by decentralised P2P technology. The discussion paper proposes two measures: a deterrent measure and seizing and destroying equipment. The proposed provision of the paper suggests,

> Criminal sanctions to be applied to (Intellectual Property Rights) infringements on a commercial scale where there are significant wilful infringements without motivation for financial gain to such an extent as to prejudicially affect the copyright owner (e.g. Internet piracy).

This paper suggests that a section needs to be incorporated into the CDPA (1988) which is independent from the circumventing technology measure and is primarily aimed at combatting the devices that possess the characteristic/architecture and is designed to encourage/facilitate/assist to infringe in mass scale. However, defence would be allowed for the technology capable of demonstrating that non-infringing use outweighs the infringing use and has the capability of offering some form of transformative use.

Conclusion

Decentralised P2P technology has brought a significant challenge to the domain of the secondary liability regime of copyright law. This is because the new context has rendered the traditional secondary liability regime entirely inoperable. To combat this challenge the US landmark case *Grokster* has devised a new theory; namely the inducement theory. While examining the prospect of implementing this new theory in the UK the paper suggests that the challenge of decentralised P2P technology should be addressed by way of device protection rather than adding a new theory (inducement theory). The rationale behind the proposal remains twofold: first, inducement theory merely emphasises ill intent/behaviour of the technology and entirely ignores the characteristic/functionality of the device. Second, the effectiveness of the theory remains doubtful beyond the era of *Grokster*. This paper alternatively suggests adoption of a device protection approach that is divorced from circumventing technology and is aimed to address both the behaviour and characteristic/functionality of the devices that facilitate infringement on a mass scale. However, defence would be allowed for the devices that can satisfy significant non-infringing behaviour coupled with some transformative use.

Notes

1. Paul Ganley, 'Surviving Grokster: Innovation and the Future of Peer to Peer', *European Intellectural Property Review* 28, no. 1 (2006): 15–25.
2. Brief of Computer Science Professors Suggesting Affirmance of the Judgment at p 15, cf Ganley, Surviving Grokster. In a brief filed with the court, several distinguished computer science professors raised the spectre of filtering and expressed their doubt about its utility in the P2P context.
3. Niva Elkin-Koren, 'Making Technology Visible: Liability of Internet Service Providers for Peer to Peer Traffic', *New York University Journal of Legislation and Public Policy* 9 (2006): 15.
4. Hasina Haque, 'Is the Time Ripe for Yet Another Exclusive Right? A Proposal', *European Intellectural Property Review* 30, no. 9 (2008) 374, see also Okechukwu Benjamin Vincents, 'Secondary Liability for Copyright Infringement in the BitTorrent Platform: Placing the Blame Where It Belongs', *European Intellectural Property Review* 30 (2008): 7: 'It is highly unlikely that a claim based on "authorising Infringement" will succeed against these BitTorrent operators'.
5. Vincents, 'Secondary Liability', 2.
6. OiNK.cd, OiNK.cd Servers Raided, 23 October 2007, Middlesbrough, http://by106w.bay106.mail.live.com (accessed June 6, 2008).
7. Elkin-Koren, 'Making Technology Visible', 15.
8. Sverker K. Hogberg, 'The Search for Intent Based Doctrines of Secondary Liability in Copyright Law', *Columbia Law Review* 106 (2006): 909, at 912.
9. Rebecca Giblin-Chen, 'On Sony, Streamcast and Smoking Guns', *European Intellectural Property Review* 29, no. 6 (2007): 215–226.
10. Bryan H. Choi, 'The Grokster Dead End', *Harvard Journal of Law and Technology* 19, no. 2 (2006): 407.
11. Michael Hart, 'Infringement and Remedies Under the Copyright, Designs and Patents Act 1988', *European Intellectural Property Review* 11, no. 4 (1989): 113–118.
12. Maureen Daly, 'Life after Grokster: Analysis of US and European Approaches to File-sharing', *European Intellectural Property Review* 29, no. 8 (2007): 319–324. Specific works means photographic negatives, moulds and the like.
13. *Philips Domestic Appliances & Personal Care BV* v. *Salton Europe Ltd, Salton Hong Kong Ltd and Electrical & Electronics Ltd* [2004] EWHC 2092 9(Ch), cf. Daly, 'Life after Grokster'.

The future of copyright in the age of convergence: Is a new approach needed for the new media world?

Neal Geach

University of Hertfordshire, St Albans, Hertfordshire, UK

In 2007 the European Commission finalised its proposals for replacing the Television without Frontiers Directive. The resultant Audiovisual Media Services Directive aims to provide a more suitable regulatory framework for the creative industries allowing it to benefit from the opportunities brought about by convergence. Convergence is the coming together of different technologies which have distinct functions to create one medium which performs each divergent function. The prime illustration of convergent technologies is arguably the coming together of telecommunications and broadcasting, through the internet and digital technology, so as to enable us to make voice telephony calls and watch television while sat at a computer. However, while convergence has created opportunities for the industry it has also created threats in that the same technology is also being used to infringe the copyright of content producers on a far greater scale. This is important as wide scale infringement may impact negatively on the creation of new works; as without protection from illegal copying the work has less economic value. It is argued that regardless of any other flaws the new Directive may have; its biggest weakness is not addressing the link between converged media platforms and the potential for increased copyright infringement. This work proceeds to evaluate whether the traditional approach to copyright protection is still the most suitable and whether in fact the arguments advanced in favour of this approach still have merit in the converged age. To this end an evaluation of a Creative Commons approach is provided in order to see whether this may have more advantages.

In 2007 the European Commission (EC) finalised its proposals for replacing the Television without Frontiers Directive. The resultant Audiovisual Media Services Directive (the AVMS Directive) aimed to provide a more suitable regulatory framework for the creative industries that are taking advantage of the opportunities brought about by convergence to transmit programs over the Internet. However, while convergence has created opportunities for the industry it has also created threats in that the same technologies are also being used to infringe the copyright of content producers on a far greater scale. This is important as wide scale infringement may impact negatively on the creation of new works; as without protection from piracy the work has less economic value. It is argued that regardless of any other flaws the new Directive may have; its biggest weakness is its failure to address the link between converged media platforms and the potential for increased copyright infringement. This work then proceeds to evaluate whether the traditional approach to copyright protection is still the most suitable and whether in fact the arguments advanced in favour of this approach still have merit in the converged age. To this end an evaluation of a Creative Commons approach is provided in order to see whether this may have more advantages.

The need for audiovisual content copyright protection

Phonographic Performance Ltd UK has described the creative industries as 'the key to prosperity in modern economies'.[1] As a body that works on behalf of performers and record companies this statement could be dismissed as mere industry self hype. However, official statistics would indicate them to be correct. In 2004 the industry contributed over £56 billion to the UK economy; growing at an average rate of 5% per year between 1997 and 2004.[2] To put this into some context; the average growth for the UK economy as a whole was only 3%.[3] As a sector the exact employment figure 'is not entirely clear' but is between 1.15 and 2 million.[4] As convergence and technological developments advance to allow more accessible access to higher quality content, over multiple platforms, these figures will surely increase. Therefore, the government argues 'it is vital that creative businesses are fully able to exploit the exciting new media technology that has opened up access to creative content, but for business to be able to make returns on their creativity and invest in new talent and innovation, it is also important that they have the necessary protection.'[5] In other words, the creative industry which provides the content for the new audiovisual media services are held up as a prime example of the traditional economic justifications for imposing strict copyright protection. The argument is that investment in design and development will not be forthcoming without the incentive that protection provides. As Bainbridge suggests, 'Why spend large sums of money to develop [content] that could be copied freely without recompense?'[6]

Threats and opportunities for audiovisual media in the converged environment

As the government quote above indicates, the new environment that audiovisual media service providers find themselves operating in offer potential huge benefits but also threats to their business viability. Converged technologies, such as Internet Protocol Television (IPTV), offer the chance to distribute content at lower costs, to wider audiences and so they are appealing business models. However, converged media platforms need high quality content to drive uptake. The increased competition for audience share between traditional broadcasters has also driven demand for higher quality content. This has led Patrick Bradley of Ingenious Media to declare that 'content is king' in today's audiovisual environment.[7] Thus, the opportunity exists for content creators to gain increased exposure through a variety of outlets that now exist for their work.[8] This could, if the quality is sufficient, lead to increase revenue to pay for further innovation. Alternatively, the Internet allows them to miss out 'the middle man' and sell their content directly to viewers and further increase revenues. Even content providers such as Sky[9] can benefit from the increased content production that arises from this demand. The House of Commons Select Committee on Culture, Media and Sport heard evidence, in preparing their report 'New Media and the Creative Industries' (the SC Report), that Sky has driven subscriptions by purchasing the rights to the show '24'.[10] Content can also be used to attract business for any complementary on-demand services being offered by the broadcaster.

However, despite these opportunities for increased exposure, and driving revenue the same technology that allows viewers greater access to content also is a threat. Internet peer to peer networks and technologies, such as BitTorrent, allow for the fast and efficient up/downloading of large files such as films and TV programmes. This in turn provides for easier distribution among individuals. This activity is a major threat to the industry as it reduces the commercial exploitation potential of content creators and providers. To take Sky again, if '24' is freely available in good quality on the internet for no cost then there is no incentive to pay a monthly subscription to the company. This threat has led to the observation that 'IPTV platforms will only succeed if companies can differentiate from the three other delivery platforms – terrestrial, cable and satellite. They need [intellectual property] rights. If those rights are secured, current TV broadcast models – and the EC's proposals – will become irrelevant.'[11]

Notwithstanding the illegal copying and distribution of audiovisual content, a problem is on-demand services themselves. The purpose of on-demand is to allow viewers to legally download a particular piece of content using the Internet. However, the Internet is obviously global and any website in the world is accessible to any person wherever they may be. This may not appear a problem at first glance. Surely this is a benefit that the Internet can provide a wider audience for content? This may be so but the flipside is that a person in for example Germany should be able to go on the website of a UK content producer and download that content after it has been transmitted in the UK. The issue is that this could be before that piece of content will have been shown in Germany, most likely under an exclusive distribution agreement between the original company and the German company providing the retransmission. Such exclusive right agreements can be extremely lucrative for the purchaser by either, helping to drive subscriptions or through generating higher value sponsorships or traditional advertisement spots. This is obviously in addition to the party selling the rights who can generate significant revenues.[12] On-demand, with the global nature of the Internet, potentially makes such agreements worthless. This dilemma is resolved by preventing access to on-demand services from foreign IP addresses, which is the situation with both the BBC's and ITV's on-demand services. This is arguably a precursor to the Balkanisation of the Internet which is widely agreed to be a detrimental development.

Copyright protection within the audio visual media services directive

In view of the economic importance of audiovisual content industry and the need for copyright protection if it is to grow;[13] it is suggested that a regulatory framework which seeks to regulate audiovisual media in order for it to flourish should have copyright close to its foundations. There would appear little logic in not coupling the copyright framework within the overall regulatory framework, if only for 'Better Regulation' purposes.[14]

However, the new European Union's (EU's) forthcoming AVMS Directive, which will provide the new regulatory framework for IPTV and traditional broadcasting, does not take this joined up approach. Article 3c is the only provision that makes reference to the issue; even then this is in the limited scope of prohibiting service providers from transmitting cinematographic works outside the periods agreed with the rights holders. Ironically this is highlighted in the SC report as something that encourages copyright infringement. In recommendation 15 they 'accept the argument, in principle, that delaying universal access to film through the use of release windows, and holding back rights to broadcast television programming via new media, contributes to a climate in which piracy flourishes.'[15]

There is a further indirect reference in the AVMS Directive through the provisions of chapter IIc, regarding exclusive rights and short news provisions. These provide in the interests of media pluralism where an event has been acquired exclusively by one 'broadcaster', they can be made to provide 'fair, reasonable and non-discriminatory' access to other broadcasters for the purpose of short news reports.[16] Compensation arrangements should be available under the member states' legal system for a breach of the access terms.[17]

No other reference to copyright is made in the framework.[18] It is worth highlighting here that the Commission's aim through its i2010 initiative is to 'foster growth and jobs in the information society and media industries' by creating a regulatory environment that encourages investment and innovation. The new framework aims to do this for the audiovisual media services industry; yet the long standing argument in favour of copyright protection is that without it, these goals will not be achieved. There is arguably a contradiction here, particularly as no significant mention of copyright is made yet the technology that has allowed the present situation to evolve is being cited as a threat to the industry's very existence. The EU may point to existing legislation that provides copyright protection and the reason for its omission here. However, this assumes that existing copyright protection is suited to the new, dynamic audiovisual environment that the new framework was a response to.

Existing EU copyright protection

EU copyright protection is provided by Directive 2001/29/EC on the harmonisation of certain aspects of copyright and related rights in the information society (the Copyright Directive). The Directive states that through a harmonised legal framework on copyright, not only will there be a higher level of protection, but also a fostering of 'substantial investment in creativity and innovation ... and lead to growth and increased competitiveness of European industry, both in the area of content provision....'.[19] This suggests a close operation between this and the broadcasting framework; particularly as it later states that intellectual property rights are 'necessary' to ensure the availability of an attractive return on the 'considerable' investment needed to produce on-demand services.[20]

The Copyright Directive provides, for present purposes, two key rights for content creators. The first is in Article 2, the reproduction right. This gives member states the ability to provide for certain creators the exclusive right to decide whether or not to allow any form of reproduction of their work. For present purposes the important group of creators that this right applies to is 'broadcasting organisations', it is also clear from the wording of the section that broadcasts transmitted over the internet are covered by this section.[21]

The second right allows for the provision of an exclusive right to determine whether a work is communicated to, and made available to the public. This includes whether to make the work available to the public in such a way that the work may be accessed 'from a place and at a time individually chosen' by a member of the public, i.e. on-demand.[22] The provision of an exclusive right to determine communication to the public applies to authors only.[23] The right for making available to the public applies to the same groups as the reproduction right, so includes 'broadcasting organisations'.

The result appears that copyright holders of audiovisual media content will have an exclusive right to determine whether their work is reproduced, communicated or made available to the public[24] and therefore, fills the gap within the new framework. For example, an individual is prevented from watching a piece of content, copying it and then placing it on a website for others to download; as this would involve the reproducing and making available of that content. It is suggested that this view is mistaken as it is only applicable to a confined range of audiovisual media situations. The Copyright Directive contains no definitions as to what constitutes the groups of recognised right holders most notably 'broadcasting organisation'. At the time of the implementation of the Copyright Directive, the meaning of the term 'broadcasting' may have been obvious, or it may have been logical to apply the definition within the old Television Without Frontiers Directive which was in force at the time. However, the concept of broadcasting is redefined by the AVMS Directive; in fact, the term 'broadcasting organisation' is completely omitted form the AVMS Directive.[25] Can it really be said that a Directive passed in 2001 can have the meaning of another Directive passed some 6 years later without the latter expressly stating that its terms are applicable? It is suggested that it cannot be, otherwise there would never be any reason to pass amending legislation to modernise terms and provisions. The problem that exists can be illustrated using the above example. If the content watched and copied was from a linear transmission there is no problem, the television broadcaster who transmits the content would clearly be a recognised right holder. Neither is there a problem where the content is transmitted by an on-demand service as long as the person behind the transmission is a 'television broadcaster' as they can still fit within a 'broadcasting organisation'. The problem arises where the transmission is performed by a person who solely operates as an on-demand service provider. The distinction made by the new framework between 'on-demand service' and 'television broadcasting'[26] means an on-demand audiovisual media service provider cannot seriously be classed as a 'broadcasting organisation'. Therefore, an equivalent to YouTube who transmits content after having the rights assigned to it, in fact has no copyright protection. If the content is produced in-house, so that they are the 'author', they could prevent the above scenario as the copying is a reproduction[27] and the putting on a website would constitute communication to the public. However, any independently sourced work, which the new framework wants to see more of, again would fall outside the Copyright Directive. The result potentially will be that these independent works are not commissioned as the economic incentive to do so is not there if they can be copied at will by the public. This in turn, hits media pluralism, a main aim of the AVMS Directive.

This void in protection could perhaps be filled by technological means. Digital Rights Management (DRM) technologies are used by copyright holders to act as access controls to content and limit the usage of digital media. They have proved controversial as they can restrict content use in ways not prohibited by existing copyright laws, primarily fair use exemptions.[28] They have also proved controversial because of software and platform interoperability issues. For example, the BBC's new on-demand demand service iplayer has generated complaints.[29] Because of the DRM used, downloaded transmissions can only be kept for 30 days (7 days once watched). This may not be such an issue for a free service such as iplayer, but it is hard to see the sustainability in a commercial model based along these lines. People who pay for downloads are surely entitled to repeat usage, as with music mp3s, yet this is the approach largely taken by Channel 4. The other complaint regarding the iplayer is that due to the DRM being jointly developed by Microsoft the service is currently only operable on Windows XP. Clearly as a public service broadcaster this has to change and a more interoperable system is due for role out in the coming months. However, this does then impact on the non-interoperability of other services. There is little incentive to develop an innovative new service, such as a broadcast equivalent of iTunes, if as a result of DRM technology within that content or content delivery platform, content cannot be viewed on certain devices needed to view the content.[30] It is somewhat surprising that at a time when the music industry is moving away from DRM,[31] broadcasters are implementing them for their on-demand services.

DRM growth and attractiveness for rights holders has flowed from the legal backing the Copyright Directive gives them.[32] Article 6 provides that member states shall provide 'adequate legal protection against the circumvention' of DRM technologies. Additional legal protection is to be offered against the 'manufacture, import, distribution, sale, rental ... or possession for commercial purposes of devices, products or components' which can be used to circumvent DRM technologies. Even the promotion, advertisement or marketing of such devices is prohibited. Further protection is given by Article 7 which provides member states to legally protect against the removal or alteration of the content's electronic rights management information, the information regarding who the rights holder is and the terms of usage.

Therefore, as things stand an individual legitimately paying to download a transmission of a programme, and then stripping away the DRM technology in order to watch the programme again, or over a longer period, or to use a different viewing platform, is committing a crime. In the UK this could potentially lead to 2 years imprisonment and/or a fine[33] for doing something which at its core level is a legitimate act.[33] Obviously, this is to act as a deterrent so that the stripped down content is then not made available to the public or distributed. However, the unequal bargaining position of viewers when accepting[35] that such an act will be copyright infringement, and thus criminal, lends weight to the view this should not be criminal behaviour and should be allowed as a private use exemption.[36]

Ultimately, the fact that legislative regulation is in place is one thing, but it is common knowledge that copyright infringement through file sharing or indeed, that solely for private individual consumption is widespread. This raises question marks over the initial justifications of copyright, content production is still occurring after all. In fact if one includes non-commercial user generated content on websites such as YouTube, it could be said to be thriving. Generally, the call is always for more robust protection with harsher penalties for infringement; as prosecutions arise the system can be said to be effective. The question must be asked however, as to whether this really is the most appropriate approach. Is there not a better way of giving protection without continually strengthening protection and increasing the deterrents? While certainly beneficial to the copyright holders, it could be argued that such a move is not beneficial to society as a whole as it does not allow as much creativity as there could be. Might instead, we adopt an approach that may allow for the easier distribution of audiovisual content, which could lead to enhanced cultural development and knowledge as well as providing inspiration for further innovation, such a scenario is after all, another aim of the AVMS Directive.

Creative Commons: a more realistic alternative?

Such an approach has in fact been advocated, the Creative Commons approach. This believes that the current copyright protection regime actually hinders creativity – the opposite outcome for its justification. As film Director Davis Guggenheim has explained before he can shoot any scene for a film he must get 'clear rights' not just for the initial story or soundtrack but also for incidental works such as billboards in the background or drinks that a character may be holding.[37] The creative idea must go through a process of scrutiny by lawyers to determine what rights may be infringed and then to gain permission for its incidental inclusion. He goes on to cite various examples of litigation that have arisen from this situation.[38] The result is a constraint on creative and editorial prerogative as the makeup of a scene is determined by copyright holders. Arguably this is no different from the influence the AVMS Directive (and its predecessor the Television without Frontiers Directive) has sought to restrict through its advertising provisions.

There are theoretical arguments to be made against the idea of a creative commons. Chander and Sunder[39] suggest that people celebrate the advent of the creative commons because of the belief that, as the resource is open to everyone, everyone will exploit it. However, they argue that this is 'naïve, idealistic and removed from reality.'[40] They highlight that, even if a regulated market exists, there will not be equal distribution of the resource. This would suggest that the possibility of greater access will not necessarily result in greater access for the masses. There is certainly merit in this view on a general level, and it would also seem to tie into the theory of the 'Tragedy of the Commons',[41] whereby resources, due to their public availability, are used to extinction or are left in ruin. However, these arguments do not appear to relate to the specific issue of broadcasting content where content is non-rivalrous. This is perhaps where the debate over the wide-spread introduction of a creative commons becomes complex. It may well be that such an approach is not suitable for certain industries; for other industries, the concept may need adaptation. Perhaps the debate over the adoption of a creative commons needs to become more sector-specific; here, the focus is on the broadcasting industry.

Arguments in favour of a new approach for copyright are vigorously resisted by the film studios and television broadcasters. The Creators' Rights Alliance has dismissed the idea as something that 'would not work in certain types of industries' and dismissed it as just the product of academics 'who do not understand the rest of the world'.[42] They frame the debate as one of maintaining protection or having none at all. However, the commons approach is about balancing the copyright system to maintain protection on the one hand while also allowing the greater distribution of ideas. The aim is to get the balance right between the degree of control that content is subject to,[43] and the extent that it is free.[44] The approach argues that this can lead to greater creativity and innovation than where the system is an attempt at perfect control through divided up proprietary rights.

The various layers that make up traditional television[45] (particularly cable and satellite) have been cited by Lessig as a system that is completely controlled, none are 'free'.[46] This can be contrasted with the Internet and its original end to end architecture[47] which means the main layers are free.[48] This can be illustrated by the vast user generated content that appears on sites such as YouTube; no station controller exists[49] to decide what can be transmitted and so creativity flourishes, creators know there is a guaranteed outlet for their work. Admittedly two points arise from this situation. First, that someone making comedy clips in their bedroom could be said to not be on the same commercial level as a multi-million pound broadcasting corporation. They are not necessarily creating work for financial gain merely for creative expression and as such are not affected by copyright infringements of their work. Second, it could be said that this lack of a body exercising editorial control encourages copyright infringement.[50]

The result for traditional television broadcasts is that the most important layer, content, is being restricted through the legislative provisions and technologies described above leaving us with a situation that is 'perfect control [, but one] that threatens to undermine the potential for innovation that the Internet promises ... [The] aim should be a system of sufficient control to give artists enough incentive to produce, while leaving free as much as we can for others to build upon and create'.[51] The rationale for this view is because '[n]othing today, likely nothing since we tamed fire, is genuinely new: culture, like science and technology, grows by accretion, each new creator building on the works of those who came before. Overprotection stifles the very creative forces it's supposed to nurture.'[52] While copyright may increase the incentives to produce for the works originator it also increases the costs of production and thus coupled with the threat of litigation can act as a barrier to the creative process. Therefore, it could be said in fact to go against its stated justifications.

The commons approach operates by way of a licence system, based on copyright, which the creator of the work uses to attach to the work. In total there are six but these are non-exclusive so that a creator can subsequently sell their work under a licence allowing for the recipient to make commercial use of that work. All of the commons licences allow file sharing provided it is not for monetary gain, if this is the case then the licence must be one which has not got a non-commercial use attached. Additionally the creator can decide whether they want derivative works to be produced from their original, although as noted the system is flexible enough to allow for a change of mind in subsequent cases. If the work is passed on then the new recipient is bound by the same licence terms and the original recipient. If the content in the above loophole scenario has a commons licence attached to it, then that work will be protected under copyright but the action would be legal and thus there is protection balanced with a greater level of access. Therefore it is suggested that this system allows for increased access to material and thus allows creativity to flourish; commercial use can be made of the work and so the financial incentives are also prevalent as the commercial use potential within the work can be reflected in the amount claimed by the creator for distributing the work to the person who seeks to have possession of it.[53]

There are criticisms that can be levied at this argument. A case can be made for arguing that people can simply circumvent payment for content use in much the same way as they do now. However, this can be countered in that it highlights the fact that the present system allows for copyright infringement now. If I lend my friend a CD they can copy it to their computer and so avoid purchasing it themselves. This new approach will simply decriminalise an act that is in fact an everyday occurrence and in fact gained support in the SC Report. Again, content is continuing to be produced regardless of such current illegal activity and by removing the existing usage restrictions, could increase further as the fear of litigation by other potential creative talents is removed.[54] This is not to say that wanton copying that is then distributed as an original piece of content should not remain prohibited. Under a commons approach the creator of the work has greater power to choose what a recipient can do, if they do not want a derivative work produced from it they can stipulate that.

However the success of adopting a wide scale commons approach is dependent on whether the potential for commercial incentives is convincing enough for the industry and the government, who would not want to negatively hit the wider economy. The British Phonographic Industry has not dismissed this idea but believe that this issue will be determined by the market.[55] There must be commercial sustainability for a content producer who operates without any content control, and before they begin production they will need to believe sufficient revenue can be generated. Research by Roger Clarke[56] suggests this is possible. In the first instance there is the typical scenario of a consumer/viewer paying for a piece of content, either per content piece or general subscription.[57] By allowing the widespread distribution of content without controls (for example by friends or download even without payment), a wider market can be generated for that content through increased awareness and interest.[58] This can then be capitalised on by providing direct access to other content that the producer has created through a payment system.[59] In this respect YouTube has been praised by the BBC as having content that while being illegal is 'good promotional content for us'.[60] Content producers also benefit from this model of deferred reciprocity in another way. This is where although initially their work may be copied or used in some way they can reciprocate this action. When producing new content a producer can use the work of others as inspiration or as a starting point, helping to reduce the production costs. This course of action, or 'wikinomics' as it has been termed is in fact gaining growing commercial acceptance as a method of adding economic value to a business.[61]

In addition to using widespread uncontrolled content for the purpose of driving subscription services, it can also be used to attract higher advertising premiums. By allowing content to be more accessible, as noted, means that more people have *the ability to watch* that content. If the product is good, more will *want to watch* that content as with any traditional television broadcast today. Wider content viewing figures which the Internet brings means therefore, wider reach for advertisers, leading in turn to higher revenues from content owners. Such an approach to monetising content has in fact been advocated by Jay Adelson, the Chief Executive of Digg.[62] However, for this benefit to be realised the content must be of sufficient value to the viewer. This is in fact the strategy being adopted by Channel 4 and has already been successfully adopted by Hulu, the joint project between NBC and News Corporation. While the content in question may not have a commons licence it can be argued that it does lend support to the argument that a more expansive commons regime can be commercially viable.[63]

Additionally, another significant benefit for content producers today comes from the fact that technology can be utilised alongside on-demand services to create a profile of the viewer.[64] This means that advertising can be targeted at people who will be more receptive to those advertisements. This is something of a holy grail for the marketing industry particularly with the lower production costs that already exist for Internet advertising. Therefore, content producers can charge a significant premium for the advertisements running on that content. The real benefit of this is that the content does not in fact need to be of mass appeal, as the advertiser is getting an interested audience they know they are more likely to instigate sales from the viewer pool.

Therefore, a commons approach would benefit content producers twofold. They can obtain access to a wider range of material to use within their content productions or as a platform that their new work builds from. As permission will already have been granted, production can start straight away and legal advice need not be sought, reducing production costs. Additionally relaxation of copyright controls can actually indirectly generate higher viewing figures or revenue by creating wider exposure from easier distribution among friends. People may watch a production on-line for free that their friend recommends; if they enjoy it they are then likely to 'tune in' to the next episode and/or perhaps buy the box set of the series – the latter being something they would not do if they have not previously seen the show for themselves. These commercial benefits are obviously in addition to the benefits to wider society that are gained by increased innovation and the greater access to those creations.

Conclusion

The proposed AVMS Directive has already been criticised in some quarters over its substantive provisions. Arguably, to any weaknesses it has, can also be added its failure to deal with the issue of copyright in the new audiovisual age. By not addressing the issue but then distinguishing between 'television broadcasts' and 'on-demand services', it has surely created a loophole in the existing copyright protection regime. If the traditional economic justifications with regard to the need for copyright protection remain valid, then the AVMS Directive is set to fail in its objective to have an innovative audiovisual media sector. Although, it is argued that the copyright framework, as well as the audiovisual media sector, would benefit from a wide scale adoption of a Creative Commons approach to copyright protection not only by solving the aforementioned loophole but also by producing more creativity than the current regime as a result of the wider flexibility and access that it provides. Whether this scenario will occur remains to be seen but is unlikely while the creative industry players remain so unconvinced by the revenue potential.

Notes

1. House of Commons, Culture, Media and Sport Select Committee, 'New Media and the Creative Industries', Fifth Report, *Sessional Papers, 2006–07*, vol. 1, p. 8; available at http://www.publications.parliament.uk/pa/cm200607/cmselect/cmcumeds/509/509i.pdf

2. Government Response to the Culture, Media and Sport Select Committee Report into 'New Media and the Creative Industries' at p. 1; available at http://www.culture.gov.uk/NR/rdonlyres/3E8E36E8-3B56-4219-89B2-0623C0AA8AF3/0/375268_GovResponse.pdf
3. Ibid.
4. Ibid. The lower figure is that suggested by research by Frontier Economics for the Department of Culture, Media and Sport, the higher figure is put forward by Ofcom. The government puts the figure at 1.8 million.
5. See note 2.
6. D. Bainbridge, *Introduction to Information Technology Law*, 6th ed. (Harlow, UK: Pearson Education 2007), 9.
7. Giving evidence to the Culture, Media and Sport Select Committee available in vol. 2 of their report 'New Media and the Creative Industries', available at http://www.publications.parliament.uk/pa/cm200607/cmselect/cmcumeds/509/6101711.htm
8. For example whereas before their consumers may have just been traditional linear broadcasters, today they could also be telecommunications companies.
9. That is, those that do not produce their own original content but buy the rights from the producers to broadcast within a define territory.
10. They then gain the secondary benefit of potentially higher advertising revenues by having the exclusive right to transmit a popular show.
11. Graham Lovelace quoted by Martin Croft, 'Will Legislation Kill off Mobile TV Before it Gains an Audience? *Marketing Week*, 5 January 2006.
12. The English Premier League Overseas rights were sold for £625 million: see BBC News Press Release, 'Premiership in New £625 m TV deal', BBC News, 18 January 2007, available at http://news.bbc.co.uk/1/hi/business/6273617.stm (accessed February 2, 2008)
13. This is not confined to the UK; the enhancement of these services is a central tenet of the EU's i2010 Initiative. Recital 4 also states that 'audiovisual media services offer significant employment opportunities . . . and stimulate economic growth and jobs'.
14. In the sense that all the regulations on one area can be found within the same document and thus making it easier for service providers and viewers to know the rights and obligations of each other.
15. Government Response, note 2, 81.
16. Art. 3j.
17. Art. 3j(5).
18. Recital 27a states the access to events for the purpose of short news reports is without prejudice to Directive 2001/29/EC.
19. Recital 4.
20. Recital 12.
21. Art. 2(e).
22. Art. 3(1)(2).
23. Art. 3(1).
24. Art. 4 also provides for a right of distribution.
25. Instead, we have the concept of a media service provider which is defined as 'the natural or legal person who has editorial responsibility for the choice of the audiovisual content of the audiovisual media service and determine the manner in which it is organised' Art. 1(6). A 'broadcaster is defined in Art. 1(d) as media service provider of television broadcasts.
26. In Art. 1.
27. This right is provided to author of works under Art. 2(a) of the Copyright Directive.
28. Naturally the ability to forward on content, even that paid for, to friends is prohibited.
29. For an overview see Bobbie Johnson, 'Test Driving the iplayer', *Guardian Unlimited*, available at http://blogs.guardian.co.uk/technolgy/arcieves/2007/07/27/test_driving_the_iplayer.html (accessed July 28, 2007).
30. Apple's iTunes store does not permit downloads to non-Apple mp3 players.
31. Jonathan Richards, 'Interview: Jay Adelson, chief executive of Digg', *Times Online*, available at http://technology.timesonline.co.uk/tol/news/tech_and_web/article3075146.ece (accessed April 20, 2008). In the interview Adelson highlights how in relation to music, media executives are moving away from DRM and monetising content in other ways. As a replacement he suggests embedding files with technologies that monitor how many times it is downloaded or streamed and then using this information to set advertising rates.

32. This is replicated in the USA with the Digital Millennium Copyright Act.
33. s. 296ZB Copyright, Design and Patents Act 1988, although the 'Gowers Review of Intellectual Property' suggests digital copyright offences should all carry the same 10 year penalty as physical infringement.
34. In that they are simply trying to watch something that they have paid for.
35. If they have in fact even read these terms and conditions.
36. Interestingly, the Copyright Directive suggests in Recital 38, 39 and 44 that member states should be able to allow private use reproduction, particularly analogue copies. It is more concerned about digital reproduction because of the economic impact on producers but in this digital audiovisual age this distinction would no longer seem valid. In the UK, the 'Gowers Review of Intellectual Property' has called for reform in this area to allow for a private copying so that format shifting can take place. A consultation period on the proposals closed on 8 April 2008.
37. In a telephone interview with Lawrence Lessig, recorded in Lawrence Lessig, *The Future of Ideas* (New York: Vintage Books, 2001).
38. For example *Woods* v. *Universal City Studios Inc.*, 920 F. Supp. 62 (SDNY 1996) concerning the film *12 Monkeys*.
39. Anupam Chander and Madhavi Sunder, 'The Romance of the Public Domain', *California Law Review*, Vol. 92 (2004).
40. Ibid at p. 1341.
41. Garrett Hardin, 'The Tragedy of the Commons', *Science* 162 (1968).
42. Giving evidence to the Department of Culture, Media and Sport Select Committee documented in 'New Media and the Creative Industries', see Government Response, note 2, 23.
43. Be it by the private sector and the market; or by the state.
44. In the sense that it can be used without permission or where permission is needed it is granted neutrally. The latter meaning without regard to the user, there is no discrimination in allowing access.
45. All communication systems have been described as having three layers by Yochai Benkler. The physical meaning the hardware that runs the system; the code layer, meaning what runs the hardware and the content layer, what is actually transmitted. Yochai Benkler, 'From Consumers to Users: Shifting the Deeper Structures of Regulation', *Federal Communications Law Journal* 52 (2000): 561.
46. Lessig, *Future of Ideas*, 25.
47. Whereby the intelligence of the system is pushed to the ends, i.e. the user's computer or application leaving the network free to simply transmit data. As such it is not intelligent enough to discriminate between different application and content.
48. Content can be added without the consent of anyone, while the code layer is neutral in not discriminating between different forms of content.
49. Such as Director General Mark Thompson at the BBC.
50. This is the charge labelled against YouTube by Viacom who are seeking US$1 billion in damages. See Anne Broache and Greg Sandoval, 'Viacom Sues Google Over YouTube Clips', *CNet News* 13 March 2007; available at http://news.com.com/Viacom+sues+Google+over+YouTube+clips/2100-1030_3-6166668.html (accessed March 13, 2008).
51. Lessig, *Future of Ideas*, 249.
52. Judge Alex Kozinski dissenting in the US case of *Vanna White* v. *Samsung Elecs. Am., Inc.; David Deutsch Assocs.*; 989 F. 2d 1512, 1514 (1993) 27.
53. For more detail as to the different licences and the operation of the Creative Commons see http://creativecommons.org (accessed April 8, 2008).
54. This threat of litigation nearly ensured that, what in the author's view is one of the most creative musical works for some time, 'The Grey Album' by the producer DangerMouse never reached the public audience that it has. The album consists of the music of The Beatles' 'White Album' mixed with the lyrics of 'The Black Album' by Jay-Z.
55. Government Response, note 2, 23.
56. Roger Clarke, 'Business Models to Support Content Commons', *SCRIPT-ed* 4, no. 1 (March 2007): 59–71.
57. The options pursued currently in the market.
58. A typical example would be a person coming across a piece of content by a producer and, as they like it so much, they go and purchase the rest of the content if it is a series.

59. An example until September 2007 would have been said to have been nytimes.com.
60. Ashley Highfield, BBC Director of Future Media and Technology quoted by Tim Weber, 'BBC Strikes Google–YouTube Deal', *BBC News*, 2 March 2007; available at http://news.bbc.co.uk/go/pr/fr/-/1/hi/business/6411017.stm (accessed March 3, 2008).
61. See for example, Don Tapscott and Anthony D. Williams, *WIKINOMICS: How Mass Collaboration Changes Everything* (London: Atlantic Books 2007).
62. See note 30.
63. Informitv News Release, 'Hulu Dawn Exploits Early Rise in Online Video Viewing', Informitv.com 17 April 2008; available at http://informitv.com/articles/2008/04/17/huludawnexploits/ (accessed April 21, 2008).
64. Especially with a subscription service although; clearly there are some data protection issues here but these are outside the scope of present discussion.

Copyright, contract and the protection of computer programs

Ruth Dawn Atkins

Department of Law & Criminology, Aberystwyth University, UK

The extent to which permitted acts under copyright law can be varied by contractual arrangement and conversely, the manner in which proprietary interests can override contrary stipulations expressed in a contractual agreement, collectively display something of the complexity facing software creators and acquirers when defining the scope of their rights and responsibilities towards each other. This paper explores the true scope of the rights granted to software users under existing legislation and considers the measures which a software creator may legitimately advance in order to vary that position. In so doing it is suggested how possible tensions between copyright and contract principles can be resolved and how a successful and suitably transparent agreement between the parties can be promoted.

Introduction

In light of decisions such as *Navitaire* v. *Easyjet Airline* and *Nova Productions* v. *Mazooma Games*,[1] the boundaries between protected expression and unprotected ideas and therefore the extent of copyright protection for computer programs has been more clearly defined. These cases reinforce the view that software houses may find it difficult to succeed in a copyright action against another for writing a computer program that emulates or imitates, by having the same 'look and feel' as an existing program, if this involves no copying of the program code.[2] Additional or alternative means of protection could be derived from other branches of intellectual property law such as the laws relating to designs, trade marks, passing off and the law of confidence and each are worthy of consideration. However, this paper considers what contribution the law of contract can make towards protecting the interests of a software supplier, given that the scope of the parties' obligations and the extent to which these may be prescribed and varied by contractual arrangement can impact upon the level of protection derived for proprietary interests. Therefore, as we continue to see the 'Law Shaping Technology; Technology Shaping the Law',[3] it can be suggested further that an assessment should be made of how one branch of law shapes another. With that purpose, this study focuses on the extent to which copyright law shapes the effect of contract law and vice versa.

Copyright and contract

Copyright is a proprietary right to prevent another from copying a work. Permission to use a copyrighted work is often granted to a software user through a licence as the licence confers permission to perform an act, in this instance, copying, which would otherwise constitute an infringement of copyright and therefore be unlawful. The scope of the permission granted will be defined by the terms and conditions of the licence. As Iain Mitchell QC expounds, the granting of a software licence is not a process by which the licensee grants contractual rights but rather is one in which the licensor surrenders the right to prevent copying.[4] Thus, although the permissions being granted may be conditional permissions, i.e. granted subject to conditions contained in the licence, nonetheless the basic premise underlying this idea remains: the rights of the licensor are not in addition to his rights but rather are in the form of conditions attaching to a subtraction from his rights. The nature of these rights and how these translate into the relationship between the parties is such that an action would not be for a breach of the licence but rather for the breach of copyright. Thus the owner of copyright and licensor will be able to pursue an action for breach of copyright on the basis that a licensee has breached the conditions that are attached to the permission and, therefore, can no longer claim the protection of that permission.

The scope of intellectual property rights can however be varied by contractual arrangement and in other circumstances, those proprietary interests can operate to override contrary stipulations expressed in a contractual agreement. As legislative controls determine the extent of the parties' proprietary interests, these operate contrary to the notion of contractual freedom for the parties to apportion the risks as they consider appropriate – an example of where the law of copyright prevails over the law of contract. From analysing the interaction of these two branches of law, an assessment can be made of the collective and precise impact upon the rights and responsibilities of software creators and users. In this paper, it is examined with reference to the acts that a lawful user is permitted by statute to perform in relation to a computer program: the making of a back-up copy; the act of decompilation; observing, studying and testing; and in certain circumstances, copying or adapting the program.[5]

Back-up copies

A licensee may wish to have a back-up copy of the program they have acquired so that they have a form of security, in the possible event that the program is corrupt or it fails. However, the licensor may be reluctant to provide, or permit to be made, another copy of the software, similarly for security reasons. This potential tension between the perceived needs of the parties is addressed through section 50A (1) of the Copyright, Designs and Patents Act 1988,[6] which provides that 'it is not an infringement of copyright for the lawful user of a copy of a computer program to make any back up copy of it which it is necessary for him to have for the purposes of his lawful use'. It is further provided that 'any term or condition in an agreement which purports to prohibit or restrict the act' will be rendered void and therefore unenforceable (section 50 (3)). Thus, the lawful user will be entitled to make a back-up copy if necessary for the licensed use of the program and by virtue of statutory provision the licensor will not be able to restrict this right.

At first glance it could be suggested that this tips the balance of interests in favour of the software acquirer, but more careful consideration reveals that the licensor does retain an element of control over the making of back-up copies of their software. In particular, it is highly relevant that the legislation states that the act of making a back-up copy by a lawful user is permitted on the basis that the making of the copy is 'necessary' for the purposes of the lawful use. Therefore, whereas it may be 'desirable' or 'sensible' to take a back-up copy, that preference does not make it strictly 'necessary' for the purposes of the lawful use of software.[7] The Act offers no definition of what constitutes 'necessary', leaving the perceived value of this defence to the lawful user somewhat uncertain. To determine what constitutes 'necessary', reference could be made to factors such as 'the relative stability of the program . . . the environment in which the program operates, and the consequences of a program failing',[8] and support for this approach can be found in *Sony Computer Entertainment Inc* v. *Owen*,[9] where it was deemed not 'necessary' to make a back up copy of a disk containing a computer game. The effect of determining the issue of necessity inappropriately and therefore making a back-up copy that is not deemed 'necessary', will be that the copyright in the computer program will be infringed. The consequence of this could be severe as by virtue of the Copyright, etc. and Trade Marks (Offences and Enforcement) Act 2002,[10] the penalties for copying computer software have been extended and a person guilty of an offence is liable on conviction on indictment to imprisonment for up to ten years or to an unlimited fine, or to both.

Of course, the potential issue of infringement will not present itself if a user receives express permission from the licensor to make a back up copy, or indeed is provided with an additional copy to be retained exclusively for back-up purposes. In the event that a licensor is reluctant to offer such a copy, a compromise between the parties' objectives could be reached, with express contractual arrangement specifying the circumstances under which a duplicate copy could be released immediately and at no extra cost to the user. Such contractual provision, if appropriately framed, could successfully avert reliance on the 'necessity' defence and therefore may operate to restrict the making of a back up copy by the licensee. Thus there are potential limits to the scope and operation of the statutory provision relating to back-up copies, which could be legitimately advanced by the licensor. Such measures could serve as safeguards employed by the licensor in order to control the circumstances under which back-up copies may be made. From a more positive stance, aiming to match the interests of both licensor and licensee, it is recommended that by addressing the issue directly through contractual provision, any potential confusion or uncertainty that the user may have relating to the scope of their permitted use could be eliminated, which undoubtedly in turn, would promote contractual clarity and certainty more generally.

Decompilation

The process of program compilation whereby the source code written by a programmer is compiled or translated into object code, can also be carried out in reverse. Reverse engineering, or decompilation, involves translating the object program, as an executable file, into a high-level language. In this form the program may be analysed to identify its components and the interrelationships between those components; it may also enable a programmer to create representations of the system in another form or at a higher level of abstraction.[11] Yet, as the very process of decompilation will require a copy of the program to be made, even a transient copy, the probability of copyright infringement is unavoidable. The 1988 Act[12] addresses this situation by specifically prescribing at section 50B the circumstances under which a lawful user of a computer program will have a valid defence to performing the act of decompilation of that program. Thus, it will not be an infringement of copyright for a lawful user of a copy of a computer program expressed in a low level language to (1) convert it into a version expressed in a higher level language, or (2) incidentally in the course of so converting the program, to copy it, i.e. to decompile it, providing two conditions are met, which are that there must be a 'permitted objective' and that the information obtained is not used for any purpose other than the 'permitted objective'. The 'permitted objective' is described as being such that 'it is necessary to decompile the program to obtain the information necessary to create an independent program which can be operated with the program decompiled or with another program' (section 50B (2)). Following on from this, there are four situations under which the conditions will not be satisfied by the lawful user and these are: first, if the lawful user has readily available to him the information necessary to achieve the permitted objective; second, if he does not confine the decompiling to acts that are necessary to achieve the permitted objective; third, if he supplies the information obtained by the decompiling to any person to whom it is not necessary to supply it in order to achieve the permitted objective; or fourth, if he uses the information to create a program which is substantially similar in its expression to the program decompiled or to do any act restricted by copyright.[13] The scope of the users' rights as permitted through legislation are qualified and limited by the identification of the four situations which will not constitute lawful use.

Although some software creators may support a utilitarian approach to software development, arguing that it offers a wider choice of programs to consumers which should outweigh the narrowing of copyright proprietor's monopoly, others may perceive their interests to be under threat if another is permitted to decompile its program.[14] A system developer may not wish to make information relating to compatibility available as accessibility to such information may be of substantial benefit to a competitor. It could enable a competitor to build a competing program; this could be compatible with the existing systems available on the market, and as the competing program had been developed relying on the information extracted from the work which had been carried out by the initial system developer, developmental costs could be substantially reduced, which in turn could be reflected in a lower sale price. As decompilation by its very nature facilitates the analysis of a system, it is apparent that some software creators will perceive it as objectionable. Although some creators may not view the situation as critical as this, many will, at the very least, wish to exercise an element of control over the process and thus it is relevant to question how effective the decompilation right is in protecting the rights of the initial creator.

In assessing the scope and effectiveness of decompilation right it is initially noted that the right is defined by reference to the act of decompilation being necessary to achieve the permitted objective. Here it can be questioned whether creating a competing program may qualify as a 'permitted objective'? As defined in the legislation, this is when 'it is necessary to decompile the program to obtain the information necessary to create an independent program which can be operated with the program decompiled or with another program' (section 50B (2)). Stipulating that the information must be 'necessary to create an independent program' clearly does not dismiss the possibility of a competitor relying on this provision, in the event that they have created a competing program following decompilation of the original program. In this instance, the initial creator would attempt to rely upon, and derive protection from, the particular situations prescribed under the legislation that are identified as being excluded from the scope of the decompilation right, notably the fourth exception – that the information should not be used to 'create a program which is substantially similar in its expression to the program decompiled' (section 50B (3)(d)). The creation by a competitor of a program that is substantially similar to the decompiled program will not be deemed to be lawful under the provisions of the 1988 Act.[15]

However, this exception could be more limited in its protection of the creator's interests. Indeed, the possibility cannot be ruled out that this exception could be narrowly interpreted to suggest that the information acquired could be used to create a competing program, with the only limitation being that the program created is not 'substantially similar', to the original program. As the legislation is limited in its definition of the parties' interests, as a consequence it is limited in its protection of those interests. For example, through defining the scope of the permitted objective, the legislation does not address the possibility that a program could be decompiled with the code being used to make a competing program and, providing this newly created program was not 'substantially similar' to the initial program there would be no infringement of the legislation. In this event the legislation may be seen to fail to protect the interests of the initial creator.

Conversely, the legislation may also be seen to fail to protect the legitimate interests of the independent software creator. For example, by defining the scope of the permitted objective with reference to a program which is 'substantially similar' the legislation fails to recognise the possibility of a program being created which may qualify as being 'substantially similar' but which could have been created completely independently of the first program. The legislation would seem to suggest that in this event the permitted objective would not be satisfied and the act of independent software development would fail to constitute lawful use of decompiled information.

This potential lack of certainty in the scope of legislative provisions may impact adversely upon the contracting parties when trying to define the scope of their rights and obligations. Moreover, the uncertainty in copyright legislation is unlikely to be clarified or improved by appropriate contractual provision. In relation to the decompilation defence, freedom of contract is restricted by the legislation which effectively removes the right to further define the scope and application of this defence. If an act is permitted within the scope of the decompilation defence, it is irrelevant whether or not there exists any contractual term that purports to prohibit or restrict the act (section 50B (4)) as any such term will be rendered void (section 296A). Thus, although in other aspects of software supply, the use of express terms in contractual documentation can facilitate the process of defining the scope of the parties' rights and obligations, this is not achievable here. Principles of copyright remain unclear and uncertain and the effectiveness of the law of contract to assist and improve the situation is curtailed through the copyright legislation.

Nonetheless, examining the issues in a practical context, since the introduction of the decompilation defence there have been indications from commentators within the computing industry that this provision is perceived as not necessary and further evidence for this view may be drawn from the fact that no claims have reached the courts, to be defended on the basis of reliance on the decompilation right.[16] However, it is possible that the apparent lack of need to rely on the decompilation defence may have come about as a result of the effectiveness of the provision, namely, in order to ensure compliance with the legislation, manufacturers are readily supplying interface information. Whether the reason for the lack of disputes arising from the decompilation right is attributable to its being a superfluous provision, or because it has proved to be a highly effective provision, it is evident that the right of decompilation is a key consideration when assessing how contract and copyright laws collectively define, protect and balance the interests of the parties.

Observe, study or test

The effectiveness of contract law to further shape and define the parties' obligations is similarly curtailed in respect of the third permitted act – the right to observe, study and test a program. A lawful user of a copy of a computer program is permitted under legislation 'to observe, study or test the functioning of that program in order to determine the ideas and principles which underlie any element of the program', when carried out while 'performing any of the acts of loading, displaying, running, transmitting or storing the program which he is entitled to do' (section 50BA (1)). This right to observe, study and test the program cannot be restricted or excluded by express contractual provision and if the contract attempts to exclude or restrict these rights then any clause purporting to do so will be considered void (section 50BA (2)). However, suppliers may be keen to define the scope of this permission more precisely and would need to exercise caution in so doing, given the potential for this type of clause to fail and be unenforceable. As a practical measure to counteract the unwanted effect of this possibility, the contract should be drafted as distinct, separate clauses, with a specific contractual provision governing severance. This should ensure that in the event any clause is considered unenforceable it may simply be subject to the blue pencil rule and severed from the contract with the remainder of the agreement continuing in force.[17] Indeed this is an approach which is to be recommended for all clauses dealing with any aspect of the permitted acts, to promote effective contract drafting practices and clarity in the contractual terms.

Copying or adapting

An act that is permitted under copyright legislation and yet which can be excluded by contractual provision relates to copying or adapting a computer program. A lawful user of a computer program can copy or adapt a program providing the copying or adapting is necessary for his lawful use (section 50C (1)(a)) and is 'not prohibited under any term or condition of an agreement regulating the circumstances in which his use is lawful' (section 50C (1)(b)). The operation of this permitted act can therefore be seen to favour freedom of contract and as such allow the parties flexibility and choice to determine where the balance of their interests should lie. The scope of this is controlled to the extent that prohibition through contract relates only to this permitted act (section 50C (3)) and thus the freedom to determine the scope of the parties' rights, in respect of copying or adapting does not extend to or impact upon the other permitted acts, for example, the making of back-up copies. The operation of the other permitted acts remain unaffected by this provision and as previously noted, any attempt to restrict or exclude those rights will be null and void under the legislation (section 296A).

Therefore, whereas in respect of other acts, copyright law prescribes how the interest of the parties should be balanced against one another, in relation to copying or adapting as necessary for lawful use, the parties are allowed to determine the scope of their rights. With more freedom being granted in this respect, the question should be raised – under which circumstances will the copying or adapting be necessary for lawful use of the computer program? In response, the legislation offers an example, stipulating that it may 'be necessary for the lawful use of a computer program to copy it or adapt it for the purpose of correcting errors in it' (section 50C (2)). To further consider the circumstances under which error correction may be permitted, it is fundamental to remember that for a user to be able to make any changes to a program, in this instance to correct errors, depends upon whether or not they have access to the program source code. Yet, the legislation does not prescribe that the supplier should supply the source code for error correction purposes and therefore the true extent of this permitted act can be restricted at the supplier's discretion. Source code provision could be the subject of negotiation between the parties for example, when defining support and maintenance provision. Retention of source code will promote a supplier's potential to be the sole maintainer of the software supplied and for this reason can represent a substantial commercial interest which will need to be met financially if it is to be passed on to the user or a third party.[18]

Early consideration in the courts, of the circumstances under which a supplier should be required to make its source code available was given in the case of *Saphena Computing v. Allied Collection Agencies*,[19] which concerned the provision of an online computer system for a debt collection agency. Here, the software that was commissioned by the agency did not function as required and despite committing considerable time and resources to the project, success was not forthcoming and the suppliers wanted to terminate the agreement. The customer agreed to this and then commissioned a third party to work on the project in an attempt to have the system running as required. The question was raised of which party was entitled to have access to the source code required for making improvements to the software: the defendant, the plaintiff or the third party. The defendant argued that it owned the copyright in the software as it had been commissioned and designed specifically for its needs but this argument was rejected by the court on the basis that commissioning a literary work did not confer ownership and also that the software was suitable for use by others. Indeed, the plaintiff had intended to sell the software to others if possible and for this reason clearly had a vested commercial interest in retaining sole access to the source code. The third party had a recognisable need for wanting access to the source code in order that it could carry out the work which it had been contracted for.

The court found in favour of the defendant on the basis that as the software was deemed not entirely fit for its purpose at the time of supply, such that Saphena was in the course of removing bugs from it in order to make it fit for its purpose, it must have been implicit that Saphena would allow the defendant use of the source programs, necessary to put the software into a condition that it was fit for its purpose. Thus the defendant was entitled to copy the source programs as required to complete the software and to make it reasonably fit for the purposes specified. The decision was founded on terms being implied as deemed necessary to give business efficacy to the agreement between the parties and through this implication of terms, the court recognised the need to protect the interests of the defendant user and to bring the relationship to an end. On the basis of the arguments advanced, the court was not willing to agree to confer ownership on the user, but it was however, prepared to rule that access to the source code should be permitted to repair existing bugs. This is surely the most appropriate result as without such access the software would not meet its requirement to be fit for purpose and aside from whether software should be treated as if it is goods or services, certain standards of quality are surely to be reasonably expected.

The introduction of statutory provisions governing error correction (section 50C (2)) has since reduced the potential need for reliance on terms implied at law. Although implied terms may serve as an appropriate mechanism for achieving a just result, it is anticipated that specific legislative provisions may offer greater certainty. However, studying the semantics of the legislation reveals some uncertainty in defining the true scope of this permission. To remind ourselves, section 50C stipulates that it is not an infringement of copyright for a lawful user to copy or adapt a program if the copying or adapting is necessary for lawful use and that it may 'be necessary for the lawful use of a computer program to copy it or adapt it for the purpose of correcting errors in it'. At first glance and from a broad interpretation, this could be seen to offer a user considerable scope to copy a program to discover errors generally. Alternatively, a more restrained interpretation would suggest that 'the right may be seen to extend only in respect of particular errors which have been discovered by the user in the course of running the program in a normal manner' and therefore although this exception to breaching copyright may indeed be referred to as a 'right', the user's right does not extend to a right for all errors to be corrected; rather, the user has the right to correct the errors without being in breach of copyright.[20]

As error correction is defined by reference to be 'necessary for lawful use' it could be implied that it will not constitute lawful use in its own right and thus the lawfulness of error correction should be determined by considering its necessity in relation to the lawful use and the end purpose of the program. Here however there are inconsistencies with the approach of the Software Directive which prescribe that there is no need to assess the necessity of error correction in relation to the program's intended purpose since error correction is to be treated as an intended purpose and a lawful use in its own right.[21] The relevant question to be posed therefore is not whether the error correction is necessary, but rather whether the infringing acts are necessary for error correction. Contractually, rather than adhering to the more restrictive approach of the national legislation derived from a literal interpretation, it could be possible to define the scope of this permission at the same level as that which is offered under the Directive, with reliance on the doctrine of indirect effect.[22] Alternatively, a supplier could attempt to restrict the permissions granted to the user more extensively, although the difficulties in framing a valid and legally acceptable contractual provision in this uncertain legal framework must be duly noted.

Conclusion

As the software industry is unlikely to achieve its desired level of protection of a creator's proprietary interests through copyright law alone, the contribution of the law of contract to offer additional layers of protection is a possibility worthy of consideration. From reviewing the existing legislative provisions it is evident that the extent to which permitted acts can be varied by contractual arrangement and conversely, the manner in which proprietary interests can override contrary stipulations presents software creators and acquirers with a complex state of affairs. Contractual obligations defined either through express terms in the contract or through the implication of terms can contribute to prescribing the extent to which copyright law will operate in a software supply context, and the effectiveness of these terms will be determined by the legal framework derived from both branches of law. It has been noted that in certain circumstances, the true effect of the interaction between the laws of copyright and the laws of contract generates tension between the two branches of law and in consequence, uncertainty in application. Awareness of these difficulties can assist the parties in planning their rights and obligations towards each other and contribute to the identification of measures that can be introduced to reduce tensions and uncertainties, thereby promoting a suitable and successful framework for the future management of the supply of computer programs.

Notes

1. *Navitaire* v. *Easyjet Airline* [2004] EWHC 1725 (Ch); *Nova Productions* v. *Mazooma Games* [2007] EWCA Civ 219.
2. Ben Allgrove and Paul McGrath, 'Pool Cues and Computer Games: The "Look and Feel" Debate Played Out in the Court of Appeal', *Computers and Law*, 18, no. 2 (2007): 5.
3. Conference theme of the 23rd BILETA Annual Conference held at Glasgow Caledonian University in March 2008. This article is an updated and expanded version of a paper presented at that conference, see further www.bileta.ac.uk.
4. For a fuller discussion of the position that the granting of a licence by a licensor is a process by which he surrenders rather than gains rights, see further Iain G. Mitchell, 'Software Licences: Should it be Getting Personal?', *Computers and Law* 15, no. 6 (2005): 21–22. Iain G Mitchell QC is Vice Chairman of the Scottish Society for Computers and Law and in his article offers an engaging discussion about the nature of licence rights and copyright.
5. The permitted acts examined in this paper are those prescribed by the Copyright, Designs and Patents Act 1988: the making of a back up copy at Section 50A; the act of decompilation at Section 50B, observing, studying and testing of computer programs at Section 50BA and in certain circumstances copying or adapting the program as set out in Section 50C. The paper does not examine acts permitted in relation to databases as set out in Section 50D, see

further L. Bently and B. Sherman, *Intellectual Property Law*, 3rd edn (Oxford: Oxford University Press, 2009), 232, 310–318.

6. Copyright, Designs and Patents Act 1988, see note 5.
7. Richard Morgan and Kit Burden, *Morgan and Stedman on Computer Contracts* (London: Sweet and Maxwell, 2001), 75.
8. Bently and Sherman, *Intellectual Property Law*, 230.
9. *Sony Computer Entertainment Inc* v. *Owen* [2002] EMLR 742.
10. Copyright, etc. and Trade Marks (Offences and Enforcement) Act 2002.
11. See further, Arie van Deursen, 'Program-Transformation.Org', 2004. Available from http://www.program-transformation.org/Transform/ReverseEngineering (accessed July 21, 2008).
12. Copyright, Designs and Patents Act 1988, see note 6.
13. The four situations are listed in Section 50B (3) (a)–(d) consecutively. It can be noted in respect of the second situation, at Section 50B (3)(b) that it could be difficult to ensure that only the relevant parts of code are decompiled and that it may be easy for a lawful user to inadvertently decompile more than was intended.
14. For example, see further, Dunn who outlines the arguments in favour of offering a wider choice to consumers – Susan A. Dunn, 'Defining the Scope of Copyright Protection for Computer Software', *Stanford Law Review* 38 (1986): 518; and Barton who discusses the conflict 'between the supporters of open source software, who argue for maximum disclosure of software code, and suppliers of proprietary software who jealously guard access to their source code' – John Barton, 'Open source and WIPO', *Computers and Law* 14, no. 5 (2003): 36–38.
15. Copyright, Designs and Patents Act 1988, see note 6.
16. For industry commentary, read the speech delivered by Christou, Chief Executive of Fujitsu Services – Richard Christou, 'Transcript of SCL's 30th Anniversary Lecture' (2004) with a link available from *Computers & Law* 14 (6): 8. To date, there have been no UK cases on reverse engineering of computer programs although cases relating to reverse engineering of other creations, e.g. drawer design, as in *LB (Plastics) Limited* v. *Swish Products Limited* [1979] RPC 551, and an exhaust system, as in *British Leyland Motor Corporation* v. *Armstrong Patents Co. Limited* [1986] RPC 279, have reached the courts. There have been decompilation cases in other jurisdictions, for example, as heard by the Singapore Court of Appeal in *Aztech Systems Pty Ltd* v. *Creative Technology Ltd* [1997] FSR 491 and the High Court of Australia in *Data Access Corporation* v. *Powerflex Services Pty Ltd* [1999] HCA 49; and in the US where the legitimacy of reverse engineering was considered in *Nintendo* v. *Atari* (1992) 975 F. 2d 832 and *Sony Computer Entertainment* v. *Connectix Corporation* 203 F. 3d 596 (2000). For a discussion on the international perspective of permitting decompilation and the approaches adopted in different jurisdictions, see further Diane Rowland and Andrew Campbell, 'Supply of Software: Copyright and Contract Issues', *International Journal of Law and Information Technology* 10, no. 1 (2002): 33–38.
17. See further, Susan E. Singleton, 'Computer Software Agreements and the Implementation of the EC Directive', *Computer Law and Practice* 9 (1993): 50 and for a sample severance clause, see Rachel Burnett and Paul Klinger, *Drafting and Negotiating Computer Contracts*, 2nd ed. (Haywards Heath, UK: Tottel Publishing, 2005), 101.
18. See further, Sherree Westell, 'Escrow Agreements: Traditional Protection for New Scenarios', *Computers and Law* 15, no. 1 (2004): 25–27; N. Swycher and M. Reberio, 'Information Technology: A Highway Code', *Practical Law Companies* 6, no. 5 (1995), 27 and also for a discussion of some of the tensions in this area see J. Yates, 'Third Party Computer Maintenance – A Legal Perspective', *Computer Law and Practice* 10, no. 1 (1994): 9–13.
19. *Saphena Computing* v. *Allied Collection Agencies* [1995] FSR 616.
20. Ian J. Lloyd, *Information Technology Law* (Oxford, Oxford University Press, 2004), 462 and see further, Diane Rowland and Elizabeth Macdonald, *Information Technology Law*, 3rd ed. (London: Cavendish, 2005), 112.
21. EC Directive on the Legal Protection of Computer Programs, 91/250/EC, which at Article 5.1 provides: 'In the absence of specific contractual provisions, the [restricted acts] . . . shall not require authorisation by the rightholder where they are necessary . . . in accordance with [the program's] intended purpose, including for error correction'.
22. Case 14/83, *Von Colson and Kamann* v. *Land Nordrhien-Westafalen* [1984] ECR 1981. As an additional comment, it can be suggested that the Software Directive itself may be more

restrictive than was intended. There is an apparent inconsistency between Article 5(1), which allows copying for error correction purposes but also allows for contractual prohibition of this, and Recital 18 which states that parties cannot prohibit copying for error correction by contract. See, further, Morgan and Burden, *Morgan and Stedman on Computer Contracts*, 78–79 and M. Sherwood-Edwards, 'Seven Degrees of Separation: The Software Directive and UK Implementation', *Computer Law and Practice* 9 (1993): 169.

Making intermediary Internet service providers participate in the regulatory process through tort law: A comparative analysis

Sophie Stalla-Bourdillon

Law Department, European University Institute, Florence, Italy

A decade after the adoption of the Communications Decency Act and the Digital Millennium Copyright Act on one side of the Atlantic and the European Directive 2000/31/EC on electronic commerce on the other side, one could have expected the role of intermediary Internet service providers (IISPs) to become clearer as regards their contribution to Internet regulation and, in particular, speech regulation. Truly, at the end of the 1990s 'self-regulation against tort law immunities' seemed to be the appropriate path to follow in order to subsidize the Information Technology and Technology industry, especially in systems where free speech is often a superseding value. Yet, such a trade-off has progressively appeared inappropriate from the perspective of victims, namely because of the growth of IISPs' regulatory capacities. This has become even more apparent with the emergence of web 2.0 applications. However, judges have not always drawn their inspiration from the originality of the regulatory models underlying the interventions of their respective legislators. This is true both within the USA and in France. This paper thus seeks to highlight the ways that the formalism of tort law has been 'instrumentalized' by the judiciary to further a particular paradigm of speech regulation in cyberspace, despite the legislative recognition of alternative paradigms.

A decade after the adoption of the Communications Decency Act (CDA) and the Digital Millennium Copyright Act (DMCA) on one side of the Atlantic and the European Directive 2000/31/EC on electronic commerce on the other side, one could have expected the role of intermediary Internet service providers (IISPs) to become clearer as regards their contribution to Internet regulation and, in particular, speech regulation in the sense of content regulation as opposed to infrastructure regulation.[1]

Truly, at the end of the 1990s 'self-regulation against tort law immunities' seemed to be the appropriate path to follow in order to subsidize the Information Technology and Technology industry, especially in systems where free speech is often a superseding value. Yet, such a trade-off has progressively appeared inappropriate from the perspective of victims, particularly because of the growth of IISPs' regulatory capacities. This has become even more apparent with the emergence of web 2.0 applications. However, judges have not always drawn their inspiration from the originality of the regulatory models underlying the interventions of their respective legislators. This is true both within the USA and in France. This paper thus seeks to highlight the ways the formalism of tort law has been 'instrumentalized' by the judiciary to further a particular paradigm of speech regulation in cyberspace, despite the legislative recognition of alternative paradigms.

In the USA, the CDA has almost gained the status of a general rule (*droit commun*), although few courts have tried to qualify the scope of the immunities granted to IISPs in the wake of the adoption of the DMCA. Even if IISPs' immunities have been questioned, it does not seem that, within the USA, the model of self-regulation has been rejected. While tort law has been used in certain cases to help 'proceduralize' self-regulation, which has thus become mandatory, voluntary self-regulation seems to be the prevailing paradigm for speech regulation.

In France, where the transposition of Articles 12 ff of the Directive on electronic commerce was finally completed in 2004, each term of the *quid pro quo* 'self-regulation against tort law immunities' has been questioned. It is true that the Constitutional Council interpreting the Act of 2004 has limited the scope of IISPs' liability so that in theory they are liable only when they disregard manifest unlawful contents. Nevertheless, it is not sure whether the rationale for the new liability regime is really to promote self-regulation given the role granted to the judge of preliminary measures (*juge des référés*) through the mechanism of injunction.

More recently, despite Article 15 of the Directive on electronic commerce, some courts have gone back to general rules such as Article 1382 of the Civil Code to impose a duty of care on IISPs and oblige them to build their systems in a way that should reduce the possibility for their users to damage third parties. Besides, because providers of hyperlinks and location tool services have not been dealt with by the European legislator, general principles of tort law still govern their activities under French law. As a result, it has been quite easy for judges to invoke a duty of care, at least in the field of trademarks.

While in France the effects of injunctive relief prevent commentators from speaking about real immunities granted to IISPs, the prevalence of the model of self-regulation depends upon the exact scope of the duties burdening IISPs: either they are simply required to improve detection mechanisms and follow up on judicial orders and the system would tend towards co-regulation, or, they are required to replace judges and the system would then tend towards mandatory self-regulation. In particular, obliging IISPs to implement filtering mechanisms is likely to give IISPs incentives to privatize the entire process of speech regulation.

1. *Specialia generalibus derogant* or tort law v. self-regulation

After the adoption of the DMCA it became clear that the CDA was to be considered as the general rule to be applied each time the liability of IISPs for third-party unlawful activity was addressed, unless intellectual property rights were at stake. The domain, as well as the effects of the CDA rule as interpreted by judges, logically bear witness to this status. However they result in the failure of tort law as a paradigm for speech regulation, whereas the DMCA shows that tort law can usefully complement self-regulation in order to avoid a situation of under regulation.

(a) The domain of the CDA rule

The CDA rule

Section 230(c)(1) of the CDA provides that 'no provider or user of an interactive computer service shall be treated as the publisher or speaker of any information provided by another information provider'. Such an exemption has been adopted in reaction to the *Stratton*

Oakmont, Inc. v. *Prodigy Servs. Co.* case,[2] in which the Court held that the bulletin board provider had to be considered as the publisher of the materials posted on its computer and thus dramatically increased the probability of IISPs being held liable for third-party unlawful contents.

The service providers entitled to benefit from the CDA rule

As to the domain of such a rule and first, the service providers entitled to benefit from section 230, the category of 'interactive computer service providers' has been broadly interpreted, and eventually completed by that of 'users of interactive computer services'. Consequently, not only are providers of transitory network communications able to benefit from the exemption of section 230(c)(1), but also hosting providers, webmasters and maybe more generally all users of individual computers.[3] That defendants exercise some editorial control does not prevent them from benefiting from section 230(c)(1).[4]

The type of speech involved

Second, as to the type of the speech involved, it is true that section 230 (c) (2) (A) provides that:

> no provider or user of an interactive computer service shall be held liable on account of – (A) any action voluntary taken in good faith to restrict access to or availability of material that the provider or user considers to be obscene, lewd, lascivious, filthy, excessively violent, harassing, *or otherwise objectionable*, whether or not such material is constitutionally protected.

Nevertheless the last part of the enumeration leaves the door largely open so that all legally objectionable contents, whatever the reason is, are potentially concerned.

This is one of the reasons why judges have made section 230(c)(1) pre-empt almost all federal as well as state causes of action amounting in one way or another to IISPs' third party liability. More precisely, inspired by the *Zeran* decision judges have not been afraid of applying section 230(c)(1) in a large variety of hypotheses involving both federal and state causes of action such as defamation, negligence, unfair competition and misleading advertising.[5]

Exceptions to the CDA rule

This said, an important field is excluded from the scope of section 230(c)(1): that of intellectual property law. Indeed, under section 230(e)(2): 'Nothing in this section shall be construed to limit or expand any law pertaining to intellectual property'. Truly, courts do not always agree on the question whether only federal intellectual property law is excluded from the scope of section 230(c)(1) of the CDA.[6] In any case, the scope of the exception is narrow and only intellectual property right holders have their interests protected through the design of a special liability regime. Yet, consumer interests as well as right holder interests are jeopardized by unlawful speech. This is why several commentators have heavily criticized section 230, before and after the multiplication of communitarian platforms.[7]

The DMCA

Contrary to the CDA, the DMCA does impose several duties upon IISPs, even if it was first adopted to clarify the law on that matter and prevent judges from extending the scope of strict liability to the detriment of IISPs. First, all IISPs have to comply with the conditions of eligibility set forth in section 512(i), which require service providers in appropriate circumstances to reasonably react against repeat copyright infringers.[8] There may be an argument though to state that such conditions do not apply to search engines because they do not have subscribers or account holders. Above all, hosting providers should react promptly and eliminate infringing materials when they are aware of the presence of 'red flags' on their systems, and they should also automatically follow up on the notification sent by the copyright holder without trying to assess the lawfulness of the contents at stake. In other words, they should comply with the notice-and-take-down procedure as described by section 512(c)(3) to make sure that content providers are informed of the elimination of the materials and are given an opportunity to send back a counter-notification to get the replacement of the removed material, unless copyright holders file an action seeking a court order. On the whole, the DMCA thus implies a model of mandatory self-regulation because alleged digital copyright infringements are dealt with through the legally forced cooperation of right holders and IISPs.

It is true that the DMCA draws a distinction between financial liability and equitable relief so that if IISPs comply with section 512 they cannot be held liable for damages. However, this does not mean that injunctions can easily be granted against IISPs. The DMCA actually makes the test for equitable relief stricter than it used to be before its adoption: plaintiffs must first establish that IISPs are secondary liable and then try to meet the requirements of section 512(j).[9]

The Lanham Act

As to the Lanham Act it does force IISPs to respond to injunctions even when they are innocent infringers. Yet, this is particularly useful in the field of trademarks because IISPs and in particular search engines are maybe more likely to be held primarily liable than secondarily liable.[10]

(b) The effects of the CDA rule

Preemption effect

The CDA exemplifies the paradigm of voluntary self-regulation against tort law immunities. Yet, it is more the result of judges' interpretation than the result of the legislator's work. Indeed, the exact boundaries of the CDA's exemption have not been carefully drawn by the legislator. In particular the latter has not expressly stated whether interactive computer service providers could be considered as distributors and thereby could be subject to notice liability.

However, judges interpreting section 230(c)(1) have not hesitated to toughen the effects of this exemption stating that they were bound by the intent of Congress. They ruled that interactive computer service providers were immune from distributor liability as well as from publisher liability. In *Zeran* (333) the Court held that 'by its plain language, §230 creates a federal immunity to any cause of action that would make service providers liable for information originating with a third-party user of the service'. Consequently, even IISPs remained passive after being informed that they would have immunity in the event of the presence of unlawful contents on their systems: notice liability is thus to be rejected. In the wake of *Zeran*, several courts have followed this path, before and after the adoption of the DMCA.[11] It is to be noted that interactive computer service providers have been exempted from liability at law and in equity. Therefore, the immunity remains if the plaintiff asks for an injunction rather than damages.[12]

The shadow of tort law

In practice, it is rare that IISPs have voluntarily committed to self-regulate their networks. Tort law immunities have thus failed to give IIPs the correct incentives. The shadow of the law has been neglected whereas the recent adoption of the User-Generated Content Principles are evidence of its relevance.[13] Strictly speaking these principles are not binding. They are said to reflect the best practices that user generated content websites should carry out, beyond what the DMCA requires. Not only should these websites contribute to the education of their users, but also they should implement effective content identification technology and cooperate with copyright holders to remove access to websites that are clearly and predominantly used for the dissemination of infringing content, as well as to enhance copyright owners' searching capacities. More correctly, these principles represent the counterpart to be performed by some IISPs in exchange of the copyright holders' declaration of intent not to assert claims of copyright infringement against websites complying with these principles. Indeed, it is not to be forgotten that section 512(m) of the DMCA provides that

> Protection of Privacy – Nothing in this section shall be construed to condition the applicability of subsections (a) through (d) on – (1) a service provider monitoring its service or affirmatively seeking facts indicating infringing activity *except to the extent consistent with a standard technical measure complying with the provisions of subsection (i)*;

Under section 512(i) by 'Standard technical measures' the legislator means technical measures that

> are used by copyright owners to identify or protect 'copyrighted works', that 'have been developed pursuant to a broad consensus of copyright owners and service providers in an open, fair, voluntary, multi-industry standards process', that 'are available to any person on reasonable and nondiscriminatory terms', and above all 'do not impose substantial costs on service providers or substantial burdens on their systems or networks'.

Contract law

Contract law has been of little help because either IISPs are not in a contractual relationship with Internet users, or above all they tend to include in user agreements clauses stipulating that IISPs have the right to take action against their users in their sole discretion. Consequently, IISPs are generally not contractually bound to take any action against those who violate their user agreements.[14]

Minority trend

It is true, that some courts have tried to go against this trend. However, all in all, such attempts have been particularly shy. Under the *Batzel* holding, users of interactive computer services and interactive computer service providers knowing that the material was not intended to be published shall be held liable. This exception to section 230(c)(2) seems nonetheless to be narrow enough not to contradict the *Zeran* holding. More interestingly, in the *Grace* case, the Court refused to immunize users of interactive computer services and interactive computer service providers from distributor liability.[15] Nonetheless, the defendant ended up exempted from liability because it had included in its contract concluded with the plaintiff a release of liability.

Two recent decisions seem to be more interesting. In *Fair Housing Council of San Fernando Valley* v. *Roommate.com*, LLC, 489 F.3d 921 (9th Cir. 2007) on rehearing 521 F.3d 1157 (9th Cir. 2008), the Court held that the operator of an online roommate-matching website was not only a provider of an interactive computer service, but that it was also a content provider since it was responsible, in whole or in part, for the creation or development of questionnaires which were intended to classify the preferences of its users. Moreover, by categorizing, channelling and limiting the distribution of users' profiles, Roommate was at least in part responsible for creating or developing the information contained in its members' profiles. As a result, it could not benefit from the CDA. Although the Court's holding ultimately seems to be grounded on the distinction between passive and active interactive computer services, which is problematic to the extent it gives IISPs incentives to remain as passive as possible, it forces active IISPs not to build their system in such a way as to encourage or solicit unlawful activities from their users. In the words of the Court, the message sent to website operators was the following: 'if you don't encourage illegal content, or design your website to require users to input illegal content, you will be immune' (1175).

The reasoning used in the second decision may be more satisfying. Although the IISP in this case was not held liable, the Court drew a distinction between causes of action treating providers of interactive computer services as publishers and other causes of action. According to the Court of Appeal in *Craigslist*, 697:

> it seems rather unlikely that, in enacting the CDA and in trying to protect Good Samaritans from filtering offensive conduct, Congress would have intended a broad grant of immunity for ICSs that do not screen any third-party content whatsoever. And because it is something less than an absolute grant of immunity, state legislatures may be able to enact, consistent with Section 230, initiatives that induce or require online service providers to protect the interests of third parties.

Further:

> To appreciate the limited role of §230(c)(1), remember that 'information content providers' may be liable for contributory infringement if their system is designed to help people steal music or other material in copyright. ... Grokster is incompatible with treating §230(c)(1) as a grant of comprehensive immunity from civil liability for content provided by a third party.

As a result, a limited duty not to induce third-party unlawful activities it is imposed upon IISPs. But state legislators are invited to intensify IISP's duties and make them participate more actively in the monitoring process.

Tort law has often been opposed to public regulation as a regulatory strategy of its own. Here, the confrontation of tort law and self-regulation in the realm of cyberspace seems to show that they are alternative regulatory strategies so that the furtherance of the latter amounts to the exclusion of the former. In othe words, self-regulation should be mainly voluntary whereas the US legislator had been particularly innovative when it enacted the DMCA, a model of mandatory self-regulation. In France, the formalism of tort law has recently been used by judges to strengthen the regulatory obligations of IISPs and sometimes undermine the original model of co-regulation set forth by the legislator with the help of the Constitutional Council.

2. *Exceptio est strectissimae interpretationis* or tort law and self-regulation

While it is true that the French transposition of the Directive on electronic commerce sets forth a special liability regime, which departs from the general rules of civil liability, judges have recently interpreted it restrictively. As a result, Articles 1382 ff are still relevant in order to grasp the behaviour of IISPs. Tort law is thus used to force the latter to self-regulate, whereas the legislator, more or less willingly, has tried to lay down the components of a strategy of co-regulation.

(a) The special liability regime of Statute no. 2004-575

Article 6 of Statute no. 2004-575

After some hesitation the French legislator finally completed the transposition of the Directive on electronic commerce with the adoption of the Statute no. 2004-575 of 21 June 2004 (*'loi no. 2004-575 du 21 juin 2004 pour la confiance dans l'économie numérique'*). At first glance the national transposition is faithful to the text of the Directive. Nevertheless, it is necessary to precise two elements concerning the liability of hosting providers.

First of all, the French legislator has tried to clarify the knowledge requirement by laying down the following presumption: the contentious facts are presumed to be known by the hosting provider once it has been notified of several elements and in particular the description of the contentious facts, their precise localization, as well as the reasons why the content should be eliminated. However, such a notification is not mandatory and hosting providers can become aware of the contentious facts by other means. One may conclude that the underlying regulatory model is that of mandatory self-regulation. An obligation to self-regulate would thus be imposed upon IISPs and non-performance would be sanctioned through the mechanism of civil liability.

The Constitutional Council's interpretation

This said, one has to interpret Article 6 of the Statute no. 2004-575 in the light of the decision of the Constitutional Council no. 2004-496 DC – 10 June 2004, which stated that inactive hosting providers could be held liable only if the content was manifestly unlawful, or if they had been enjoined by the judge to react. As a result, self-regulation is mandatory solely in the case of manifest unlawful contents. Of course, the scope of the obligation of hosting providers depends upon the way judges interpret the adverb 'manifest'. The Constitutional Council's interpretation of this term seems to be quite narrow.[16] If one looks at Case law, such a requirement has been initially interpreted in favour of hosting providers.[17] However, this is not always the case anymore, as several decisions from the Paris Court of Appeal show it in the field of privacy, although such a trend has been heavily criticized.[18]

Role of injunctions

Reducing the domain of the obligation imposed on hosting providers, which in theory have to react only when the content is manifestly unlawful, may be justified by the function granted to the mechanism of injunction intended to complement the process of self-regulation. It is true that on its face the national transposition seems to go less far than the text of the Directive on electronic commerce. Indeed, while the judge of preliminary measures may enjoin Internet access providers or hosting providers to stop or prevent unlawful activities on their systems, the former shall be enjoined only subsidiarily (see Article 6(I)(8)). This said, judges, interpreting this requirement, have not been particularly demanding, so that hosting providers as well as Internet access providers have been several times enjoined to make access to the unlawful content impossible, sometimes under penalty payment.[19] In part because the plaintiff asking for an injunction does not have to prove the negligence of the IISP, nor its knowledge of the unlawful act, and in part because stop orders are considered to be a more satisfying remedy than damages in many cases, the judge of preliminary measures has been a key intermediary between IISPs and victims. Furthermore, his decisions are most of the time aimed to be definitive.[20] As a result, the injunction is not necessary temporary as the Paris Court of Appeal explains.[21]

Despite the defects of judicial proceedings, one could thus see in the refinement of the mechanism of injunction, a traditional remedy of civil liability, an attempt to set up a system of co-regulation necessary to safeguard freedom of expression on the Internet and avoid censorship on the part of IISPs and, generally speaking, to make sure that third-party interests are taken into consideration. This is all the more true that it seems that it can be used for manifest and non-manifest unlawful content.[22]

This said, using the mechanism of injunction against IISPs is another way to make them contribute to the regulatory process at the stage of monitoring, or even more to undertake the whole regulatory process. Truly, everything depends upon the way injunctions are calibrated and it is doubtful whether judges will always try to carefully identify the future infringing activities at issue to reduce IISPs' leeway as in two recent first-instance cases.[23]

The recent agreement between public authorities and some IISPs in the framework of the Olivennes mission may at first glance seem to further the model of co-regulation through the intervention of an independent administrative authority supposed to frame private enforcement.[24] However, nothing is provided for in the case of preventive filtering, which as such amounts to self-regulation and, besides, this agreement aims only at protecting intellectual property right holders.

(b) The general rule of Articles 1382 ff

Article 6 as a narrow exception to Articles 1382 ff

Among the recent judicial decisions rendered in the field of civil liability,[25] several tend to qualify the scope of the liability regime of 2004.[26] At least three types of reasoning have been used to extend the obligations imposed on hosting providers. Two of them are of particular interest.

IISPs as editors of contents

First, judges have tried to include some hosting providers into the category of editors of contents. This is what happened in several cases.[27] In the *Tiscali* case,[28] according to the Paris Court of Appeal, a hosting provider who commercially exploited its website by offering advertising space to be paid for on its users' personal web pages, also acted as an editor and was thus liable for copyright infringement committed by its users. To be sure, such reasoning is not without problems. Indeed, within the French statute or within the Directive on electronic commerce there is no distinction drawn between information society services that are commercially exploited and free information society services. Moreover, although there is no statutory definition of an editor in this field, it is difficult to affirm that a hosting provider, which offers advertising space on personal web pages, does make a choice as to the content of the personal web pages themselves. Furthermore, adopting such a restrictive definition of 'hosting provider' would oblige all hosting providers, which commercially exploit their sites, to monitor the information stored on their systems and actively search for unlawful activities not to be liable each time an unlawful content is posted on their systems. Yet, this seems to be *contra legem*.

IISPs bound by an obligation of loyalty in the course of their commercial activity

As to the second route, it has been used by the Paris Court of Appeal in the *Meridien* case. It consisted of 'discovering' on the ground of Article 1382 an obligation of loyalty to be performed by all IISPs in the course of their commercial activities in order to make sure that their activities did not lead to unlawful acts damaging other economic operators. The Court derived such a principle from that of loyalty and that of free competition associated with the exercise of all commercial activities. In the *eBay* case, the Court of Appeal acknowledged that eBay, as a hosting provider, had to ensure, as far as possible, that its site was not unlawfully used. The Court referred to such an extra-contractual obligation to justify the termination by the hosting provider of a user account. The same is true in two recent first instance decisions but this time eBay was finally held liable for not performing its obligation of loyalty.[29] While the language of the tribunals is sometimes close to that of liability for risks, a form of strict liability, they tried to establish the wrongs committed by eBay, which could not be considered as a mere intermediary in the meaning of the Statute no. 2004-575 because its activity was that of a broker. It seems that the judges would have been satisfied if eBay had made its best efforts to prevent its users from damaging trademark holders' interests at stake. However, according to the Paris Tribunal of Commerce, terminating accounts of alleged infringers on the request of the victims should have been spontaneously undertaken by eBay.

The contours of the obligation of loyalty are relatively blurred, and it might thereby undermine the equilibrium set by the Statute no. 2004-575 if it does more than ask hosting providers to build their system and thereby organize the communities of their users in a way that reduces unlawful activities, i.e. if it asks hosting providers to actively and systematically search for unlawful materials and/or replace judges in the event of non-manifest unlawful contents.

As regards search engines whose activity is covered neither by the Directive on electronic commerce nor by Statute 2004-575 although the Court of Cassation has recently questioned the European Court of Justice about their exact status,[30] it has been easier for courts to impose an obligation of loyalty on IISPs. Truly, there is no consensus concerning the ground of this obligation.[31] It is sometimes more implicit than explicit and its effects may thus be overreaching. Nonetheless, they bear witnesses in several cases to the vitality of general rules of tort law such as Articles 1382 ff as a component of the regulatory strategy that aims at making IISPs participate into the monitoring of the information transmitted through the Internet, if not more.

Conclusion

Private law rules are malleable and they can serve contrary regulatory objectives. *Specialia generalibus derogant* and the CDA becomes the general rule while the DMCA is only an exception so that generally speaking IISPs are not burdened with any duty of care. *Exceptio est strictissimae interpretationis* and Statute no. 2004-575 is narrowly construed so that articles 1382 ff are applicable to IISPs, which should take into account third-party interests in the course of their commercial activity.

Therefore, the only way to tackle the problem of IISPs' liability is to proceed through two successive stages. The first question to answer is whether self-regulation or co-regulation should be advanced given the interests to be protected. The second question is then how to make the elected regulatory model effective and one must consider each regulatory activity separately: that of standard setting, that of monitoring and that of enforcement. At this stage it is important to bear in mind that private regulation, public regulation and tort law are complementary strategies and not to stop at the formalism of tort law rules. It remains to be determined who is better fitted to address the question of the appropriate regulatory model for speech regulation: the judicial or the legislative branch.

Notes

1. L. Rapp, 'L'avenir de la régulation – réflexions libres autour d'un concept-clé', *Revue Lamy Droit de l'Immatériel*, 17 (2006): 51–55.
2. *Stratton Oakmont, Inc.* v. *Prodigy Servs. Co.*, 1995 WL 323710 (N.Y.Sup.Ct. 1995).
3. *Perfect 10, Inc.* v. *CCBill*, LLC, 340 F.Supp.2d 1077, (C.D.Cal. 2004) (provider of transitory network communications); *Schneider* v. *Amazon.com, Inc.*, 108 Wash. App. 454 (Washington Court of Appeal 2001); Blumenthal v. Drudge, 992 F. Supp. 44 (US District Court, District of Columbia 1998); Stoner v. eBay, Inc., 2000 WL 1705637 (Cal. Super. 2000); *Gentry* v. *eBay, Inc.*, 99 Cal. App. 4th 816 (Court of Appeal 4th District, Division 1, California 2002) (hosting providers); *Batzel* v. *Smith*, 333 F. 3d 1018, 1021–1022 (Court of Appeal, 9th Cir. 2003); *Barrett* v. *Rosenthal*, 40 Cal. 4th 33, 59 (Supreme Court of California 2006) (webmasters); *Grace* v. *eBay Inc.*, 16 Cal.Rptr.3d 192, (Court of Appeal, Second District, California 2004) (obiter dictum) (users of individual computers).
4. *Zeran* v. *America Online, Inc.*, 129 F.3d 327 (4th Cir.1997) (*Zeran*); *Blumenthal* v. *Drudge*, 992 F. Supp. 44 (US District Court, District of Columbia 1998).
5. See e.g. *Barrett* v. *Rosenthal*, 40 Cal. 4th 33 (Supreme Court of California 2006) (defamation); *Carafano* v. *Metrosplash.com, Inc.*, 339 F. 3d 1119 (Court of Appeal, 9th Cir. 2003) (invasion of privacy, misappropriation of right of publicity, and negligence); *Gentry* v. *eBay, Inc.*, 99 Cal. App. 4th 816 (Court of Appeal 4th District, Division 1, California 2002) (unfair competition); *Perfect 10, Inc.* v. *CCBill*, LLC, 488 F.3d 1102 (9th Cir. (Cal.) 2007) *certiorari* denied by 128 S.Ct. 709 (U.S. 2007) (unfair competition and misleading advertising); *Novak* v. *Overture Services, Inc.*, 309 F.Supp.2d 446 (E.D.N.Y. 2004) (tortious interference with prospective economic advantage); *Doe* v. *Bates*, 2006 WL 3813758 (E.D. Tex., 2006) (violations of federal child pornography laws); *Doe* v. *SexSearch.com*, 502 F.Supp. 2d 719 (N.D. Ohio, 2007) (common law of contract, fraud, negligent infliction of emotional distress, negligent misrepresentation, breach of warranty, violation of consumer law and failure to warn); *Doe* v. *MySpace, Inc.*, 474 F.Supp.2d 843 (W.D.Tex. Feb 13, 2007) affirmed by 2008 WL 20680664 (5th cir. 2008) (negligence, gross negligence, fraud, and negligent misrepresentation); *Chicago Lawyers' Comm. for Civ. Rights Under the Law, Inc.* v. *Craigslist, Inc.*, 461 F. Supp. 2d 681 (N.D. Ill. 2006) affirmed by 519 F.3d 666 (C.A.7, 2008) (*Craiglist*) (violation of the federal Fair Housing Act). This is true even after the emergence of web 2.0 applications. See *Doe* v. *Bates*, 2006 WL 3813758 (E.D.Tex. 2006); *Doe* v. *SexSearch.com*, 502 F. Supp. 2d 719 (N.D. Ohio 2007); *Doe* v. *MySpace, Inc.*, 474 F.Supp.2d 843 (W.D.Tex. 2007); *Universal Communications Systems* v. *Lycos, Inc.*, 2007 U.S. App. LEXIS 3946 (1st Cir. 2007).
6. See in particular *Perfect 10, Inc* v. *CCBill*, LLC 488 F.3d 1102 (9th Cir.(Cal.) 2007): 'In the absence of a definition from Congress, we construe the term "intellectual property" to mean "federal intellectual property"'. Compare with *Universal Communication System, Inc.* v. *Lycos, Inc.*, 478 F.3d 413, 422–423 (1st Cir. 2007): '[Plaintiff]'s remaining claim against [Defendant] was brought under Florida trademark law, alleging dilution of the "UCSY" trade name under Fla. Stat. §495.151. Claims based on intellectual property laws are not subject to Section 230 immunity'.

7. C. Butler, 'Plotting the Return of an Ancient Tort to Cyberspace: Towards a New Federal Standard of Responsibility for Defamation for Internet Service Providers', *Michigan Telecommunications & Technology Law Review*, 6 (2000): 247–272; R.W. King, 'Online Defamation: Bringing the Communications Decency Act of 1996 in Line with Sound Public Policy', *Duke Law & Technology Review* (2003): 24–34; B.C. McManus, 'Rethinking Defamation Liability for Internet Service Providers', *Suffolk University Law Review* (2001): 647–669; C.J. Ottenweller, 'Cyberbullying: The Interactive Playground Cries for a Clarifying of the Communications Decency Act', *Valparaiso University Law Review* 41 (2007): 1285–1334; S.K. Patel, 'Immunizing Internet Service Providers from Third-party Internet Defamation Claims: How Far Should Courts Go?', *Vanderbilt Law Review* 55 (2002): 647–691; E. Posner and D. Lichtman, 'Holding Internet Service Providers Accountable', *Supreme Court Economic Review* 14 (2006): 221–259; D.R. Sheridan, 'Zeran v. AOL and the Effect of Section 230 of the Communications Decency Act upon Liability for Defamation on the Internet', *Albany Law Review* 61 (1997): 147–179; K. Siver, 'Good Samaritans in Cyberspace', *Rutgers Computer and Technology Law Journal* 23 (1997): 1–45.
8. *CoStar Group Inc.* v. *LoopNet, Inc.*, 164 F.Supp.2d 688, 702, 703 (D.Md. 2001), aff'd on other grounds, 373 F.3d 544 (4th Cir. 2004); *Corbis Corp.* v. *Amazon.com, Inc.*, v 351 F.Supp. 2d 1090, 1108 (W.D. Wash. 2004); *Perfect 10, Inc.* v. *CCBill*, LLC, 488 F.3d, 1102, 1114 (9th Cir 2007). See also H.R. REP. 105-551(I), 25 and T.E. Reese, 'Wading through the Muddy Waters: The Courts' Misapplication of Section 512(c) of the Digital Millennium Copyright Act', *Southwestern University Law Review* 34 (2004): 287–323.
9. See *Perfect 10* v. *Google, Inc.*, 416 F.Supp.2d 828 (C.D.Cal.2006) reversed in part by *Perfect 10, Inc.* v. *Amazon.com, Inc.*, 487 F.3d 701 (9th Cir. 2007) and H.R. REP. 105-551(I), 25.
10. See for example *Playboy Enterprises, Inc.* v. *Netscape Communs. Corp.*, 354 F.3d 1020 (9th Cir. 2004); *Government Employees Ins. Co.* v. *Google, Inc.*, 77 U.S.P.Q.2d 1841 (E.D. Va. 2005); *800-JR Cigar, Inc.*, v. *GoTo.com, Inc.*, 437 F.Supp.2d 273, 284 (D.N.J 2006); *Google Inc.* v. *American Blind & Wallpaper*, 2007 WL 1159950 (N.D.Cal. 2007). Compare with *Rescuecom Corp.* v. *Google, Inc.* 456 F.Supp.2d 393 (N.D.N.Y. 2006). Besides, secondary liability doctrines are particularly restrictive in the field of trademark. See M. Bartholomew and J. Tehranian, 'The Secret of Life of Legal Doctrine: The Divergent Evolution of Secondary Liability in Trademark and Copyright Law', *Berkeley Technology Law Journal* 21 (2006): 1363–1419.
11. See e.g. *Kathleen R.* v. *City of Livermore*, 87 Cal. App. 4th 684 (Court of Appeal, California, 2001); *Gentry* v. *eBay, Inc.*, 99 Cal. App. 4th 816 (Court of Appeal 4th District, Division 1, California 2002); *Doe* v. *America Online, Inc.*, 783 So. 2d 1010 (Fla. 2001); *Barrett* v. *Rosenthal*, 40 Cal. 4th 33 (Supreme Court of California 2006); *Beyond Systems, Inc.* v. *Keynetics, Inc.*, 422 F.Supp.2d 523, 536+ (D.Md. Feb 14, 2006); *Global Royalties, Ltd.* v. *Xcentric Ventures*, LLC, 2007 WL 2949002 (D. Ariz. October 10, 2007).
12. *Noah* v. *AOL Time Warner, Inc.*, 261 F.Supp.2d 532 (E.D.Va., 2003): 'Given that the purpose of §230 is to shield service providers from legal responsibility for the statements of third parties, §230 should not be read to permit claims that request only injunctive relief. After all, in some circumstances injunctive relief will be at least as burdensome to the service provider as damages, and is typically more intrusive.' See also Ben Ezra, 206 F.3d 980, 983–986 (Court of Appeal, 10th circuit 2000); *Smith* v. *Intercosmos Media Group, Inc.*, 2002 WL 31844907 (E.D.La. 2002). Compare with *Mainstream Loudoun* v. *Board of Trustees of the Loudoun County Library*, 2 F.Supp.2d 783, 790 (E.D.Va.1998).
13. *Harvard Law Review*, 'The Principles for User Generated Content Services: A Middle-ground Approach to Cyber-Governance', *Harvard Law Review* 121 (2008): 1387–1408.
14. S. Freiwald, 'Comparative Institutional Analysis in Cyberspace: The Case of Intermediary Liability for Defamation', *Harvard Journal of Law and Technology* 14 (2001): 569–655. See for example *Noah* v. *AOL Time Warner, Inc.*, E.D.Va.2003, 261 F.Supp.2d 532, affirmed 2004 WL 602711.
15. See also *Barrett* v. *Rosenthal*, 9 Cal.Rptr.3d 142 (Cal.App. 1 Dist. 2004), as modified (3 February 2004).
16. L. Thoumyre, 'Les hébergeurs en ombres chinoises – Une tentative d'éclaircissement sur les incertitudes de la LCEN', *Revue Lamy Droit de l'Immatériel* 5, no. 58 (2005): 58–65.
17. See for example, CA Paris, 11e ch., 8 November 2006, Comité de défense de la cause arménienne c/ S. Aydin et a., confirming TGI Paris 15 November 2004, www.juriscom.net

(negationism); TGI Paris, réf., 19 October 2006, www.juriscom.net (violation of privacy right); TGI Paris, réf., 29 October 2007, M.B., P.T., F. D., c/ Widimedia Foundation Inc., www.legalis.net (violation of privacy right, defamation).

18. CA Paris, 14e ch., A, 6 December 2006, M. Adbelhadi et Société Dounia c/ Société iEurope et Société Lyocs, no. 06/09805, http://global.lexisnexis.com/fr (violation of right to privacy); CA Paris, 14e ch. A, 12 December 2007, Google Inc. et Google France c/ Benetton Group et Bencom no. 07/10036, www.juriscom.net (trademark infringement). For a criticism of this trend see L. Thoumyre, 'Précisions contrastées sur trois notions clés relatives à la responsabilité des hébergeurs', *Revue Lamy Droit de l'Immatériel* 35 (2008): Actualités; the report presented before the Parliament on the application of the Statute no. 2004-575, Rapport D'information sur la mise en application de la loi no. 2004-575 du 21 juin 2004 pour la confiance dans l'économie numérique enregistré à la Présidence de l'Asssemblée nationale le 23 janvier 2008, www.juriscom.net. See also TGI Paris, ch. 3, sect. 2, 15 April 2008, Omar et Fred c/ SA Dailymotion et Lafesse c/ SA Dailymotion, www.juriscom.net (copyright infringement).

19. TGI Paris réf., 2 November 2005, http://www.legalis.net (injunction under penalty payment); TGI Paris, réf., 19 October 2006, Mme H. P. c/SARL Google France et Sté Google Inc., no. 06/58312, http://www.foruminternet.org; Tribunal de commerce de Paris Ordonnance de référé 26 juillet 2007, Kenzo et autres / DMIS (I) et Tribunal de commerce de Paris Ordonnance de référé 31 octobre 2007 Kenzo et autres / DMIS (II), www.legalis.net (hosting providers); TGI Paris, réf., 25 March 2005, Communication commerce électronique 2005, comm. 118, note Grynbaum L.; TGI Paris, réf., 20 April 2005, UEJF, SOS Racisme, J'Accuse et a. c/ OLM-LLC, The Planet.com Internet Services Inc. et a.; TGI Paris, réf., 13 June 2005, L'Union des étudiants juifs de France et autres c/ Sté OLM, LLC et autres, no. 05/553871, www.juriscom.net, Revue Lamy Droit de l'Immatériel (7)2005, no. 203, p. 43, obs. Costes; Cour d'Appel de Paris 24 November 2006, St Tiscali Accès et autre c/ Associations UEJF, MRAP, SOS Racisme et autres, http://www.legalis.net and C. cass, civ. 1, 19 June 2008, no. 07-12244 (Internet access providers). For a comment on the role of Internet access providers in the regulatory process see P. Stoffel-Munck, 'Le rôle des fournisseurs d'accès dans la régulation du réseau n'est pas complètement subsidiaire', *Communication Commerce Electronique* 9 (2005): comm. 140.

20. B. Gorchs, 'Vers un référé de l'Internet autonome', *Communication Commerce Electronique* 12 (2007): Etude no. 31

21. See Case Cour d'Appel de Paris 24 November 2006, St Tiscali Accès et autre c/ Associations UEJF, MRAP, SOS Racisme et autres, http://www.legalis.net.

22. See TGI Paris, réf., 19 October 2006, Mme H. P. c/SARL Google France et Sté Google Inc., http://www.foruminternet.org

23. TC Paris, réf., 26 July 2007 and 31 October 2007, Société Kenzo et autre c/ DMIS, www.legalis.net

24. See 'Le développement et la protection des oeuvres culturelles sur les noveaux réseaux', Novembre 2007, Rapport au ministère de la culture et de la communication, Mission confiée à Denis Olivennes, www.culture.gouv.fr; the agreement concluded between public authorities, author associations and IISPs such as Internet access providers and communitarian platform providers, 'Accord pour le développement et la protection des oeuvres et programmes culturels sur les nouveaux réseaux', Friday 23 November 2007, www.culture.gouv.fr. However, 2.0 platforms have refused to sign the agreement, such as Dailymotion. They have nevertheless formed an association to enhance the dialogue with public actors. See the 'Association des Services Internet Communautaires' (ASIC), www.lasic.fr. See also Projet de Loi relatif à la Haute Autorité pour la diffusion des oeuvres de la protection des droits sur Internet autrement dénommé Projet de Loi Olivennes (Projet de Loi Olivennes). The legislative plan has however been criticized at the national level and the European level because the main sanction consists in shutting down users' Internet access. See for example Rapport à Monsieur le Ministre de la Culture et de la Communication, 'Le téléchargement illicite d'oeuvres protégées par le droit d'auteur', Jean Cédras, April 2007; the amendment adopted by the European Parliament on 10 April 2008 but rejected later on; the note sent by the ASIC to the President, the Prime Minister and several ministers; the critical opinion of the *Autorité de Régulation des Communications Electroniques et des postes* (ARCEP) and the CNIL of 27 and 30 May 2008.

25. Generally speaking, the emergence of the web 2.0 has lead to a new wave of Case law on the liability of IISPs in France. See TGI Paris, réf., 22 June 2007, Lambert c/ sté Myspace, www.legalis.net; TGI Paris, réf., 2 July 2007, UDAF de l'Ardèche et autre c/ Linden Research et

autres, www.legalis.net, TGI Paris, 3e ch., 1re sect., 18 December. 2007, J.-Y. L. et a. c/ Sté Dailymotion, no. 06/18289, www.juriscom.net; TGI Paris, 3e ch., sect. 2, 13 July 2007, Carion c/ SA Dailymotion, www.legalis.net; TGI Paris, 3e ch., sect. 2, 19 October 2007, SARL Zadig Productions c/ sté Google, www.legalis.net, TGI Paris, 3e ch., 1re sect., 18 December 2007, J.-Y. L. et a. c/ Stés Google, no. 07/02707, www.juriscom.net, TGI Paris, réf., 9 January 2008, no. 07/58913, R. Mezrahi et a. c/ SARL Google Inc. et a., TGI Paris, réf., 9 January 2008, no. 07/58929, R. Magdane et a. c/ SARL Google Inc. et a. . Revue Lamy Droit de l'Immatériel (35)2008; TGI Paris, réf, 29 October 2007, M.B., P.T., F. D., c/ Widimedia Foundation Inc., www.legalis.net; TGI Paris, réf., 9 January 2008, no. 07/58929, R. Mezrahi et a. c/ Sté Youtube Inc. and TGI Paris, réf., 9 January 2008, no. 08/50112, R. Magdane et a. c/ Sté Youtube Inc. Revue Lamy Droit de l'Immatériel (35)2008.

26. CA Paris, 4e ch., A, 7 June 2006, Tiscali Media c/ Dargaud Lombard, Lucky Comics, www.legalis.net (*Tiscali*); CA Paris, 4e, A, 7 March 2007, Hôtels Meridien c/ Sedo, Stéphane H. www.legalis.net (*Meridien*); CA Paris, 14e ch., B, 9 November 2007 eBay Europe c/ DWC, www.legalis.net (*eBay*); TGI Paris, 3e ch., sect. 2, 13 July 2007, Carion c/ SA Dailymotion, www.legalis.net; TGI Paris, réf., 22 June 2007, Lambert c/ sté Myspace, www.legalis.net; TC, Paris, 1e ch, B, 30 June 2008, Parfums Christian Dior et autres c/ eBay Inc., eBay International AG, www.legalis.net; TGI Troyes, Ch. Civ., 4 June 2008, Hermès International c/ eBay et autres, www.legalis.net.
27. *Tiscali*, *Meridien*, TGI Paris, réf., 22 June 2007, Lambert c/ sté Myspace, www.legalis.net. Compare with CA Aix-en-Provence, 13 March 2006, Lucent Technologies c/ Escota, www.legalis.net.
28. *Tiscali*, see note 27 above.
29. TC, Paris, 1e ch, B, 30 June 2008, Parfums Christian Dior et autres c/ eBay Inc., eBay International AG, www.legalis.net; TGI Troyes, Ch. Civ., 4 June 2008, Hermès International c/ eBay et autres, www.legalis.net
30. Cass. com, 20 May 2008, no. 06-20230, 05-14331, 06-15136.
31. See e.g. CA Paris, 4e ch., B., 1 February 2008, Gifam et atures c/ Google, www.legalis.net; TGI Paris, 3ème ch, du 12 July 2006, Gifam et autres c/Google France, www.legalis.net; TGI Paris, 3e ch. 3e, 12 December 2007, Syndicat Français de la literie c/ Google France, www.legalis.net; CA Aix-en-Provence, 6 December 2007, TWD Industrie c/ Google France, Google Inc, www.legalis.net; TC Paris, 15e ch., 24 November 2006, One Tel c/ Google, Olfo, www.legalis.net; CA Paris, 4e ch., A, 28 June 2006, Google France c/ Louis Vuitton Malletier, www.legalis.net; CA Versailles, 12e ch., 1, 2 November 2006, Overture c/ Acor, www.legalis.net; CA Versailles, 12e ch., 23 March 2006, Google c/ Cnrrh, www.legalis.net; TGI Nanterre, 1e ch., 2 March 2006, Hôtels Méridien c/ Google France, www.legalis.net, TGI Paris, 3e ch., 2e, 8 December 2005, Kertel c/ Google, Cartephone, www.legalis.net; CA Versailles, 10 March 2005 Google France c/ Viaticum et Luteciel, www.legalis.net; TGI Paris, 24 June 2005, Amen c/ Espace 2001 et Google France, www.legalis.net. Compare with TC Paris, 8e ch., 31 October 2007, Trednet c/ Bodxl, Google France, www.legalis.net; TGI Strasbourg, 2e civ., 20 July 2007, Atrya c/ Google France et autres, www.legalis.net; TGI Paris, réf., 12 May 2003, http://www.juriscom.net; CA Paris, 15 May 2002, Altavista c/ Matelsom, www.juriscom.net. Compare in particular TGI Paris, 3ème ch, du 12 July 2006, Gifam et autres c/ Google France, www.legalis.net; TC Paris, 15e ch., 24 November 2006, One Tel c/ Google, Olfo, www.legalis.net; TGI Paris, 3e ch., 2e, 8 December 2005, Kertel c/ Google, Cartephone, www.legalis.net and CA Paris, 4e ch., B., 1 February 2008, Gifam et atures c/ Google, www.legalis.net; CA Aix-en-Provence, 6 December 2007, TWD Industrie c/ Google France, Google Inc, www.legalis.net; CA Paris, 4e ch., A, 28 June 2006, Google France c/ Louis Vuitton Malletier, www.legalis.net; CA Versailles, 12e ch., 1, 2 November 2006, Overture c/ Acor, www.legalis.net; CA Versailles, 12e ch., 23 March 2006, Google c/ Cnrrh, www.legalis.net; TGI Nanterre, 1e ch., 2 March 2006, Hôtels Méridien c/ Google France, www.legalis.net; TGI Paris, 24 June 2005, Amen c/ Espace 2001 et Google France, www.legalis.net.

Index

Page numbers in *Italics* represent tables.

For Product Safety Concerns and Information please contact our EU representative GPSR@taylorandfrancis.com Taylor & Francis Verlag GmbH, Kaufingerstraße 24, 80331 München, Germany